Preface

This book is mainly targeted for the exam of Security Analysis & Portfolio Management for all Universities. It has been introduced in market after seeing the huge demand of ready to grasp material for exams with high level of quality, and its un-availability in market. We the GullyBaba Publishing House took a step ahead to publish the quality material focusing on exams at the same time giving you indepth knowledge about the subject.

GPH Book is the pioneer effort that provides a unique methodology so as to perform better in exams. If your goal is to attain higher grade use this powerful study tool independently or along with your text.

On the Web : ***www.gullybaba.com*** *is the vital resource for your exams acting as catalyst to boost up your preparation. Now you can access us on the net through* ***www.doeacconline.com, www.ignouonline.com, and www.astrologyeverywhere.com.***

We gratefully acknowledges the significant contributions of Mr. S.K. Goel, Mr. Dinesh Verma, Mr. Mahesh Chand, Mrs. Bimla Devi, Mrs. Bhawna Verma and our experts in bringing out this publication.

New Delhi

Dear Reader, You are welcome in the world of GullyBaba Publishing House.

By long, in deep study & Research, we assure / guarantee you the most reliable, latest & accurate information on the subject.

We still believe that there is always a scope for improvement.

You a reader can be our best guide in making this book more interesting & user friendly.

We welcome your valuable suggestions.

***Feedback about the book can be sent at* feedback@gullybaba.com.**

Publisher.

TOPICS COVERED

Security Analysis and Portfolio Management

MS-44

For

Master of Business Administration [MBA]

By

Kanu Jain

BFIA, M.Com

Useful For

IGNOU, KSOU (Karnataka), Bihar University (Muzaffarpur), Nalanda University, Jamia Millia Islamia, Vardhman Mahaveer Open University (Kota), Uttarakhand Open University, Kurukshetra University, Seva Sadan's College of Education (Maharashtra), Lalit Narayan Mithila University, Andhra University, Pt. Sunderlal Sharma (Open) University (Bilaspur), Annamalai University, Bangalore University, Bharathiar University, Bharathidasan University, HP University, Centre for distance and open learning, Kakatiya University (Andhra Pradesh), KOU (Rajasthan), MPBOU (MP), MDU (Haryana), Punjab University, Tamilnadu Open University, Sri Padmavati Mahila Visvavidyalayam (Andhra Pradesh), Sri Venkateswara University (Andhra Pradesh), UCSDE (Kerala), University of Jammu, YCMOU, Rajasthan University, UPRTOU, Kalyani University, Banaras Hindu University (BHU) and all other Indian Universities.

Closer to Nature  We use Recycled Paper

GULLYBABA PUBLISHING HOUSE PVT. LTD.

ISO 9001 & ISO 14001 CERTIFIED CO.

Published by:
GullyBaba Publishing House Pvt. Ltd.

Regd. Office:
2525/193, 1st Floor, Onkar Nagar-A,
Tri Nagar, Delhi-110035
(From Kanhaiya Nagar Metro Station Towards Old Bus Stand)
Call: 9991112299, 9312235086
WhatsApp: 9350849407

Branch Office:
1A/2A, 20, Hari Sadan,
Ansari Road, Daryaganj,
New Delhi-110002
Ph.011-45794768
Call & WhatsApp:
8130521616,8130511234

E-mail: hello@gullybaba.com, **Website**:GullyBaba.com

New Edition

ISBN: 978-93-81638-46-0

Contents

Question Papers

Block – 1

An Overview

Chapter – 1

Nature and Scope of Investment Process

Q1. Define Investment? How is it different from speculation?

Ans. The term 'Investment' refers to exchange of money wealth into some tangible wealth. The 'money wealth' refers to the money (savings) which an investor has and the term tangible wealth refers to the assess the investor acquires by scarifying the money wealth. By investing, an investor commits the present funds to one or more assets to be need for sometime in expectation some future returns in terms of interest or dividend (revenue) or capital gain. In speculation, there is an investment of funds with an expectation of some return in the form of capital profit resulting from the price change and sale of investment.

Basis	**Investment**	**Speculation**
1. Degree of Risk	Relatively Lesser	Relatively Higher
2. Basis of Return	Income of the Investee	Change in market place
3. Basis for Decision	Analysis of Fundamentals	Rumours, tips, perception of investors etc.
4. Position of Investors	Ownership	Party to an agreement
5. Investment Period	Long-term	Short-term

Q2. Define speculator. Why are they important for proper functioning of any market?

OR

'Speculation is a necessary evil'. Comment. [Dec 2007, Q7(a)]

Ans. Speculators invest in high risk securities for a short period and hence exposed to high level of risk. Speculators essentially provide liquidity for the securities and often match the demand and supply of the market. For example, positive news on a firm may attract a large demand for the stock. In the absence of any sellers, the price will shoot up. Some speculators may take a different view and willing to sell the stock to meet the excess demand of the market. Similarly, a mutual fund may wants to sell 1 lakhs shares of a company. If there are limited buyers for the stock, the stock price would crash. Again, speculators would buy the stock in anticipation of selling the same at a small profit once the demand for the stock picks up in the market.

Q3. Distinguish between a speculator and an investor.

Ans. We can distinguish the two operators as follows:

(i) The time-horizon of a speculator is short while that of the investor is long.

(ii) The investor expects a 'good' return and a consistent performance over time but the speculator expects abnormal returns earned quickly over short periods.

(iii) The investor generally sticks to his investment, but the speculator makes rapid shifts to greener pastures. He moves from one stock to other for a small profit.

(iv) The investor is risk-averse but the speculator takes greater risks. Often, speculators take risk by entering into margin trading to increase the volume and his exposure in the market.

Q4. What do you mean by 'risk'? What do you mean by 'risk-return tradeoff'? Why do different investments have varying degree of expected return? Explain with the help of a diagram. [Dec 2006, Q1(a)]

Ans. Risk is defined as the probability that the realized return would be different from the anticipated return of an investment.

Investment decisions are premised on an important assumption that investors are rational and hence prefer certainty to uncertainty. They are risk-averse which implies that they would be unwilling to take risk just for the sake of risk. They would assume risk only if an adequate compensation is forthcoming. Figure below depicts the risk-return trade-off available to rational investors. The line R_F_M shows the risk-return function i.e., a trade-off between expected return and risk that exists for all investors interested in financial assets. The R_f M line always slopes upward because it is plotted against expected return, which has to increase as risk rises.

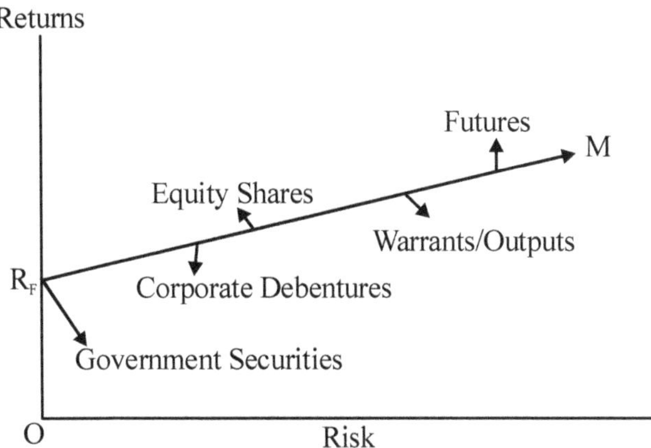

Fig : The Expected Returns-risk trade-off functions

The point RF is the expected return on government securities where risk is zero and is recognized as the risk-free rate. As you move on the R_{F}_M line, you find successive points, which show the increase in expected return as risk increase. Thus, equity shares, which carry lot more of risk than government securities and company debentures are plotted higher on the line. Company debentures are less risky than equity because of the mortgages and assurances made available to the investor but more risky than government securities where the default risk is zero because government generally does not fail. They are placed between the two securities viz., government securities and equity shares. Warrants, options and financial futures are other specialized financial assets ranked in order of rising risk.

Investors need to strike a balance when they allocate their wealth under various investments. If some one invests their entire savings only in government securities or only in highrisk securities like equity or derivatives, it may not yield desired result. Investors need to balance the investments by partly investing in equities and partly in government securities.

Q5. Explain the 'Investment Decision Process'. How is it going to help investor in making sound investment decision? [June 2005, Q1]

Ans. The investor decision process is concerned with as to how an investor should proceed in making decision about

(i) What marketable securities to invest in?

(ii) How diversified the investment should be?

(iii) When the investment should be made?

There is a well-knit investment decision process involved therein.

A typical investment decision undergoes a five-step procedure, which in turn forms the basis of the investment process. These steps are:

(1) Determine the investment objectives and policy

(2) Security Analysis

(3) Portfolio Construction

(4) Portfolio Revision

(5) Portfolio Performance Evaluation

(1) Determine the investment objectives and policy

The investor will have to work out his investment objectives first and then evolve a policy with the amount of investible wealth at his command.

The objective should be in clear and specific terms. It can be expressed in terms of expected return or expected risk. Suppose, an investor can aim to earn 12% return against the risk-free rate of 9%.

The investor can set her or his preference on risk by stating that the risk of investment should be below market risk. It is desirable to set one of the two parameters (risk or return) and find the other one from the market. If necessary, an investor can revise the objective if sheik finds the risk is too high for her/ him to bear a desired return.

The next step in formulating the investment policy of an investor would be the identification Of categories of financial assets he/she would be interested in. It would depend on the objectives, amount of wealth and the tax status of the investor.

(2) Security Analysis

After defining the investment objective and broadly setting the proportion of wealth to be invested under different categories, the next step is selecting individual securities under each category. For instance, a long-term government bond is much riskier than short-term bonds. Similarly, investment in equities requires identification of companies stocks, in Which the investment can be made. Security analysis is often performed in two or three stages. The first stage, called economic analysis, would be useful to set broad investment objective. If the economy is expected to do well, investor can invest more in stocks. On the other hand, if the economic slowdown is expected to continue, investor can invest less in stocks and more in bonds. In stage two, investors typically examine the industries and identify the industries, in which investment can be made.

The issue is an analysis of broad trends of industry and future outlook is essential to proceed further on security analysis.

At the last step, one has to look into the fundamentals of specific companies and find whether the stock is desirable for investment and investors need to match the risk-return objective she/he has set in the previous stage. Company specific analysis includes examination of historical financial information as well as future outlook.

Through such analysis, analysts quantify the intrinsic value of the stock and compare the same with current market price. If the intrinsic value is greater than the current market price, the stock qualifies for investment.

(3) Portfolio Construction

Under portfolio construction stage, the investor has to allocate the wealth to different stocks. A couple of principles guide such allocation of wealth. Investors need to appreciate that the risk of portfolio comes down if the portfolio is diversified. Diversification here doesn't mean more than one stock but stocks whose future performance are not highly correlated. Further, too much diversification or too many stocks may also create problem in terms of monitoring.

While including stocks in the portfolio, the investor has to watch its impact on the overall portfolio return and risk and also examine whether it is consistent with the initial investment objective.

Since investors saving take place over a period of time, portfolios are also constructed over a period of time. It is a continuous exercise. Sometime, timing of investment may be critical. For instance, if an investor saves Rs. 30,000 during the first quarter and the desired portfolio includes both bonds and stocks, the issue before the investor is whether the amount has to be used for bonds or stocks or both.

(4) Portfolio Revision

Under portfolio construction, investor is matching the risk-return characteristics of securities with the risk-return of investment objective. Under two conditions, the securities, in which investment was made earlier, require liquidation and investing the amount in a new security. The risk or expected return of the security might have changed over a period of time when the business environment changes.

Another reason for selling some of the securities in the portfolio and buying a new one in its place is a change in investment objective. For instance, when you are young and have less family commitments, then your investment objective may aim for higher return even if it amounts to higher risk. You may invest more of your savings in equity stocks and derivatives. When your family grows, you might want to reduce the risk and change the investment objective. Or when the macro-economic condition changes, you may want to shift part of your investment from equity to debt or vice versa depending on the future economic outlook.

(5) Portfolio Performance Evaluation

The value of your investment changes over a period of time and it reflects the current market value of the securities in the portfolio.

At the end of each period, you may like to compute the portfolio return and risk and compare the same with your investment objective as well as certain benchmark risk-return. The objective of this exercise is to evaluate the efficiency in construction and management of portfolio.

Q6. Define 'Return'? Differentiate between expected return and realized return.

Ans. Investors always wish to earn a return on the funds invested in assets. Because there is always an opportunity cost of funds. Return from an investment helps the investor realizing that opportunity cost. The return from an investment is the sum of revenue return (dividends or interest) and/or capital return (capital appreciation or increase in the price of the security).

Expected Return: refers to the anticipated return for some future period. It is estimated on the basis of actual returns in the past period while the

Realised Return: is the net actual return earned by the investor over the holding period. It refers to the actual return over some past period.

The actual or the realized return may be more or less than the expected return. The difference between the expected and the realized return give rise to the risk attached with the return.

Q7. Discuss the effect of investment environment on investment decisions.

OR

What are the different elements constituting investment environment? Why are they important?

Ans. The investment environment is a complicated network of number of institutions, participants, instruments and the regulatory bodies. Different components of the investment environment are interdependent and operate in cohesiveness to produce a competitive, healthy and efficient structure and environment in which the investors undertake the investment activities. The flow of funds from the funds-surplus units to fund-deficit units is smoothened and facilitated by the presence of competitive investment environment. Investors have to be fully aware of this environment for making optimal investment decisions.

a) Financial Instruments

Investors invests through financial assets or financial instruments or securities. Financial assets or instruments can be classified in a variety of ways.

i) Debt instruments furnish an evidence of indebtedness of the issuer to the buyer. Periodic payments on such instruments are generally mandatory and all of them provide for the eventual repayment at maturity of the principal amount. Securities may also be sold at a price below the eventual redemption price, the difference between the redemption price and the sale price constituting the interest.

ii) Ownership Securities : These instruments are called `equities' because investors who invest in them get a right to share residual profits. Equity investment may be acquired indirectly or directly or even through a hybrid instrument known as preference shares.

b) Financial Intermediaries

Financial intermediaries perform the intermediation function i.e., they bring the users of funds and the suppliers of funds together. Many of them issue financial claims against themselves and use cash proceeds to purchase the financial assets of others. The Unit Trust of India and other mutual funds belong to this category.

Most financial institutions underwrite issues of capital by non-governmental public limited companies in addition to directly subscribing to such capital either under a public issue or under a private placement.

The financial institutions engaged in intermediary activities include the Industrial Development Bank of India, Industrial Finance Corporation of India, Industrial Credit and Investment Corporation of India, Unit Trust of India, Life Insurance Corporation, and General Insurance Corporation. Two institutions, which have broadened financial services activities in India, deserve a special mention. They are: The Credit Rating Information Services of India Ltd., (CRIS1L) and other credit rating agencies, and the Stockholding Corporation of India Ltd. (SHCIL).

c) Securities market can be seen as primary and secondary market.

i) Primary Market : The primary market or the new issues market is an informal forum with national and even international boundaries.

Individuals, trusts, banks, mutual funds, financial institutions, pension funds, and for that matter any entity can participate in such markets. Companies enter this market with initial and subsequent issues of capital. They are required to follow the guideline prescribed by the regulating agencies like SEBI from time to time unless they are expressly exempted from doing so. Some companies would use the primary market by using their `in house' skill but most of them would employ brokers, broking and underwriting firms, issue managers, lead managers for planning and monitoring the new issue.

(ii) Secondary Market : Secondary markets or stock exchanges are set up under the Securities Contracts (Regulation) Act, 1956. They are known as recognized exchanges and operate within precincts that possess networks of communication, automatic information scans, and other mechanized systems. Members are admitted against purchase of a membership card whose official prices vary according to the size and seniority of the exchange.

Today, all exchanges in India have introduced screen-based trading where the members of the exchange transact the business (purchase and sale of securities) through computer terminals.

The Securities and Exchange Board of India (SEBI) is now responsible to monitor and control the stock market operations, new capital issues, working of mutual funds, merchant bankers and other intermediaries. SEBI has issued separate guidelines for each of the above entities and requires all the intermediaries to register with the SEBI and periodically submit the reports on their operations.

Q8. Write short note on

(a) Zero-interest Bond **[Dec 2007, Q7(c)]**

Ans. Sometimes when a security is sold at a price below the eventual redemption price, the difference between the redemption price and the sale price constituting the interest. This is called zero-interest bonds. E.g. If the buyer pays Rs. 94:30 at the beginning and receives Rs. 100 at maturity i.e., The buyer receives 6 per cent of Rs. 94.30 that is equal to the difference between Rs. 100 (redemption price) and Rs. 94.30 (issue price). Then this arrangements is known as zero-interest bonds.

(b) Nominal or Coupon Rate of Interest

Ans. The interest amount in rupees measured as a percent of the par value of a debt instrument is known as nominal or coupon `rate of interest. For example, Rs. 28 payable per year on a debenture whose face/par value is Rs. 200 yields a coupon rate of 14 per cent per annum.

(c) Public Debt Instruments/Gilt Edged Securities

Ans. Government issues debt instruments for long and short periods. They are rated the best in terms of quality and are risk-free. A common term used to designate them is 'gilt-edged-securities'. The 182-day treasury bills issued by the Government of India are examples of short-term instruments. Government also borrows, money for long-term and 11.5 percent Loan 2009 (V issue) of the Government of India is an example of long-term instruments. State governments and local bodies also issue series of loans and bonds.

(d) Private Debt Instruments

Ans. These are issued by private business firms, which are incorporated as companies under the Companies Act, 1956. Generally these instruments are secured by a mortgage on the fixed assets of a company. In addition to plain debt instruments, there are several variations. A very popular variety of such debentures are `convertible' whereby either the whole or a part of the par value of a debenture is convertible (either automatically or at the option of investors) on the expiry of a stipulated period after issue. The terms of conversion are stated in advance. There may be a series of conversions and conversion price may differ from period to period.

Selected Indian companies are now raising short-term funds by issuing a debt instrument known as Commercial paper (CP).

(e) Special Debt Instruments

Ans. With a view to mop up resources and innovating the spectrum of debt-instruments, two new debt instruments are, Public Sector Undertaking (PSU) Bonds (long-term) and Certificate of Deposit (shortterm). The PSU bonds are issued to the general public and financial institutions by public sector undertakings, usually with tax incentive. A large proportion of PSU bonds is privately placed with banks, their subsidiaries, and financial institutions. Commercial banks are permitted to issue CDs within a ceiling equal to 2 per cent of their fortnightly average outstanding aggregate deposits.

Interest rates for CDs are normally higher than the interest rate offered by the bank for similar maturity period deposits.

(f) Indirect Equities

Ans. The investor acquires special instruments of institutions, who take the buy-sell decisions on behalf of investors. Such institutions are Unit Trust or Mutual Funds. An individual who buys Unit gets a dividend from the income of the Trust/Mutual Fund after meeting all expenses of management. The Units can be bought from and sold to the institution at sale and repurchase prices announced from time to time (on a daily basis).

The objective of Trusts and Mutual Funds is to use their professional expertise in portfolio construction and pass on the benefits to the small investor who cannot repeat such a performance if left alone to subscribe to equity shares directly.

(g) Direct Equities

Ans. The investor can subscribe directly to the equity issues placed on the market by the new companies or by the existing companies. If she/he is already a shareholder of an existing company, which enters the capital market for additional issue of equity shares, such an investor would get a pro rata right to subscribe, on a preemptive basis, to the new issue. Such offerings are known as ‘rights shares'. Established companies' reward their shareholders in the form of 'bonus shares' as well. They are given out of the accumulated reserves and shareholders need not pay any cash consideration as happens in the case of `right shares'.

(h) Financial Intermediation

Ans. A function, which brings the savers and users of funds together, usually performed by specialized agencies and institutions like banks and underwriters for art agreed/stipulated commission.

(i) CRISIL

Ans. CRISIL, the first credit rating agency of the country, was set up jointly by ICICI, UTI, LIC, GIC, and Asian Development Bank. It started operations in January 1988 and has rated a large number of debt instruments and public deposits of companies. CRISIL ratings provide a guide to investors as to the risk of timely payment of interest and principal on a particular debt instruments and preference shares on receipt of request from a company. Ratings relate to a specific instrument and not to the company as a whole. They are based on factors like industry risk, market position and operating efficiency of the company, track record of management, planning and control system, accounting, quality and financial flexibility, profitability and financial position of the company, and its liquidity management.

(j) Risk Free Rate of Return

Ans. The monetary rate of return obtainable on financial assets with zero probability of default on principal and periodic payments, e.g. government or gilt edged securities.

Chapter – 2

Components of Investment Risk

Q1. How the return of an investment can be measured?

Ans. The return may be measured as the total gain or loss to the holder over a period of time and may be defined as a percentage return on the initial amount invested. With reference to investment in equity shares, return is consisting of the dividends and the capital gain/loss at the time of sale of these shares and may be defined as

$$k = \frac{P_1 - P_o + D_1}{p_o}$$

where, k = rate of return from the investment

P_o = market price at time 0

P_1 = market price at time 1

D_1 = cash dividend for the period 1

This is also known as 'Holding Period Rate of Return'.

Q2. Differentiate between risk and uncertainty.

Ans. Risk is defined as a situation where the possibility of happening or non-happening of an event can be quantified and measured, while uncertainty is defined as a situation where this possibility can't be measured. Thus, risk is a situation when probabilities can be assigned to an event on the basis of facts and figures available regarding the decision. Uncertainty, on the other hand, is a situation where either facts and figures are not available or the probabilities can't be assigned.

Q3. How the risk of a security can be measured? Explain different methods to measure risk.

Ans. Statistical as well as non-statistical measures can be used to make more precise measurement of risk about the estimated returns, to gauge the extent to which the expected return and actual return are likely to differ.

Statistical measures for computing risk are :

(1) Range: The range is the difference between the highest and lowest expected return. For e.g., the return from an investment may fluctuate between 20% to 25%. The expected rate of return from the investment has a range of variation of 5%.

(2) Standard Deviation: A reliable and convenient way to quantify the risk is to measure the degree of spread of possible returns around the expected return. This is called the standard deviation, σ, of possible returns.

$$\sigma = \sqrt{\sum_{i=1}^{n}\left[P(x_i)(x_i - \in V)^2\right]}$$

where $\in V$ = Expected value
x_i = Possible returns
$P(x_i)$ = Related probabilities

Also, the squared standard deviation $(\sigma)^2$ is known as 'variance' and is an equally useful measure of risk.

Non-statistical measures for computing risk are :–

(1) Debt Ratio : Analysts used financial statement data for evaluating the risk of securities of a company. The broad indicators used by them were the amount of debt employed by the firm. Their rule was: `the higher the amount of debt the greater the, riskiness of security & this is called debt ratio.

(2) Margin of Safety : The difference between `intrinsic value' and `market price' was called the `margin of safety' and the rule used for assessment of risk was `the higher the margin of safety, the lower the risk.'

Q4. Define the 'expected value of returns'? How is it calculated?

Ans. Expected value of returns is the sum of products of possible returns with their respective probabilities

$$\text{Expected Value (EV)} = \sum_{i=1}^{n} x_i P(x_i)$$

where x_i = Possible returns
$P(x_i)$ = Related probabilities

It is also known as the 'weighted average return'.

Q5. Distinguish between Systematic and Unsystematic Risk.

[June 2007, Q1(a)]

Ans. Systematic Risk: It refers to that portion of the variability of return which is caused by the factors affecting all the firms. It refers to fluctuation in return due to general market factors such as money supply, inflation, economic recessions, interest rate policy of the government, tax reforms etc. These are the factors which affect almost all the firms. The effect of these factors is to cause the prices of all securities to move together. This part of the risk arises because every security has a built-in tendency to move in line with the fluctuations in the market. No investor can avoid or eliminate this risk, whatever precautions or diversification may be resorted to. The systematic risk is also called the "non-diversifiable risk" or "general risk".

Unsystematic Risk: It represents the fluctuations in return from an investment due to factors which are specific to the particular firm and not the market as a whole. These factors are same which are responsible for business risk or financial risk. Since these factors are unique to a particular firm, these must be examined separately for each firm and for each industry. The unsystematic risk results from random events. It is also called specific risk or diversifiable risk.

Total Risk = Systematic Risk + Unsystematic Risk

Q6. How the systematic and unsystematic risk can be measured?

Ans. Total risk is equal to Systematic risk plus Non-systematic risk. Systematic risk is normally measured by comparing the stock's performance vis-a-vis market's performance under different conditions.

This is done by measuring a value called `beta'. The beta of the stock is equal to beta of the regression coefficient when stock's of returns are regressed on return of market - index. If the beta of stock is 1.50, then the stock is expected to show a price increase of 1.5 times of stock returns in a good period. At the same time, if the market declines by some percentage in a bad period, the stock is. expected to decline 1.5 times more than market's negative return.

Q7. How the changes in interest rates affects stock prices? What can be done to avoid interest rate risk and duration risk?

Ans. Interest rate risk arises from variations in interest rates, which cause changes in market prices. A rise in market interest rates causes a decline in market prices of securities and vice versa.

It affects the expected or required rate of return because investors always compare risk-free return with the expected return of an investment.

Since stocks have no maturity, the interest rate changes affect the stock prices more than bonds. Secondly, increase in interest rates also reduces the profit of the companies and hence securities prices are negatively affected. The market prices (or present values) of securities would be inversely related both to market interest rates (or yield to maturity) and duration.

With a view to avoid the interest rate and duration risk, the investor, may like to invest in short-term securities. Rather than buying a 5-year debenture, he may buy a one-year security every time the earlier one-year security matures.

Q8. Define market risk. What are the causes of market risk? How can it be avoided? [June 2005, Q7(f)]

Ans. Market risk is demonstrated by the increased variability of investor returns due to alternating bouts to bull and bear phases. Efforts to minimize this component of total investment risk require a fair anticipation of a particular phase.

Business cycles are a major determinant of the timing and extent of the bull and bear market phases. The ups and downs in securities markets would follow the cycle of expansion and recession in the economy. A bear market triggers pessimism and price falls on an extensive scale.

Investors can protect their portfolios by withdrawing invested funds before the onset of the bear market. A simple rule to follow would be: `buy just before the security prices rise in a bull market and sell just before the onset of the bear market', that is, buy low and sell high. This is called good investment timing but often difficult to practice.

Q9. What is coupon interest rate risk?

Ans. Variability in coupon rates in successive short term securities leads to coupon interest rate risk or the probability of the coupon rate of interest printed on the face of a debt security as a percentage of its face value being changed in successive short periods.

Q10. Distinguish between purchasing power risk and inflation risk.

Ans. Inflation risk is the variability in the total purchasing power of an asset. It arises from the rising general price level. The interest rate on bonds and debentures and dividend rates on equity and preference shares are stated in money terms and if the general price level rises during some future period, the buying power of the cash interest/dividend income is likely to be received for that period would decline. And if the rate of inflation is equal to the money rate of return, the investor does not add anything to his existing wealth since he obtains a zero rate of return.

The purchasing power risk arises even if the market prices of assets rise. Likewise, this risk may emerge even if the asset prices do not fluctuate. The reason for these relationships is that the purchasing power risk arises from fluctuations in the purchasing power of real income and/or real price of assets and not from fluctuations in buying power of their nominal income and/or nominal prices.

Q11. If a security is expected to yield a nominal rate of return of 12% and the rate of inflation is expected to be 15%. Should an investor stop investing in such situation?

Ans. If the investor decides to invest, his real rate of return would be

$$R_f = \frac{1+r}{1+q} - 1$$

where R_f = Real rate of return
r = coupon rate or nominal rate of return
q = inflation rate

$$\therefore R_f = \frac{1+0.12}{1+0.15} - 1$$

= – 0.026
It works out to a negative 2.6% return.
If the investor keeps the idle cash, then the real rate of return would be :

$$R_f = \frac{1+0.00}{1+0.15} - 1$$

= – 0.131
So, it would be better to have a negative return of 2.6% than to end with a negative return of 13.1% by keeping cash idle.

Q12. Distinguish between Real Assets and Financial Assets.
Ans. (1) Investment assets are real assets like land, real estate, gold, diamonds and financial or monetary assets like shares, bonds, and debentures.
(2) Prices of real assets move with inflation and are positively correlated with it. In contrast, prices of monetary assets are relatively rigid and are negatively correlated with inflation.
(3) Real assets are good inflation hedges but monetary assets are not. Hence, monetary assets cannot form part of a portfolio, which already has got a high degree of purchasing power risk. Such a portfolio can be diversified with real assets.

Q13. Write short notes on:
(a) Default Risk
Ans. The default risk arises from a deterioration of financial strength of the company that issues securities. Holders of such securities have to experience greater variability of returns when financial strength begins to worsen. Since the basic parameter is `financial health', default risk is also known as financial risk.

(b) Business Risk
Ans. Firms operate in an environment, which often changes and such changes causes variation in expected income and this. For example, a change in

government policy on fertilizer subsidy may affect a group of companies in the fertilizer industry. Similarly, an action by a competitor, domestic or from outside may also affect other companies. While the above changes in the environment are caused by certain entities, there are several factors, which change the operating environment but can't be attributed to anyone. For instance, many firms are exposed to business cycle and the income of such firms significantly differs from period to period.

(c) Financial Risk

Ans. Financial risk arises when the firm uses debt in its capital structure. Debt brings fixed liability and hence increases the variability of income available to the equity shareholders. Use of debt is not always bad. It will increase the profitability when the company performs well and equity holders get a return more than what is available otherwise. Debt creates problem in bad times because of the fixed liability. If the company fails to meet the debt obligation, the managers need to spend a lot of time in convincing the lenders to accept delayed payment and in meanwhile loose valuable managerial time.

The impact of financial risk upto a limit is restricted only to the equity holders. But too much of debt creates problems even to existing debt security holders unless the debt is fully secured.

(d) Liquidity Risk

Ans. Liquidity risk of securities results from the inability of a seller to dispose them off except by offering price discounts and commissions. It is easy to rank assets according to liquidity. Government securities and blue chip shares are the next highly liquid group of assets. Debt securities and equity shares of some small and less known companies are less liquid or even illiquid. Lack of liquidity forces investors to sell the securities at a price below to the existing price, particularly when the quantity to be sold is large.

(e) Trough

Ans. It occurs when general business activity has bottomed out at the end of a recession. The usual timing of a trough is at the end of a recession and the beginning of a recovery in business activity.

Q14. How is agency cost associated with management risk? Which factors can be used to evaluate the management team of a company?

[June 2007, Q7(a)]

Ans. Management risk is that part of total variability of return which is caused by managerial decisions in firms where owners are not managers.

Management errors are the main reasons, which give rise to management risk component of total investor risk.

Nevertheless, some potential areas of management errors can be highlighted. The one great blunder that management might commit is to ignore product obsolescence.

Another risk is the dependence of a firm on a single large customer. Management must adequately diversify customer groups.

Yet one more area of management errors could be the wrong handling of a correct decision when it is subjected to unfair criticism and is even fought out in a court.

A recent development in the area of explaining management risks is concerned with research that seeks to explain the basic motivations of owners and managers.

The emerging theory hypothesizes that owner-non-managers delegate all authority to non-owner managers, who then operate under a principal-agent relationship. Since ex-post rewards and punishments are not perfect and just, hired executives may not make, as much ex ante effort to generate profitable investment opportunities than they would if they owned the firm. Thus, there is a conflict of interest between owners and managers and the latter may abuse the authority delegated to them much to the detriment of owners. In consequence, investors, who are rational individuals, would pay a higher price for shares of owner-managed firms than for shares of employee managed firms. The difference between the two sets of prices has been termed as `agency cost'.

Factors that can be used for evaluating management are :–

(1) Age, health, and experience profile of executives

(2) Growth-orientation and aggressiveness of management

(3) Composition of Board of Directors and the number of outside directors; Effectiveness of the Board.

(4) Management depth of the firm i.e., extent of delegation and decentralization and development of managers at all levels with a strong middle-management team.

(5) Dynamism and flexibility of management.

(6) Compensation to managers including special arrangements like stock option plans.

Practical Questions :

Q1. The market price of an equity share is Rs. 100. Following information is available in respect of dividends, market price and the expected market condition after one year :

Market Condition	Probability	Market Price	Dividend
Good	.25	Rs. 115	Rs. 9
Normal	.50	107	5
Bad	.25	97	3

Find out the expected return and variability of returns of the equity share.

Ans. The expected return of the equity share may be found as follows:

Condition	Probability	Total Return	Cost	Net Return
Good	.25	Rs. 124	Rs. 100	Rs. 24
Normal	.50	112	100	12
Bad	.25	100	100	0

Expected Return = (24 × .25) + (12 × .50) + (0 × .25)
= 12%

The variability of return can be studied in terms of the standard deviation as follows :–

$$\sigma^2 = .25(24-12)^2 + .50(12-12)^2 + .25(0-12)^2$$

= 36 + 0 + 36
= 72

$$\sigma^2 = \sqrt{72} = 8.49$$

Q2. An investment is currently available for Rs. 40. The revenue return and the year-end price of this investment depend upon the economic conditions. Three such conditions are likely with equal probabilities. The return and year-end prices are expected as follows:

Condition	Return	Year-end price
Boom	Rs. 2.00	Rs. 50
Normal	1.00	43
Recession	0.50	34

Find out the expected value of return for one-year period and the standard deviation of the return.

Ans. The expected value of return and standard deviation can be calculated as follows:

Condition	Prob.	Return	Year-end Price	Total Return	Prob. × Return
Boom	1/3	Rs. 2.00	Rs. 50	2 + (50 – 40) = 12.0	4.000
Normal	1/3	1.00	43	1 + (43 – 40) = 4.0	1.333
Recession	1/3	0.50	34	.5 + (34 – 30) = -5.5	-1.833
Expected Return					3.500

Prob.	Return	P. (Ret. – Exp. Value)^2
1/3	2.00	1/3 $(12 - 3.500)^2 = 24.083$
1/3	1.00	1/3 $(4 - 3.500)^2 = 0.083$
1/3	0.50	1/3 $(-5.5 - 3.500)^2 = 27.000$
		= 51.166

Standard Deviation $= \sqrt{51.166}$

= 7.15%

So, the expected return is 8.75% (i.e., $3.50 \div 40$) with standard deviation of 7.15%.

Chapter – 3

Valuation of Securities

Q1. What are the different approaches to the valuation process of making investments?

Ans. There are two general approaches to the valuation process when you make an investment decision: (1) the top-down, three-step approach and (2) the bottom-up stock valuation, stock picking approach. The difference between the approaches is the perceived importance of economy and industry influence on individual firms and stocks. The three-step approach believes that a firm's revenue is considerably affected by the performance of economy and industry and thus, the first step in valuation of process is to examine the economy and industry and their impact on the firm's cash flow. On the other hand, bottom-up approach believes that it is possible to find stocks that offer superior returns regardless of the market or industry outlook.

Thus, the three-step approach is also called economy-industry-company (E-I-C) approach. Figure below illustrates the E-I-C approach.

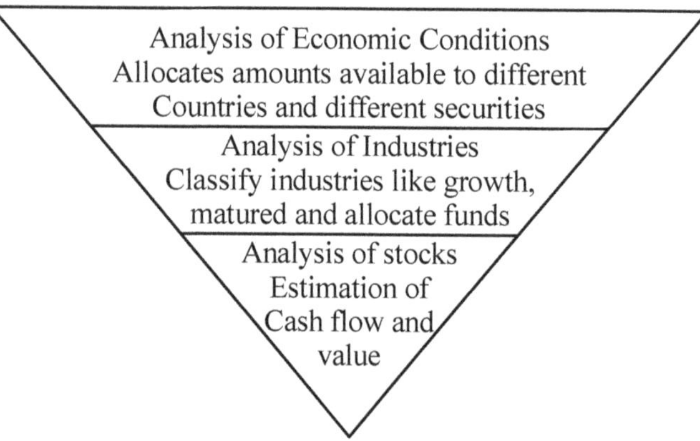

Fig : The Investment Process (E-I-C Approach)

Q2. Explain dynamic valuation process with the help of a diagram.

Ans. Estimates of present value, riskiness and discount rates, future income, and buy-sell action have to be reviewed from time to time in response to new bits and sets of information. Figure below depicts the dynamic valuation process which is an ever continuing phenomenon. The investors start with their estimates of intrinsic value using the present value procedure. Working on the trading rules, they buy sell or don't trade. In the process, buying and selling pressures are generated and prices either move up or down. In either case, Future return will be influenced by the latest market price reacting to buying/selling pressures. This will require present values to be reworked. The process will thus go on.

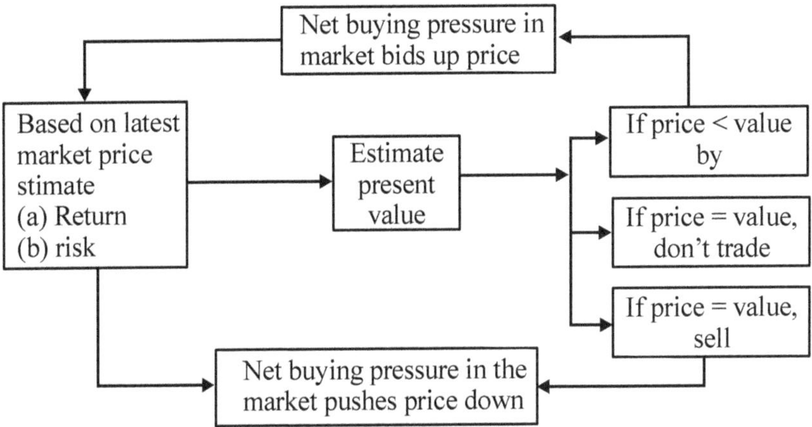

Fig : The dynamic Valuation Model

Q3. How does an investor decide to buy/sell or hold on the basis of value-price relationship?

OR

After determining the intrinsic value of a share, how does an investor makes investment?

Ans. Present value, also known as intrinsic value or economic value, determines price. Given a risk adjusted discount rate and the future expected earning two of a security in the form of interest, dividend earnings or cash flow, one can always determine. The present value as follows:

$$PV = \frac{CF_1}{1+r} + \frac{CF_2}{(1+r)^2} + \frac{CF_3}{(1+r)^3} + \ldots + \frac{CF_n}{(1+r)^n}$$

where PV = Present value

CF = Cash flow, interest, dividend or earnings per time period upto 'n' number of periods

r = Risk-adjusted discount rate (generally the interest rate)

The role of 'buying and selling pressures' which make prices more towards value is very important. Now, you would ask: 'what these pressures are and how do they occur? You will briefly understand that 'investor action' in the wake of revisions of values spurs such pressures.

You would recall that investment strategies can be 'passive' or 'active'. Following this, investors and investment managers can also be broadly grouped in 'passive' and 'active' categories. You should note that buying and selling pressures dominantly originate with active investors. And they follow certain rules of the game which are outlined below:

Rule 1: Buy when value is more than price. This underlines the fact that shares are underpriced and it would be a bargain to buy now and sell when prices move up toward value.

Rule 2: Sell when value is less than price. In a situation like this, shares would be overpriced and it would be advantageous to sell them now and avoid less when price later moves down to the level of the value.

Rule 3: Don't trade when value is equal to price. This is a state when the market price is in equilibrium and is not expected to change.

Q4. How is the intrinsic value of a bond or debenture calculated?

Ans. The intrinsic value of a bond or debenture is equal to the present value of its expected cash flows. The coupon interest payments, and the principal repayment are known and the present value is determined by discounting these future payments from the issuer at an appropriate discount rate or market yield. The usual present value calculations are made with the help of the following equation :–

$$\text{PV} = \sum_{i=1}^{n} \frac{C}{(1+r)^{`}} + \frac{TV}{(1+r)^{``}}$$

Where PV = the present value of the security today (i.e., time period zero)
C = coupons or interest payments per time period `t'
TV = the terminal value repayable at maturity; this could be at par, premium, or even at discount (in extraordinary cases)
r = the appropriate discount rate or market yield
n = the number of years of maturity

Now, consider a bond (Bond-B) with a face value of Rs. 1,000 issued five years ago at a coupon of 6%. The bond had a maturity period of ten years and as of today, therefore, five more years are left for final repayment at par. The current discount rate is 10 per cent and interest is paid annually.

The present value of bond-B will be determined as follows :

$$PV_B = \frac{Rs.60}{1+.10} + \frac{Rs.60}{(1+.10)^2} + \frac{Rs.60}{(1+.10)^3} + \frac{Rs.60}{(1+.10)^4} + \frac{Rs.60 + Rs.1000}{(1+.10)^5}$$

$= 60\times.9091+60\times.8264+60\times.7513+60\times.6830+1060\times.6209$

$= 54.55+48.59+45.08+40.98+658.15$

= Rs. 847.35

If the interest payments are made semi-annual, the PV equation will have to be modified as follows: divide 'C', and `r' both by 2 and multiply `n' by 2. The resultant equation will be:

$$PV = \sum_{t=1}^{2n} \frac{C_{t/2}}{(1+r/2)^t} + \frac{TV}{(1+r/2)^{2n}}$$

Q5. Explain the concept of:

(a) Current Yield

Ans. Current yield : This is calculated as follows :

$$\text{Current yield} = \frac{\text{Stated (coupon) interest per year}}{\text{Current market price}}$$

For example, if a 15% Rs. 200 debenture is currently selling for Rs. 220 the annual current yield would be:

$$\frac{Rs.30}{Rs.220} = 13.64\%$$

Current yield is a superior measure to coupon rate because it is based on the current market price. However, it does not account for the difference between the purchase price of the bond/debenture and its maturity value.

(b) Yield to Maturity

Ans. Yield-to-maturity (YTM): It may be defined as the indicated (promised) compounded rate of return an investor will receive from a bond purchased at the current market price and held to maturity. Computing YTM involves equating the current market price of a bond with the discounted value of future interest payments and the terminal principal repayment; the YTM is IRR of initial investment (market price) and periodic payments including principal amount received at the end of the period.

Assume that an investor purchases a 15%, Rs. 500 fully secured non-convertible debentures at the current market price of Rs. 400. The debenture is to be repaid at the end of five years from today. The yield-to-maturity can be estimated as follows :

$$MP = \sum_{t=1}^{n} \frac{C_t}{(1+YTM)^t} + \frac{TV}{(1+YTM)^n}$$

$$\text{or, Rs.}400 = \sum_{t=1}^{5} \frac{Rs.75}{(1+YTM)^t} + \frac{Rs.500}{(1+YTM)^5}$$

By trial & error, we get YTM=22.07%

YTM is just a promised yield and the investor cannot earn it unless the bond/ debenture is held to maturity. Secondly, the YTM concept is a compound interest concept with the investor earning interest-on-interest at YTM throughout the holding period till maturity. If intermediate cash flows are not reinvested at YTM, the realized yield actually earned will differ from the promised YTM.

YTM can be approximated and tedious calculations be avoided using the following formula :–

$$\text{Approximate YTM} = \frac{\text{Coupon Interest } + [(MP_n - MP_t)]/N}{[(MP_n - MP_t)]/2}, \text{ where } MP_n \text{ is}$$

market price at maturity and MP_t is market price (or cost) at beginning. In the above example, the approximate YTM is

$$= \frac{75 + [(500\text{–}400)/5]}{(500+400)/2} = \frac{95}{450} = 21.11\%$$

(c) Preference Shares

Ans. Preference shares are a hybrid security. They have some features of bonds and some of equity shares. Theoretically, preference shares are considered a perpetual security but there are convertible, callable, redeemable and other similar features, which enable issuers to terminate them within a finite time horizon. In the case of redeemable preference shares, legal mandates require creation of redemption sinking funds and their earmarked investments to ensure funds for repayment.

Preference dividends are specified like bonds. This has to be done because they rank prior to equity shares for dividends.

Preference shares are less risky than equity because their dividends are specified and all arrears must be paid before equity holders get dividends. They are, however, more risky than bonds because the latter enjoy priority in payment and in liquidation. Bonds are secured also and enjoy protection of principal, which is ordinarily not available to preference shares. Investors' required returns on preference shares are more than those on bonds but less than on equity shares.

(d) Active Investment Strategy

Ans. Active Investment Strategy : A form of investment management which involves buying and selling financial assets with the objective of earning positive risk-adjusted returns.

(e) Passive Investment Strategy

Ans. Passive Investment Strategy: A strategy whereby investors do not actively seek out trading possibilities in an attempt to out perform the market.

(f) P/E Ratio

Ans. P/E Ratio : The ratio of share price to earnings using historical, current or estimated data. This ratio is also referred to as multiplier.

Q6. How is the intrinsic value of preference shares estimated?

Ans. Since dividends from preference shares are assumed to be perpetual payments, the intrinsic value of such shares will be estimated from the following equation

$$V_{ps} = \frac{D}{K_{Ps}}$$

where D = Preference Dividend

K_{Ps} = required rate of return

V_{ps} = value of preference share

Consider Firm-A issuing preference shares of Rs. 100 each with a specified dividend of Rs. 11.5 per share. Now, if the investors' required rate of return corresponding to the risk-level of Firm-A is 10% the value today of the share would be :

$$V_{ps} = \frac{\text{Rs.}11.50}{.10} = Rs.115.00$$

Q7. Explain dividend valuation model which is used to estimate the value of equity shares.

Ans. Dividend Valuation Model

Under dividend valuation model, future dividends are discounted at the required rate to get the value of share. There are three possible situations on future dividend.

(a) Dividends do not grow in future i.e., the constant or zero growth assumption,

(b) Dividends grow at a constant rate in future, i.e., the constant-growth assumption, Dividends grow at varying rates in future time periods i.e., multiple-growth assumption.

(c) The dividend valuation model is now discussed under the above three situations

(a) The zero-growth Case :

The value of equity share will be $V = \frac{D_t}{K}$

where V = value of equity share

D_t = dividend

K = dividend capitalisation rate

(b) The Constant Growth Case : When dividends grow in all future periods at a uniform rate 'g',

$$V = \frac{D_0(1+g)}{K-g} = \frac{D_t}{K-g}$$

(c) The Multiple-Growth Case : The multiple-growth assumption has to be made in a vast number of practical situations. The infinite future time-period is viewed as divisible into two or more different growth segments. The investor must forecast the time `T' upto which growth would be variable and after which only the growth rate would show a pattern and would be constant. This would mean that present value calculations will have to be spread over two phases viz., one phase would last until time 'T' and the other would begin after `T' to infinity.

The present value of all dividends forecast upto and including time `T' $V_{T(i)}$ would be: (3.15)

$$V_{T(i)} = \sum_{t=1}^{T} \frac{D_t}{(1+K)^t}$$

The second phase present value is denoted by $V_{T(2)}$ and would be based on constant growth dividends forecast after time `T'.

The present value of the second phase stream of dividends can, therefore, be estimated at time 'T':

$$V_T = D_{T+1}\left(\frac{1}{K-g}\right)$$

Hence, when this value has to be viewed at time `zero', it must be discounted to provide the present value at `zero' time for the second phase present value.

The latter can also be viewed at time `zero' as a series of cash dividends that grow a constant rate as already stated. The resulting second phase value $V_{T(2)}$ will be given by the following equation:

$$V_{T(2)} = V_T\left(\frac{1}{(1+K)^T}\right)$$

$$= \frac{D_{T+1}}{(K-g)(1+K)^T}$$

Now, the two present values of phase 1 and phase 2 can be added to estimate the intrinsic value of an equity share that will pass through a multiple growth situation. The following describes the summation procedure of the two phases:

$$V_0 = V_{T(1)} + V_{T(2)}$$

$$= \sum_{t=1}^{T} \frac{D_t}{(1+K)^t} + \frac{D_{T+1}}{(K-g)(1+K)^T}$$

Q8. How the P/E ratio is used to estimate the value of equity shares?

Ans. The PIE approach is fairly simple widely followed in the stock market. The first step under this model is estimating future earnings per share. Next, the normal price-earnings ratio will be found. Product of these two estimates will give the expected price. The most practical way of using P/E model is first computing the industry average P/E or P/E of similar firm and then multiplying the same with the expected or actual earning of the stock. P/E of an industry is expected to be high when the industry is in high growth industry. P/E will be low if the industry or firm is expected to show a low growth rate. P/E is also affected by the risk associated with the earnings.

Value = EPS × P/E Ratio

$$\text{where EPS} = \frac{\text{Profits after tax - Preference Dividend}}{\text{Number of Equity Shares}}$$

Practical Questions :

Q1. A bond of Rs. 10,000 bearing coupon rate 12% and redeemable in 8 years at par is being traded at Rs. 10,600. Find out the YTM of the bond.

Ans. The given situation can be presented as follows:

$$10,600 = \sum_{i=1}^{8} \frac{1200}{(1+YTM)^i} + \frac{Rs.10,000}{(1+YTM)^8}$$

or $10,600 = 1200 \times PVAF_{(YTM,8)} + 10,000 + PVF_{(YTM,8)}$

Now, the value of right-hand side of this equation is to be found for different values of YTM.

At YTM = 10%, the value is = 1,200 × 5.335 + 10,000 × .467

= Rs. 11,072

At YTM = 11%, the value is = 1,200 × 5.146 + 10,000 × .434

= Rs. 10,515

The above calculation shows that at 10%, the value is 11,072 and at 11%, the value is Rs. 10,515. But what is the discount rate at which the value comes to 10,600. This can be found by interpolating between 10% and 11% as follows:

$$YTM = 10\% + \frac{11,072 - 10,600}{11,072 - 10,515}$$

= 10.85%

So, the YTM of the bond is 10.85%.

Q2. A bond of Rs. 1,000 bearing a coupon rate of 12% payable half yearly is redeemable after 5 years. Find out the value of the bond and compare with the value of the bond if the interest is payable annually. The required rate of return of the investor is 14%.

Ans. Basic information Annual Interest = Rs. 120

k_d = 14%

n = 5 years

RV = Rs. 1,000.

Value of the bond is :

= 60 ($PVAF_{7\%,\ 10}$) + 1,000 ($PVF_{7\%,\ 10}$)

= 60 (7.024) + 1,000 (.508)

= Rs. 929.

So, the value of the bond is Rs. 929. In the same case, if the interest is payable on yearly interval, then the value of the bond is as follows:

= 120 ($PVAF_{14\%,\ 5y}$) + 1,000 ($PVF_{14\%,\ 5y}$)

= 120 (3.433) + 1000 (.519)

= Rs. 931.

Q3. A Rs. 1,000 bond matures in 20 years and offers a 9% coupon rate. The required rate of return is 11%. Compute the bond's value.

Ans. The annual interest payment is Rs. 90. At the end of the year 20, the bondholder receives Rs. 90 interest payment and the Rs. 1,000 par value. The present value of the interest payment is obtained by using the present-

value annuity factor for 11% and 20 payments:
PV = Interest × ($PVAF_{11\%,\ 20\ y}$)
PV = Rs. 90 × (7.693)
= Rs. 719.67
The present value of the Rs. 1,000 principal repayment is obtained by using the present value, single-payment factor for 11% and 20 years:
PV = Amount × ($PVF_{11\%,\ 20\ y}$)
= Rs. 1,000 × (.124)
= Rs. 124
Therefore, the bond's value is Rs. 840.67 (Rs. 716.67 + 124.00).
In this example, the discount rate exceeds the coupon rate. As a consequence, the bond's intrinsic value is less than its par value.

Q4. A Rs. 5,000 bond with a 10% coupon rate matures in 8 years and currently sells at 97%. Is this bond a desirable investment for an investor whose required rate of return is 11%.
Ans. The present value of the bond is:
PV = Interest × ($PVAF_{11\%,\ 8y}$) + Face Value × ($PVF_{11\%,\ 8y}$)
= Rs. 500 × (5.146) + Rs. 5,000 × (.434)
= Rs. 4,743
Current Price = Rs. 5,000 × 97% = Rs. 4,850
Since, the bond is available at a price higher than its present value of returns, the investment in bond is not desirable.

Q5. Large Events Ltd. has recently paid a dividend of Rs. 3.50 per share. The dividends are growing at 10% p.a. and the equity capitalization rate applicable to the company is 12%. Find the implicit PE ratio if the EPS of the company is Rs. 7.
Ans. The value of the share as per constant growth rate is:

$$P_0 = \frac{D_1}{k_e - g}$$

$$= \frac{Rs.3.50(1.10)}{.12 - .10} = \frac{Rs.3.85}{.02} = Rs.192.50$$

EPS = Rs. 7 (given)

$$\text{P/E Ratio} = \frac{MP}{EPS} = \frac{Rs.192.50}{7} = 27.5$$

So, the P/E ratio for the company is 27.5.

Q6. The current market price of a share is Rs. 65 and it is expected to be Rs. 90 after 1 year. Dividend expected after 1 year from now is Rs. 2.90. Find out the equity capitalization rate.

Ans. As per discounted cash flow model:

$$P_0 = \frac{Div_1}{(1+k_e)^1} + \frac{P_1}{(1+k_e)^1}$$

$$Rs.65 = \frac{Rs.2.90}{(1+k_e 1)^1} + \frac{Rs.90}{(1+k_e)^1}$$

$$k_e = \frac{Rs.2.90 + Rs.90}{Rs.65} - 1$$

= 42.9%

So, the equity capitalization rate is 42.9%.

Q7. Air Mail Ltd. has just paid a dividend of Rs. 2 per share. In view of the rapid growth of company, the dividend is expected to grow at 20% p.a. for next 3 years. After that the process will slow down and the earnings are expected to grow only at 7% p.a. In view of the risk involved in the investment, a return of 22% is considered. Find out the price an investor should be ready to pay for the shares.

Ans. The case can be taken up as a multiple growth rate case, where

$$P_0 = \sum_{i=1}^{n} \frac{Div_i}{(1+k_e)^i} + P_n \times \frac{1}{(1+k_e)^m}$$

In the given situation the PV of Dividend for first 3 years is:

Year	Dividend	$PVF_{(22, n)}$	PV
1	$2\,(1.20)^1$ = Rs. 2.40	.820	Rs. 1.97
2	$2\,(1.20)^2$ = 2.88	.672	1.94
3	$2\,(1.20)^3$ = 3.46	.551	1.91
			5.82

Value of the share at the end of year 3, $P_3 = \frac{D_4}{k_e - g} = \frac{3.46(1.07)}{.22 - .07}$

$$= \frac{3.70}{.15} = Rs.24.67$$

Value of the share today, P_0 = Rs. 5.82 + Rs. 24.67 × $PVF_{(22, 3)}$

= Rs. 5.82 + Rs. 24.67 × .551
= Rs. 19.41

Q8. GullyBaba.com Ltd. has just paid its annual dividend of Rs. 3 per share on the equity shares having face value of Rs. 10. The dividend rate is expected to grow at the rate of 8% p.a. forever. The company belongs to a risk-group for which the equity capitalization rate of 14% is found to be consistent.
What is the intrinsic value of the share? Would the value be different if the company belongs to a risk class of 16%?

Ans. In the given case, the value of equity shares may be found as per the constant growth formula as follows:

D_0 = Rs. 3
g = 8%
D_1 = 3 (1 + .08) = Rs. 3.24

$$P_0 = \frac{D_1}{k_e - g} = \frac{Rs.3.24}{.14 - .08} = Rs.54$$

However, if the company belongs to risk class of 16%, the value would be:

$$P_{0-} = \frac{Rs.3.24}{.16 - .08} = Rs.40.50$$

Q9. GullyBaba.com Ltd. is currently paying dividend of Re. 1 and it is expected to grow at 7% p.a. infinitely. What is the value if:
(i) The equity capitalization rate is 15%,
(ii) The equity capitalization rate is 16%,
(iii) The growth rate is 8% instead of 7%, and
(iv) The equity capitalization rate is 16% and the growth rate is 4%.

Ans. (i) The Basic Information
D_0 = Re. 1
g = 7%
k_e = 15%
Now, D_1 = 1 (1 + .07) = Rs. 1.07

$$P_0 = \frac{D_1}{k_e - g} = \frac{1.07}{.15 - .07} = Rs.13.38$$

(ii) If k_e = 16%

$$P_0 = \frac{D_1}{k_e - g} = \frac{1.07}{.16 - .07} = Rs.11.89$$

(iii) If g = 8% (k_e = 15%)

$$P_0 = \frac{D_1}{k_e - g} = \frac{1(1.08)}{.15 - .08} = \frac{1.08}{.07} = Rs.15.43$$

(iv) If k_e = 16% and g = 4%

$$P_0 = \frac{D_1}{k_e - g} = \frac{1(1.04)}{.16 - .04} = \frac{1.04}{.12} = Rs.8.67$$

Q10. The earning per share of Gullybaba Couriers Ltd. is Rs. 1.50. The investors expect that a PE ratio of 32 is appropriate for this company. What should be the price of the share? If the share is currently available for Rs. 45 or Rs. 50, should an investor buy?

Ans. In the given case, EPS = Rs. 1.50

PE = 32

Value = 32 × 1.50

= Rs. 48

Now, if the share is available for Rs. 45, it should be purchased by an investor. However, at a price of Rs. 50, it is not recommended.

Q11. Equity shares of Gullybaba Gas Ltd. are currently selling at Rs. 60. The company is expected to pay a dividend of Rs. 3 after 1 year, with a growth rate of 8%. Find out the implied required rate of return of the equity investors.

Ans. As per constant growth model, $P_0 = \frac{D_1}{k_e - g}$

or $k_e = \frac{D_1}{P_0} + g$

$$= \frac{Rs.3}{Rs.60} + .08$$

= .13 or 13%

Q12. Following information is available in respect of a bond:

Face Value	**Rs. 1,000**	**Coupon Rate**	**8%**
Life	**3 Years**	**Maturity**	**At par**
Expected Yield	**10%**		

How much price an investor should be ready to pay for the bond if the interest is payable half yearly or yearly basis?

Ans. Valuation of bond if interest is payable half yearly :

$$B_0 = \sum_{i=1}^{6} \frac{Rs.40}{(1+.05)^i} + \frac{Rs.1,000}{(1+.05)^6}$$

= Rs. 40 × $PVAF_{(5, 6)}$ + Rs. 1,000 × $PVF_{(5, 6)}$

= Rs. 40 × 5.076 + Rs. 1,000 × .746

= Rs. 949.04

Valuation of bond if the interest is payable yearly:

B_0 = Rs. 80 × $PVAF_{(10, 3)}$ + Rs. 1,000 × $PVF_{(10, 3)}$

= Rs. 80 × 2.487 + Rs. 1,000 × .751

= Rs. 949.96

It may be noted that different values are obtained for annual and semi-annual interest payments. In both the cases, the value is less than the par value because the required yield (10%) is more than the coupon rate (8%).

Q13. An investor is considering the purchase of the following bond:

Face Value	**Rs. 100**
Coupon Rate	**11%**
Maturity	**3 years**

(i) If he wants a yield of 13%, what is the maximum price he should be ready to pay for?

(ii) If the bond is selling for Rs. 97.60, what would be his yield?

Ans. Calculation of Maximum Price: The price which will give a yield of 13% to the investor may be found as follows :

B_0 = Rs. 11 × $PVAF_{(13, 3)}$ + Rs. 100 × $PVF_{(13, 3)}$

= Rs. 11 × 2.361 + Rs. 100 × .693

= Rs. 95.27

Calculation of Yield: If the bond is selling at Rs. 97.60 which is more than the fair value, the YTM of the bond would be less than 13%.

At 12%, the value = Rs. 11 × $PVAF_{(12, 3)}$ + Rs. 100 × $PVF_{(12, 3)}$

= Rs. 11 × 2.402 + Rs. 100 × .712

= Rs. 97.62

∴ YTM = 12%

BLOCK – 2

Securities Market in India

Chapter – 4

Indian Stock Market: Organisation and Functioning

Q1. Write a lucid note on the structure of primary and secondary markets in India?

OR

What are the different types of securities markets? What are their role and functions? [June 2005, Q2(a)] [Dec 2005, Q1(b)]

Ans. Securities of various companies, from time to time, to raise funds in order to meet their financial requirements for modernization, expansion and diversification programmes, are issued directly to the investor (both individual as well as institutional) through the mechanism called primary market or new issue market. The primary market refers to the set up which helps the industry to raise funds by issuing different types of securities. This set up consists of the type of securities available, financial institutions and the regulatory framework. The structure of primary markets has two distinguishing features:
(i) It is the segment of the capital market where capital formation occurs, and
(ii) In order to obtain required financing, new issue of shares, debentures and other securities are sold in the primary market. Subsequent trading in these securities occurs in other segment of the capital market, known as secondary market.

In the primary market, new issues May be made in three ways, namely, public issue, rights issue, and private placement. Public Issues involves sale of securities to members of public. Rights issue involves sale of securities to the existing shareholders/debenture holders. Private placement involves selling securities privately to a selected group of investors. In the primary market, equity shares, fully convertible debentures (FCD), partially convertible debentures (PCD), and nonconvertible debentures(NCD) are the securities commonly issued by non-government public limited companies. Government companies issue equity shares and bonds. Primary market has become very active in India after the abolition of Controller of Capital Issue. You can refer In the primary market, issues are made either 'at par' or `at premium'. Pricing the new Issues is regulated under `Guidelines on Capital Issues' or what are also known as "Guidelines for Disclosure and Investors Protection" issued by the Securities and Exchange Board of India (SEBI).

Some of the steps involved in a public issue are : –

(a) Appointment of underwriters: The underwriters are appointed who commit to shoulder the liability and subscribe to the shortfall in case the issue is undersubscribed. For this commitment they are entitled to a commission upto maximum of 2.5 % on the amount underwritten.

(b) Appointment of Bankers: Bankers along with their branch network act as the collecting agencies and process the funds procured during the public issue. The Banks provide temporary loans for the period between the issue date and the date the issue proceeds becomes available after allotment, which is referred to as a `bridge loan'.

(c) Appointment of Registrars: Registrars process the application forms, tabulate the amounts collected during the Issue and initiate the allotment procedures.

(d) Appointment of the brokers to the Issue: Recognized members of the Stock exchanges are appointed as brokers to the Issue for marketing the Issue. They are eligible for a maximum brokerage of 1.5%.

(e) Filing of prospectus with the Registrar of Companies: The draft prospectus along with the copies of the agreements entered into with the Lead Manager, Underwriters, Bankers, Registrars and Brokers to the issue is filed with the Registrar of Companies of the state where the registered office of the company is located.

(f) Printing and dispatch of Application forms: The prospectus and application forms are printed and dispatched to all the merchant bankers, underwriters, brokers to the issue.

(g) Filing of the initial listing application: A letter is sent to the Stock exchanges where the issue is proposed to be listed giving the details and stating the intent of getting the shares listed on the Exchange.

(h) Statutory announcement: An abridged version of the prospectus and the Issue start and close dates are published in major English dailies and vernacular newspapers.

(i) Processing of applications: After the close of the Public Issue all the application forms are scrutinized, tabulated and then shares are allotted against these applications.

(j) Establishing the liability of the underwriter: In case the Issue is not fully subscribed to, then the liability for the subscription falls on the underwriters who have to subscribe to the shortfall, in case they have not procured the amount committed by them as per the Underwriting agreement.
(k) Allotment of shares: after the Issue is subscribed to the minimum level, the allotment procedure as prescribed by SEBI is initiated.
(l) Listing of the Issue: The shares after having been allotted have to be listed compulsorily in the regional stock exchange and optionally at the other stock exchanges.

Secondary Market : The secondary market is the segment in which outstanding issues are traded and thus provide liquidity. Investors, who seek both profitability and liquidity, need both primary and secondary markets. There is thus a direct and complementary interface between the primary and secondary markets. Secondary market exists both for short-term (money market) securities and long-term securities. It exists for debt, equity and a variety of hybrid securities. While the secondary market activities in money market securities are conducted over phone or through market makers, the trading is more organized for long-term securities and conducted through stock exchanges. Buying and selling securities in secondary market is fairly simple. Investors have to open an account with a member of stock exchange and then place orders through the member.
Technology has converted stock exchanges into a virtual institution. Thanks to development in telecommunication and information technology, the physical constraint was removed during the last few years. National Stock Exchange today has its presence everywhere in the country. Bombay Stock Exchange has also expanded its network. This new development has improved transparency of operations and brought down the cost. Today, stockbrokers are operating from their office through computer network and investors can see the price at which the transactions are settled. Internet based stock braking allows investors to enter into transactions by themselves without contacting their brokers directly. Competition has brought down the brokerage from 2% to in India around 0.5% and today the brokerage rate in India is one of the lowest in the world.

Q2. What are the different entities/players operating in secondary markets? [Dec 2007, Q2(a)]
Ans. Members of stock exchanges, called stock brokers, are intermediary between buyers and sellers. Buying and selling securities through members of

stock exchange is beneficial, legally and functionally. Entry of major institutions like ICICI, Kotak Mahindra, into brokerage services and development in technology including internet based broking service have improved the quality of service.

Clearing corporation enables the members to settle the transactions entered among themselves on behalf of their client-investors. Earlier when securities are traded in physical form, a large number of securities have to be exchanged between members and clearing corporation had a major work on this part. Today, after depository facility was introduced, the workload of the clearing corporations has come down significantly. Clearing corporation today facilitate the members to transfer (or receive) securities to (or from) depositories and also settle monetary part of the transactions. It is an institution exclusively serving the brokers.

Depository service is another major development in the Indian stock market. It allows investors to hold securities in electronic form (like you are holding cash in your bank account) and transfers electronically when they sell the shares. Investors have to open a depository account with a member of depository service provider (we have two depository service providers in India - National Securities Depository Ltd and Central Depository Services (India) Limited). Investors can give physical securities that they are holding for cancellation (provided depository facility is available for the securities/ company) and convert them in to electronic holding. A large number of companies have depository holding facility and SEBI has put it compulsory to trade certain stocks only under depository mode. When an investor apply new shares next time in the primary market, they can ask the issuer to credit the depository account in the event of successful allotment. Any new purchases in the secondary market can also be credited in the depository account. Investors will get periodical statement on their holding from the member with whom the depository account is maintained.

Under depository mode, the shares are transferred in a short period of time without any further action from your side.

Transfer agents maintains the members register of the companies. On the instructions of the company, they transfer the shares from the existing members to new member. When an investor buys a share in a physical mode and intend to transfer the share in her/his name, she/he has to send the transfer deed along with share certificate to the Transfer Agent.

After initial verification, they will place the shares received for transfer for the approval of company's Board. The shares are transferred in the name of investors after the approval of the Board and investor will receive communication to this effect along with share certificates from the Transfer Agent. Some companies perform this transfer of shares internally whereas many leading companies have outsourced this service by appointing one of these transfer agents. The process of verification and other formalities connected with transfer has been simplified after the introduction of depository services.

Securities and Exchange Board of India (SEBI) regulates the Institutions and Intermediaries connected with the securities to protect the interest of investors.

Some of the major achievements of SEBI so far are bringing transparency in the securities market operation, speeding up the technological progress and improving disclosure norms. SEBI is struggling hard to prevent insider trading and price rigging. Since regulation is a complex task, it will take time to complete the process.

Q3. Give salient features of SEBI guidelines for IPO. What is the eligibility criteria for an IPO?

Ans. An Indian Company is allowed to make an IPO if : –

(1) The company has a track record of dividend paying capability for 3 out of the immediately preceding 5 years;

(2) A public financial institution or scheduled commercial bank has appraised the project to be financed through the proposed offer and the appraising agency participates in the financing of the project to the extent of at least 10% of the Project cost. Typically a new company has to compulsorily issue shares at par, while the companies with a track record can issue shares at a premium.

The salient features of SEBI guidelines on IPO are given below :–

(1) Promoters should contribute a minimum of 20% of the total issued capital, if the company is an unlisted one.

Promoter's contribution is subject to a lock-in period of 3 years.

(2) Net Offer to the General Public has to be at least 25% of the Total Issue size for listing on a Stock Exchange.

(3) Minimum of 50% of the Net offer to the Public has to be reserved for Investors applying for 10 or less than 10 marketable lots of shares.

(4) In an Issue of more than Rs. 100 crores the issuer is allowed to place the whole issue by book-building.

(5) There should be at-least 5 investors for every 1 lakh of equity offered.

(6) Allotment has to be made within 30 days of the closure of the Public Issue and 42 days in case of a Rights Issue.

(7) All the listing formalities for a Public Issue has to be completed within 70 days from the date of closure of the subscription list.
(8) Indian Development Financial Institutions and Mutual Funds can be allotted securities upto 75% of the Issue Amount.

Indian Stock Market :
(9) Allotment to categories of FII's and NRI's/OCB's is upto a maximum of 24% which can be further extended to 30% by an application to the RBI - supported by a resolution passed in the General Meeting.
(10) 10% individual ceiling for each category a) Permanent employees b) Shareholding of the promoting companies
(11) Securities issued to the promoter, his group companies by way of firm allotment and reservation have a lock-in period of 3 years. However shares allotted to FII's and certain Indian and Multilateral Development Financial Institutions and Indian Mutual Funds are not subject to Lock-in periods.
(12) The minimum period for which a Public Issue has to be kept open is 3 working days and the maximum for which it can be kept open is 10 working days. The minimum period for a Rights Issue is 15 working days and the maximum is 60 working days.
(13) A public issue is effected if the issue is able to procure 90% of the Total issue size within 60 days from the date of earliest closure of the Public Issue. In case of over-subscription the company may have the right to retain the excess application money and allot shares more than the proposed Issue which is referred to as the `green-shoe' option.
(14) A Rights Issue has to procure 90% subscription in 60 days of the opening of the Issue.

Q4. Briefly explain the role and function of stock exchanges in India? [June 2007, Q1(b)]

OR

Discuss the importance of stock exchanges in India?

OR

'Stock exchanges serve the role of a barometer of the nations economy'. Comment.

Ans. There are 23 stock exchanges in India, some of them being regional ones with allocated areas. Three others set up in the reforms era, viz., National Stock Exchange (NSE), the Over the Counter Exchange of India Limited (OTCEI), and Interconnected Stock Exchange of India Limited (ISE) have mandate to nationwide trading network.
Stock exchanges have a very important function to fulfil in the country's

economy. The Supreme Court of India has enunciated the role of the stock exchanges in these words:

"A Stock Exchange fulfils a vital function in the economic development of a nation: its main function is to `qualify' capital by enabling a person who has invested money in, say a factory or a railway, to convert it into cash by disposing off his shares in the enterprise to someone else. Investment in joint stock companies is attractive to the public, because the value of the shares is announced day after day in the stock exchanges, and shares quoted on the exchanges are capable of almost immediate conversion into money.

The stock exchange is really an essential pillar of the private sector corporate economy. It discharges three essential functions in the process of capital formation and in raising resources for the corporate sector. They are :

First, the stock exchange provides a market place for purchase and sale of securities viz., shares, bonds, debentures, etc. It, therefore, ensures the free transferability of securities which is the essential basis for the joint stock enterprise system. At the same time those who wish to invest their surplus funds in securities for long-term capital appreciation or for speculative gain can also buy stocks of their choice in the market.

Secondly, the stock exchange provides the linkage between the savings in the household sector and the investment in corporate economy. It mobilizes savings, channelises them as securities into those enterprises which are favoured by the investors on the basis of such criteria as future growth prospects, good returns and appreciation of prevalence on the Indian scene of such interventionist factors as industrial licensing, provision of credit to private sector by public sector development banks, price controls and foreign exchange regulations. The stock exchanges discharge this function by laying down a number of regulations which have to be complied with while making public issues. The broker community provides an organic linkage between the primary and the secondary markets in India

Thirdly, by providing a market quotation of the prices of shares and bonds, a sort of collective judgement simultaneously reached by many buyers and sellers in the market-the stock exchanges serves the role of a barometer, not only of the state of health of individual companies, but also of the nation's economy as a whole. It is often not realised that changes in share prices are brought about by a complex set of factors, all operating on the markets simultaneously. Share values as a whole are subject to secular trends set by the economic progress of the nation, and governed by factors like general economic situation, financial and monetary policies, tax changes, political environment, international economic and financial developments, etc. These trends are influenced to some extent by periodical cycles of booms and depressions in the free market economies.

These factors, both long-term and short-term, act as macro influences on the corporate sector and the level of stock prices as a whole, there is also a set of micro influences relating to prospects of individual companies such as the reputation of the management, the state of industrial relations in the enterprises, the volume of retained earnings and the related prospects of capitalization of reserves, etc., which have a bearing on the level of prices.

Another important function that the stock exchanges in India discharge is of providing a market for gilt-edged securities i.e. securities issued by the Central Government, State government, Municipalities, Improvement Trusts and other public bodies. These securities are automatically listed on the stock exchanges when they are issued and transactions in these take place regularly on the stock exchanges.

Q5. Describe the trading system followed by National Stock Exchange (NSE).

Ans. NSE operates on the 'National Exchange for Automated Trading' (NEAT) system, a fully automated screen based trading system, which adopts the principle of an order driven market. NSE consciously opted in favour of an order driven system as opposed to a quote driven system. This has helped reduce jobbing spreads not only on NSE but in other exchanges as well, thus reducing transaction costs. Till the advent of NSE, an investor wanting to transact in a security not traded on the nearest exchange had to route orders through a series of correspondent brokers to the appropriate exchange. This resulted in a great deal of uncertainty and high transaction costs. NSE has made it possible for an investor to access the same market and order book, irrespective of location, at the same price and at the same cost.

The best buy order is matched with the best sell order. An order may match partially with another order resulting in multiple trades. For order matching, the best buy order is the one with the highest price and the best sell order is the one with the lowest price. This is because the system views all buy orders available from the point of view of a seller and all sell orders from the point of view of the buyers in the market.

Members can proactively enter orders in the system which will be displayed in the system till the full quantity is matched by one or more of counter-orders and result into trade(s) or is cancelled by the member. Alternatively, members may be reactive and put in orders that match with existing orders in the system. Orders lying unmatched in the system are `passive' orders and orders that come in to match the existing orders are called `active' orders. Orders are always matched at the passive order price. This ensures that the earlier orders get priority over the orders that come in later.

Q6. Explain the different order conditions that a trading member can enter depending upon his requirements.

Ans. A Trading Member can enter various types of orders depending upon his/her requirements. These conditions are broadly classified into three categories: time related conditions, price-related conditions and quantity related conditions.

Time Conditions

• **DAY** - A Day order, as the name suggests, is an order which is valid for the day on which it is entered. If the order is not matched during the day, the order gets cancelled automatically at the end of the trading day.

• **GTC** - A Good Till Cancelled (GTC) order is an order that remains in the system until it is cancelled by the Trading Member. It will therefore be able to span trading days if it does not get matched. The maximum number of days a GTC order can remain in the system is notified by the Exchange from time to time.

• **GTD** - A Good Till Days/Date (GTD) order allows the Trading Member to specify the days/date up to which the order should stay in the system. At the end of this period the order will get flushed from the system. Each day/date counted is a calendar day and inclusive of holidays. The days/date counted are inclusive of the day/date on which the order is placed.

• **IOC** - An Immediate or Cancel (IOC) order allows a Trading Member to buy or sell a security as soon as the order is released into the market, failing which the order will be removed from the market. Partial match is possible for the order, and the unmatched portion of the order is cancelled immediately.

Price Conditions

• **Limit Price/Order** - An order which allows the price to be specified while entering the order into the system.

• **Market Price/Order** - An order to buy or sell securities at the best price obtainable at the time of entering the order.

• **Stop Loss (SL) Price/Order** - The one which allows the Trading Member to place an order which gets activated only when the market price of the relevant security reaches or crosses a threshold price. Until then the order does not enter the market.

Quantity Conditions

• **Disclosed Quantity (DQ)**- An order with a DQ condition allows the Trading Member to disclose only a part of the order quantity to the market. For example, an order of 1000 with a disclosed quantity condition of 200 will mean that 200 is displayed to the market at a time. After this is traded, another 200 is automatically released and so on till the full order is executed. The Exchange may set a minimum disclosed quantity criteria from time to time.

• **MF** - Minimum Fill (MF) orders allow the Trading Member to specify the minimum quantity by which an order should be filled. For example, an order of 1000 units with minimum fill 200 will require that each trade be for at least 200 units. In other words, there will be a maximum of 5 trades of 200 each or a single trade of 1000. The Exchange may lay down norms of MF from time to time.

• **AON** - All or None orders allow a Trading Member to impose the condition that only the full order should be matched against. This may be by way of multiple trades. If the full order is not matched it will stay in the books till matched or cancelled.

Q7. Write short notes on :

(a) Right Issue [June 2005, Q2(a)] [Dec 2006, Q1(b)]

Ans. The rights Issue involves selling of securities to the existing shareholders in proportion to their current holding. When a company issues additional equity capital, it has to be offered in the first instance to the existing shareholders on a pro-rata basis as per Section 81 of the Companies Act, 1956. The shareholders may by a special resolution forfeit this right, partially or fully by a special resolution to enable the company to issue additional capital to the public or alternatively by passing a simple resolution and taking the permission of the Central Government. There is no restriction on pricing of rights Issues.

(b) Private Placement [June 2005, Q2(a)] [Dec 2006, Q1(b)]

Ans. A private placement results from the sale of securities by the company to one or few investors. The issuers are normally the listed public limited companies or closely held public or private limited companies which cannot access the primary market. The securities are placed normally with the Institutional investors, Mutual funds or other Financial Institutions. In a number of cases, Indian companies have also offered shares to promoters under this route. SEBI has issued a separate guideline for pricing of such preferential offers.

(c) Dematerialisation

Ans. The depositories system enables the conversion of physical securities (i.e., the certificates) into electronic from through a process of dematerialisation of certificates. The securities in the depositories mode are fungible and cease to have any distinctive number.

(d) Rematerialisation

Ans. When the investors convert their shares from depository mode to physical mode then the process involved is known as 'rematerialisation'.

(e) Odd Lot Theory

[June 2005, Q7(b)] [Dec 2006, Q7(d)] [Dec 2007, Q7(e)]

Ans. Odd Lot Market : All orders whose order size is less than the regular lot size are traded in the odd-lot market. An order is called an odd lot order if the order size is less than regular lot size. These orders do not have any special terms attributes attached to them. In an odd-lot market, both the price and quantity of both the orders (buy and sell) should exactly match for the trade to take place. Currently the odd lot market facility is used for the Limited Physical Market as per the SEBI directives.

(f) Auction Market

Ans. Auction Market : In the Auction Market, auctions are initiated by the Exchange on behalf of trading members for settlement related reasons.

There are 3 participants in this market :

- **Initiator :** The party who initiates the auction process is called an initiator.
- **Competitor :** The party who enters orders on the same side as of the initiator is called a Competitor.
- **Solicitor :** The party who enters orders on the opposite side as of the initiator is called a Solicitor.

(g) Stop Loss Book

Ans. Stop Loss orders are stored in this book till the trigger price specified in the order is reached or surpassed. When the trigger price is reached or surpassed, the order is released in the Regular lot book. The stop loss condition is met under the following circumstances:

Sell Order - A sell order in the Stop loss book gets triggered when the last traded price in the normal market reaches or falls below the trigger price of the order.

Q8. What is NSE and OTCEI? What are the benefits of getting OTCEI listing for companies & investors.

Ans. National Stock Exchange : The National Stock Exchange of India Limited (NSE) was incorporated in November 1992 by IDBI and other All-India Financial Institutions and became recognized stock exchange with effect from April 26, 1993 to provide nationwide stock trading facilities. The NSE has a fully automated screen-based trading system. It operates on the principles of an order-driven market. It was a part of the financial market sector reforms being undertaken in the economy. The basic idea of setting up of NSE was to facilitate computerized trading in debt market instruments. And resources on a cost-effective manner.

Market Segments of NSE : The NSE was intended to establish a viable and vibrant debt market which was in an underdeveloped stage. Now, it provides the traditional retail market for securities and also operates a Wholesale Debt Market (which may be termed as money market segment). The NSE consists of three mutually exclusive segments :

(1) Wholesale debt market segment.

(2) Capital market segment.

(3) Futures and Options Segment.

(1) Wholesale Debt Market Segment : The wholesale debt market segment of the NSE is a facility for institutions including subsidiaries of banks engaged in financial services and corporate bodies including companies to enter into high value transactions in instruments such as Public Sector Undertaking (PSUs) bonds, Treasury Bills (T-Bills), Governments Securities, Units of UTI, Commercial Papers (CPs), Certificate of Deposits (CDs), Floating yields bonds, etc. Members on the Wholesale Debt Market segment can trade on their own behalf and on behalf of their clients. NSE trading system facilitates making of two ways quotes in a highly flexible manner.

(2) Capital Market Segment : The capital market segment covers trading in equities and retail trade in convertible or non-convertible debentures and hybrids. This particular segment comprises the securities of medium and large companies with nation-wide investors base. These will also include securities which are being traded on their stock exchanges. By virtue of equal access nation wide, such securities can be traded at the same price from any part of the country. This provides good trading and investment opportunities, increases the volume of the trade and increases the liquidity considerably.

(3) Futures and Options Trading : Besides the capital market segment, the NSE also provide opportunity to the investors to deal in the derivative products, i.e. futures and options. At present, NSE provides facility to trade in Nifty Futures. Nifty Options, Individual Stock Options and Individual Stock Futures.

Over the Counter Exchange of India (OTCEI) : It is recognized as a stock exchange under Section 4 of the Securities Contracts (Regulations) Act, 1956. It was set up to provide investors with a convenient, efficient and transparent platform for dealing in shares and stocks; and to help enterprising promoters set up new projects or expand their activities, by providing them an opportunity to raise capital from the capital market in a cost-effective manner. Trading in securities takes place through OTCEI's network of members and dealers spanning the length and breadth of India.

Salient Features of OTCEI :

(a) Ringless and Screen-based Trading : The OTCEI was the first stock exchange to introduce automated, screen-based trading in place of conventional trading ring found in other stock exchanges. The network of on-line computers provides all relevant information to the market participants on their computer screens. This allows them the luxury of executing their deals in the comfort of their own offices.

(b) Sponsorship : All the companies seeking listing on OTCEI have to approach on the members of the OTCEI for acting as the sponsor to the issue. The sponsor makes a through appraisal of the project; as by entering into the sponsorship agreement, the sponsor is committed to making market in that scrip (giving a buy-sell quote) for a minimum period of 18 months. Sponsorship ensures quality of the companies and enhance liquidity for the scrips listed on OTCEI.

(c) Transparency of Transactions : The investor can view the quotations on the computer screen at the dealer's office before placing the order. The OTCEI system ensures that trades are done at the best prevailing quotation in the market. The confirmation slip/trading document generated by the computers gives the exact price at which the deals has been done and the brokerage charged.

(d) Liquidity through Market-making : The sponsor-member is required to give quotes (buy and sell) for the scrip for 18 months from commencement of trading. Besides the compulsory market maker, there is an additional market maker giving two way quotes for the scrip. The idea is to create an environment of competition among market makers to produce efficient pricing and narrow spreads between buy and sell quotations.

(e) Listing of Small and Medium-sized Companies : Many small and medium-sized companies were not able to enter capital market due to the listing requirement of Securities Contracts (Regulation) Act, 1956 regarding the minimum issued equity of Rs. 10 crores in case of the Mumbai Stock Exchange and Rs. 3 crores in case of other stock exchanges. The OTCEI provides an opportunity to these companies to enter the capital market as companies with issued capital of Rs. 30 lakhs onwards can raise finance from the capital market through OTCEI.

(f) Technology : OTCEI uses computers and telecommunications to bring members/dealers together electronically, enabling them to trade with one another over the computer rather than a trading floor in a single location.

(g) Nation-wide Listing : OTCEI network is spread all over India through members, dealers and representative office counters. The company and its securities get nation-wide exposure and investors all over India can start trading in that scrip.

(h) Bought-out Deals : Through the concept of a bought-out deal, OTCEI allows companies to place its equity with the sponsor-member at a mutually agreed price. This ensures swifter availability of funds to companies for timely completion of projects and a listed status at a later date.

The Benefits of getting OTCEI Listing for Companies : The OTCEI offers facilities to the companies having an issued equity capital of more than Rs. 30 lakhs. The benefits of listing at the OTCEI are :

(1) Small and medium closely-held companies can go public.

(2) The OTCEI encourages entrepreneurship.

(3) Companies can get the money before the issue in cases of Bought-out-deals.

(4) It is more cost-effective to come with an issue of OTCEI.

(5) Nation-wide trading by listing at just one exchange.

The Benefits of Trading on OCTEI for Investors :–

(i) The OTCEI trading counters are easily accessible.

(ii) The OTCEI provides greater confidence because of complete transparency in deals.

(iii) At the OTCEI, the transactions are fast and are completed quickly.

(iv) The OTCEI ensures security, liquidity by offering two-way quotes.

(v) The OTCEI is an investor friendly exchange with Single Window Clearance for all investor requests.

Q9. Explain the following.

(a) Negotiated Trade Book (b) Odd Lot Book (c) Auction Book

Ans. (a) Negotiated Trade Book : The Negotiated Trade book contains all negotiated order entries captured by the system before they have been matched against their counterparty trade entries. These entries are matched with identical counterparty entries only. It is to be noted that these entries contain a counterparty code in addition to other order details.

(b) Odd Lot Book : The Odd lot book contains all odd lot order (orders with quantity less than marketable lot) in the system. The system attempts to match an active odd lot order against passive orders in the book. This is referred as the Limited Physical Market (LPM).

(c) Auction Book : This book contains orders that are entered for all auctions. The matching process for auction orders in this book is initiated only at the end of the solicitor period.

Chapter – 5

Regulation

Q1. Discuss the importance of investor protection regulations?

Ans. There are a number of investor protection regulations. All regulatory agencies in the financial sector claim that the primary objective of the regulation by them is to protect the interest of investors. It is generally perceived that investors are the weakest participants of the financial markets and hence need protection from malpractice, fraud and collapse. The information asymmetry between the investors and financial intermediary or institution affects the investors and thus regulatory agencies step-in to protect the interest of the investors. Thus, investor protection regulations are often in the nature of demanding larger disclosure information.

The regulations in general aim to ensure the soundness and safety of financial institutions, maintain the integrity of the transmission mechanism and protect the consumers of financial services. The regulations also ensure freedom of operation to improve the efficiency and provide adequate scope for innovation that benefit the investors and other participants. The success of the regulation thus not only depends on its ability to ensure investors protection but also determined by the level of advancement and sophistication the system has achieved. In other words, regulation should not block the development of financial service industry.

Q2. Which act governs the functioning of stock exchanges in India? Discuss the main points of this Act?

Ans. Securities Contracts (Regulation) Act 1956 and the rules made there under, namely in Securities Contracts (Regulation) Rules, 1957 are the main laws governing stock exchanges in India.

The preamble to the Securities Contracts (Regulation) Act states that it is 'an act to prevent undesirable transactions in securities by regulating the business of dealing therein, by prohibiting options and by providing certain other matters connected therewith". This Act provides for the direct and indirect control of virtually all aspects of securities trading and the running of the stock exchanges. The Act makes every transaction in securities in any notified State or area illegal and punishable by fine and/or imprisonment if it is not entered into between or with members of a recognized stock exchange in the state or area. It also makes every such securities contracts void.

It thus prohibits the existence of other than recognized stock exchanges and provides the mechanism of recognizing stock exchanges.

After it recognizes a stock exchange, the Central Government exerts regulatory control over it. Periodic reports are furnished to the Central Government. Certain books and records are maintained for a period of five years. All officers, directors, members and others who have had dealings in the matter under inquiry are required to produce requested documents, statements, or information.

The Securities Contract (Regulation) Act grants the Central Government power to supercede governing body of a recognized exchange. The suspension of business may be complete or subject to conditions. Suspensions may not last more than seven days initially but may be extended from time to time. The Central Government may supercede the governing body of any exchange by declaration and then appoint any person or group of persons to exercise and perform all the power and duties of the governing body. Other powers granted to the Central Government include the ability to stop further trading in specified securities for the purpose of preventing undesirable speculation, and the power to compel a public company "in the interest of the trade or in the public interest" to list its securities on any of the recognized exchanges.

Q3. Briefly explain the importance & future of Self-regulation in monitoring security market dealings?

Ans. In addition to legislative regulation, self-regulation is equally important. There exist a number of self-regulatory organizations (SROs) which really complement legislative regulation.

The spirit of self-regulation had been prevalent in the Indian securities market as well. If one looks at the powers given to recognized stock exchanges in India to make and enforce bye-law under the Securities Contracts (Regulation) Act, 1956, one tends to conclude that Indian stock exchange have been envisaged as self-regulatory organizations.

Any recognized stock exchange may, subject to the previous approval of the Central Government (till 1991) and Securities and Exchange Board of India (since 1992) make bye-laws for the regulation and control of contracts.

In particular, without prejudice to the generality of the foregoing power, such bye-laws may provide for :–

(a) The opening and closing of markets and the regulation of the hours of trade;

(b) A clearing house for the periodical settlement of contracts and difference thereunder, the delivery of the payment for securities, the passing on of delivery orders and the regulation and maintenance of such a clearing house;

(c) The submission to the Central Government (till 1991) and Securities and Exchange Board of India (since 1992) by the clearing house as soon as may be after each periodical settlement of all or any of the following particulars as the Central Government (till 1991) and Securities and Exchange Board of India (since 1992) may, from time to time to another.

(i) The total number of each category of security carried over from one settlement period to another;

(ii) The total number of each category of security contracts which have been squared up during the course of each settlement period;

(iii) The total number of each category of security actually delivered each clearing etc.

Of late, merchant banks and mutual funds have also been envisaged as SROs. Unfortunately, the record of Indian stock exchanges as SROs has been dismal. Despite various malpractices prevalent in stock exchanges, hardly any disciplinary action had been initiated against any member of the stock exchange. Recent inspection by SEBI of some of the stock exchanges have clearly brought out that their bye-laws relating to margins, etc. have been observed more in breach. Nevertheless it can't be denied that self-regulation is a necessary complement to legislative regulation of securities market in any country.

Q4. "The emergence of SEBI on the horizon of Indian Capital market has heralded an era of protections of investors". Explain giving the functions & activities of SEBI.

OR

"In a short span of its existence, SEBI has been able to fully meet its objectives". Critically comment.

OR

Discuss the objectives & functions of SEBI.

[June2005, Q3, June2007,Q2(b), Dec 2007, Q2(b)]

Ans. The SEBI was given a statutory status on 30th January, 1992 by an Ordinance to provide for the establishment of SEBI. A Bill to replace the Ordinance was introduced in Parliament on 3rd March, 1992 and was passed by both houses of Parliament on 1st April, 1992. The Bill became on Act on 4th April, 1992 the date on which it received the President's assent.

Under Section 11 of the SEBI Act it is provided that subject to the provisions of this Act, it shall be the duty of the Board to protect the interest of investors in securities and to promote the development of and to regulate the securities market, by such measures as it thinks fit. It is further provided that without prejudice to the generality of the foregoing provisions, the measures referred to therein any provide for :

(a) regulating the business in stock exchanges and any other securities markets;

(b) registering and regulating the working of stock broker, sub-brokers, share transfer agents, bankers to an issue, trustee of trust deeds, registrars to an issue, merchant bankers, underwriters, portfolio managers, investment advisors and such other intermediaries who may be associated with securities markets in any manner;

(c) registering and regulating the working of collective investment schemes, including mutual funds.

(d) promoting and regulating self-regulatory organizations;

(e) prohibiting fraudulent and unfair trade practice relating to securities markets.

(f) promoting investors education and training of intermediaries of securities markets;

(g) prohibiting insider trading in securities;

(h) regulating substantial acquisition of shares and take-over of companies;

(i) conducting research for the above purpose;

(j) performing such other functions as may be prescribed.

In sum and substance, Securities and Exchange Board of India has been constituted to promote orderly and healthy development of the securities market and to provide adequate investor protection. It aims to remove the unhealthy practices prevalent in the Indian capital market and create an environment to facilitate mobilization of resource through the securities market. Thus the Board plays a dual role by adopting regulatory functions as well as playing an important development role. Its functions include :–

(1) to deal with all matters relating to development and regulations of the securities market.

(2) To administer various legislation affecting securities market.

(3) Regulation of the market intermediaries viz. stock exchanges, stock brokers, merchant bankers, mutual funds, etc.

(4) To provide adequate investor protection.

For day to day functions the activities of SEBI have been divided into five operational departments viz.,

(1) Primary markets-policy, intermediaries, investor grievances and guidance, etc.

(2) Issue Management & Intermediary department

(3) Secondary market-policy, operations and exchange administration, new investment products and insider trading, etc.

(4) Secondary market-exchange administration, inspection and non-member intermediaries, etc.

(5) Institutional investment Mutual funds and FIIs, mergers and acquisitions, research & publications and internal regulation.

Q5. 'SEBI is an independent Board' Do you agree? Why or Why not?

Ans. Yes, SEBI is an independent Board. The management of SEBI vests in the Board which consists of the following members, namely :

(a) a Chairman;

(b) two Members from amongst the officials of the Ministries of the Central Government dealing with Finance and Law;

(c) one Member from amongst the officials of the Reserve Bank of India.

(d) two other members, to be appointed by the Central Government.

The general superintendence, direction and management of the affairs of the SEBI vests in a Board of Members, which may exercise all powers and do all acts and things which may be exercised or done by the Board.

The Chairman and the Members referred to a (a) and (d) above shall be appointed by the Central Government and the members referred to at (b) and (c) above shall be nominated by the Central Government and the Reserve Bank of India respectively.

Block – 3

Analysis for Equity Investment

Chapter – 6

Economy & Industry Analysis

Q1. Discuss the relevance of fundamental analysis in efficient market set up?

Ans. Economic and industry analyses are part of fundamental analysis. In the fundamental approach, various fundamental or basic factors that affect the risk-return of the securities are examined. Effort, here, is to identify those securities, which are perceived to be mispriced in the stock market. The assumption in this case is that the 'market price' of the security and the price as justified by its fundamental factors called 'intrinsic value' are different and the market place provides an opportunity for a discerning investor to detect such discrepancy. The moment such a discrepancy is identified the decision to invest or disinvest is taken. The decision rule under this approach is as follows.

The price prevailing in the market is called 'market price' (MP) and the one justified by its fundamental is called 'intrinsic value' (IV).

Decision Rule				Recommendation
(1)	If IV	>	MP,	Buy the Security
(2)	If IV	<	MP,	Sell the Security
(3)	If IV	=	MP	No action

The fundamental factors mentioned above may relate to the economy or industry or company or all/some of them. Thus, economy fundamentals, industry fundamentals and company fundamentals are considered while analyzing the security for taking investment decision.

Fundamental analysis is not free from criticism. It is pertinent to mention that doubts are expressed about the utility of this approach in the context of efficient stock market, which already incorporates the information about the economy, industry and company in the share price. It is claimed that stock market incorporates such information in the share price rather instantaneously. The result of this assumption is that price prevailing at the market place can be taken to represent the price of the share justified by its fundamental i.e., intrinsic value (IV). The quality of MP and IV makes the fundamental analysis or any other analysis useless or redundant. The above given view about share market efficiency implies that no one would be able to make abnormal gains given such a set up.

In fact, stock market is not efficient to the extent the researchers proclaim. There are many operational inefficiencies and structural deficiencies in stock market. Though the market is fairly efficient in the long run in a sense that only information leads price changes, operational and structural inefficiencies cause time lag between arrival of information and its impact on the security prices. It is a fact of life that earning abnormal profits is not the only and final goal for most of the investors. Rather, it has been observed that earning the normal returns, (i.e., the return commensurate with risk prevalent in the market) is a nutshell, fundamental analysis has an important role to play for making investment decisions in an efficient set up, too.

Q2. "Economic-Industry-Company framework provides a useful approach to equity investment decision". Discuss. [June 2007, Q7(c)]

Ans. The analysis of economy, industry and company fundamental is the main ingredient of fundamental approach. The analysis should take into account all the three constituents which form different stage in the investment decision making process and are depicted graphically with three concentric circles as shown in fig. below. The process of investment analysis starts with an evaluation of economic outlook. After getting some confidence on economic outlook, the analysis is moved to industry specific to identify industries, which are worth for further analysis to pick up good stocks. The last stage is identifying specific stocks from selected industry. Operationally, to base the investment decision on various fundamentals, all the three stages must be taken into account.

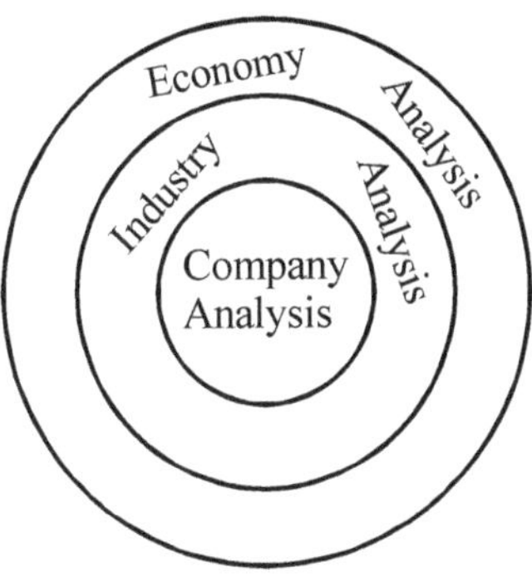

Q3. "Economic forecasting is the heart of economy analysis". Comment & briefly explain the various techniques of economic forecasting .

OR

Discuss the Barometric or Indicator approach.

Ans. In order to perform economic analysis, it is essential to forecast economic performance with the help of some of the economic factors. Depending upon the duration, forecasting can be made for short term, intermediate and long term. Some short term forecasting techniques are :

(1) Anticipatory Surveys : This is a very simple method through which investor can form their opinion/expectations with respect to the future state of the economy. As is generally understood, this is the survey of expert opinions of those who are prominent in the government, business, trade and industry. Generally, it incorporates expert opinion with regard to construction activities, plant and machinery expenditures, level of inventory, etc. which have important bearing on the economic activities. Despite the valuable inputs provided by this method, care must be exercised in using the information generated through this method. Precautions are needed because :

(i) Survey results can not be regarded as forecasts *per se* A consensus of opinion may be used by the investor in forming his own forecasts.

(ii) There is no guarantee that the intentions of surveys would certainly materialize. To this extent, the investors can not rely solely on these.

(2) Barometric or Indicator Approach : In this approach, various types of indicators are studied to find out how the economy is likely to perform in the future. For meaningful interpretations, these indicator are classified into leading, roughly coincidental, and lagging indicators.

Leading Indicators : As the name suggests, these are indicators that lead the economic activity in terms of their outcome. That is, these are those time series data of the variables that reach their high points as well as their low points in advance of the economic activity.

Roughly Coincidental Indicators : These are the indicators that reach their peaks and the troughs at approximately the same time as the economy.

Lagging Indicators : These are time series data of variables that lag behind in their consequence vis-à-vis the economy. That is, these reach their turning points after economy has already reached it own.

Indicator approach is quite useful in suggesting the direction of a change in the aggregate economic activity. However, it tells nothing about the magnitude of change. In developed countries, data relating to various indicators are published at short intervals. For example, U.S. Department of Commerce publishes data regarding various indicators in each of the following categories :

Leading Indicators

– Average weekly hours of manufacturing production workers.
– Average weekly initial unemployment claims
– Contracts and orders for plant and machinery
– Index of S&P stock prices
– Money supply (M2)

Coincidental Indicators :

– Index of industrial production
– Manufacturing and trade sales
– Employment on non-agricultural payrolls.
– Personal income less transfer payments

Lagging Indicators :

– Average duration of unemployment
– Ratio of manufacturing and trade inventories to sales
– Average prime lending rate
– Commercial and industrial loans outstanding
– Change in consumer price index for service.

Various indicators under broad category of leading indicators, its various measuring may give conflicting signals in terms of future direction of the economy.

To overcome the limitations, the use of diffusion index or composite index had been suggested. This takes care of the problems by combining several indicators into one index in order to measure the strength or weaknesses in the movement of a particular kind of indicators. Care has to be exercised even in this case because diffusion are not without problems either. Apart from the fact that its computations are difficulties, it does not eliminate the irregular movements in the series.

Econometrics : This is another approach in determining the precise relationship between the dependent and the Independent variables. In fact, econometrics is a discipline where in application of mathematics and statistical techniques is made to economic theory. It presupposes the precise and clear relationship between the dependent and independent variables. Thus by using econometrics, the analyst is able to forecast a variable more precisely than by any other approach. But forecasts thus derived would be as good as the data inputs used and assumptions made.

Opportunistic Model Building or GNP Model Building or Sectional Analysis is frequently used in practice and is most eclectic method. **Various steps while using this approach are :–**

(1) Hypothesize the total demand in the economy as measured by its total income (GNP) based on likely scenarios in the country like war, peace, political instability, economic changes level and rate of inflation, etc.

(2) Forecast the GNP figure by estimating the levels of its various components like :

– Consumption expenditure

– Gross private domestic investment

– Government purchases of goods and services.

– Net exports

(3) After forecasting the individual components of GNP, the analyst adds them up and get a figure of the forecasted GNP.

(4) The analyst compares total of GNP so arrived with an independently arrived at, a priori Forecast of GNP and test, the overall forecast for internal consistency. This is done to ensure that both his total forecast and subcomponents' forecast make sense and fit together in reasonable manner.

This opportunistic model building involves all the details described above with a vast amount of judgement and inequity.

Q4. Explain the relevance of economy analysis? How does the investor assess the future of economic activity?

OR

What are the different measures of economic activity?

Ans. All investment decisions are made within the economic environment after taking into account the economic prospect of the country. This environment varies as the economy goes through stages of prosperity. When the economy is booming, companies over invest in projects and create excess capacity and thus lead to slow down of the economy. Further, government policies and external pressures also create complications to the economy. Different stages of economic prosperity are also referred to as the business cycle. The cycle moves on without any definite length of time between the stages because government and other agencies would like to extend the expansion stage while trying to cut down the recession or speed up the recovery phase. Figure illustrates the common characteristics that are applicable to different business cycles.

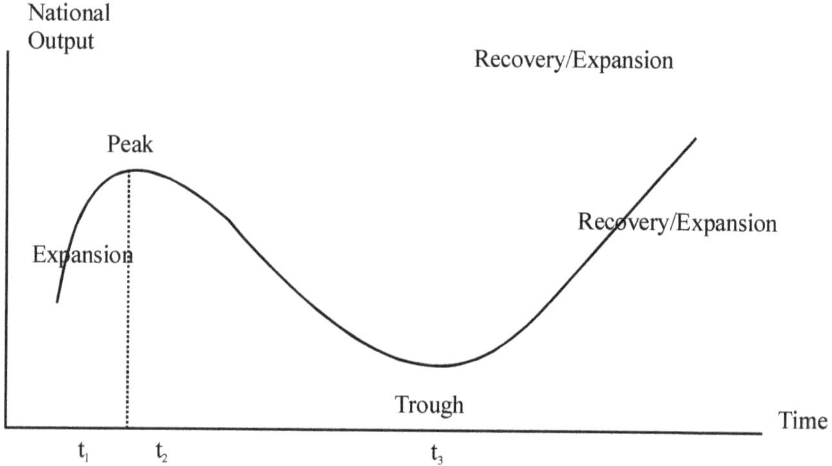

Economists all over the world have developed a fair amount of understanding on factors leading to different phases of the economy and also developed necessary monetary and fiscal policies to speed up the process of recovery and extend the period of expansion. Despite such efforts, the government fails to achieve desired results because of new factors emerging in the economy and ever-changing social and political events.

It is possible by forecasting a few widely used economic measures. Different measures of economic activity are :

Gross Domestic Product : Economic activity is measured by aggregate indicators such as the level of production and national output. The most widely and commonly quoted measure is Gross Domestic Product (GDP), which is the total value of all final good and services newly produced within the country's boundaries with domestic factors of production. A similar measure is Gross National Product, which measures the total value of all final goods and services newly produced by an economy and includes income generated abroad. GDP and GNP and particularly the growth rate of GDP or GNP are relevant for investment for two reasons. One, a good GDP growth means continuous income for individuals and hence surplus money can be deployed for investments. Two, corporate growth is directly influenced by the GDP growth.

Measures of Consumer Confidence : This type of survey is not available unfortunately in India at this stage. Consumer confidence index is one of the strong short-term economic indicators used by the investors to assess whether there is any change of direction in the economy. Consumer confidence affects spending, which has an impact on corporate profit and levels of employment. A positive change in the consumer confidence index or consumer sentiment index in the U.S. indicates a strong impact on the profitability of firms in general and in particular for firms dealing with consumer items. Since such surveys are not conducted in India, what is useful is estimate of personal disposable income. A correlation analysis between GDP growth rate and Personal Disposal Income shows a strong correlation of 0.98.

Inflation of Consumer Price Index : In addition to aggregate measures of economic activity and leading indicators, measures of inflation can have an important impact on investors' behavior. Inflation in general denotes a general change in the price levels and measured in terms of index. Two commonly used indexes are Consumer price index (CPI) and the Wholesale price index (WPI). Inflation in general is not bad as long as it comes along with the growth of the economy. When the economy is expanding fast, it is natural that money supply also increases along with disposable personal income of individuals and thus cause an increase in prices. Under this condition, stock market is favorably affected on account of increase in profitability of firms. Nevertheless, inflation affects interest rates and hence adversely affects the stock prices. An increase in rate of inflation will cause an increase in rate of interest of all kinds of securities. An increase in interest rate affects the value of stock as well as other securities in two ways. One, it affects adversely the profitability of firms because of higher outflow on interest cost. Two, it also increases the expected rate of return of investors and directly affects the discount rate. An increase in discount rate has an adverse impact on value of securities of different types. Such an adverse impact may ultimately lead to a recession and hence government and central banks are concerned with inflation. A typical reaction from the central banks (in our case Reserve Bank of India) is controlling money supply through appropriate monetary policies.

Interest Rates : The level of interest rates is perhaps the most important macro economic factor to consider in one's investment analysis. Forecast of interest rates directly affect the forecast of returns in the fixed income market. The following factors would help investors in forecasting the future direction of the interest rates :–

(1) The supply of funds from savers, primarily households.

(2) The demand for funds from businesses to be used to finance physical investments in plant, equipment, and inventories.

(3) The monetary policy of the Reserve Bank of India.

(4) The expected rate of inflation.

There is a close linkage between the above variables. For instance, the supply of funds from savers depends on the level of economic growth. The same economic growth determines the demand for funds from businesses. The monetary policy of RBI is the outcome of inflation and inflation of the country is influenced by monetary policy as well as economic performance. The Government and the Central Bank influence the interest rates significantly. For example, an increase in the government's budget deficit increases the government borrowings. An increase in the demand for funds pushes the interest rates. The Central Bank can reduce the impact of government borrowing by increasing the supply of money through monetary policy. While this will temporarily arrest an increase in the interest rates, increased money supply pushes the inflation, which in turn decreases the interest rates. Many times, the Central Bank also uses interest rates directly to control the economy.

Government Policy : The government has two broad classes of macro economic tools – those that affect the demand for goods and services and those that affect their supply. In practice, supply-side economists have focused on the appropriateness of the incentives to work, innovate, and take risks that result from the system of taxation. The thrust is creating infrastructure and skills among people to increase the economic activity. Such policies may have little impact in the short run but they produce sustainable long-run growth in the economy.

Fiscal Policy : Fiscal policy refers to the government's spending and tax action and is part of demand-side management. It is the most direct way to influence the economy. For instance, when the government increases spending, it creates more demand in the economy and similarly, when the government reduces spending, it causes slow down in the economy. It must be noted that government is a major direct buyer of several core sector products. The government can also increase or decrease the demand for the products by reducing or increasing the tax rates. Changes in tax rates directly increase or decrease the disposable income of the public.

Monetary Policy : Monetary policy, in the form of changing CRR and SLR is also demandside management of economy. The Central Bank Changes the money supply (rather adjust the growth rate of money supply) through variety of policies and thus influence the economy. One of the reasons for inflation being under control during the last two years is slow down in the growth of money supply. The Central Bank by reducing the money supply can slow down the growth and prevent the economy to create over capacity in several industries. However, monetary policy affects the economy in more roundabout way than fiscal policy.

Q5. Define & explain the importance of industry analysis? How can the industries be classified from the investment decision point of view? [Dec 2006, Q3, June 2007, Q2(a), Dec 2007, Q3]

Ans. An industry is a homogenous group of companies. That is, companies with the similar characteristic can be grouped into one industrial group. There are many other bases on which grouping of companies can be done. For example, traditional classification is generally done product wise like pharmaceutical, cotton, textile, synthetic fiber industry, etc. Such a classification though useful does not help much in investment decision making. Some of the more useful bases for classifying industries from the investment decision point of view are as follows :

Growth industry : This is the industry, which is expected to grow persistently and its growth is likely to exceed the average growth of the economy.

Cyclical industry : In this category of the industry, the firms included are those which move closely with the rate of industrial growth of the economy and fluctuate cyclically as the economy fluctuates.

Defensive industry : It is a grouping that includes firms which move steadily with the economy and decline less than the average decline of the economy in a cyclical downturn.

Declining industry : This is that category of firms, which either generally decline absolutely or grow less than the average growth of the economy.

Q6. Give the different stages in the life cycle of an industry? What are its implications on investment decisions?

Ans. The stages in the life cycle of an industry are :–

Pioneer's Stage : This is the first stage in the industrial life cycle of a new industry. Being the first stage, the technology and its products are relatively new and have not reached a stage of perfection. Experimentation is the order both in product and technology. However, there is a demand for its products in the market, thereby, the profit opportunities are in plenty. This is a stage where the venture capitalists take a lot of interest and enter the industry and sometimes organize the business. At this stage, the risk of many firms being out of the industry is also more; hence, mortality rate is very high in the industry, with the result that if an industry withstands the risk of being out of the market, the investors would reap the rewards substantially or else substantial risk of loss of investment exist. This period saw many companies that could not survive the onslaught of competition. Only those which tolerate this onslaught of price war could remain in the industry.

Fast growing stage : This is the second stage when the chaotic competition and growth that were the hallmark of the first stage is more or less over. Firms that could not survive this onslaught have already died down. The surviving large firms now dominate the industry. The demand for its products still grows faster in the market leading to an increase in profits to the companies. This is the stage where companies grow orderly and rapidly. These companies provide a good investment grow faster, they sometimes break the records in various areas like payments of dividends, etc., thus becoming more and more attractive for investments.

Maturity and Stabilization stage : This third stage where industries grow roughly at the rate of the economy and are fully developed to reached a stage of stabilization. Looked at differently, this is a stage where the ability of the industry to grow appears to have more or less lost. As compared to the competitive industries, rate of growth in the industry in slower. Sales may still be rising, but a lower rate. It is at this stage that the industry is facing the problem of what Grodinsky called "latent obsolescence" a terms used to describe a situation where earliest signs of decline has emerged. Investors have to be very cautions to examine and interpret these signs before it is too late.

Relative Decline stage : The fourth stage of industrial life cycle development is the relative decline stage. Industry at this stage has grown old. New products and new technology have come in the market. Customers have changed their habits, styles, liking, etc. Its products are not much in demand as was in the earlier stages. Still, the industry can continue to exist for some more time.

Consequently, the industry would grow less than the average growth of the economy during the best of the times of the economy. But as it expected, the industry would decline much faster than the decline of the economy in the worst of times.

The specific characteristics of different stages of life cycle development of industries have a number of implications for investment decision. For example, Pioneering stage is very risky stage. As you know that risk and returns are positively correlated, investment at this stage is quite rewarding. However, for an investor looking for steady long-term returns with risk aversion, it is suggested that he should in general avoid investing at this stage. These are good for venture capitalists. But if he is still keen to invest, he should try to diversify or disperse his investment in companies that are in the second stage of development i.e., fast growth. This probably explains the prevalent higher stock prices of the companies of this industry.

From the investment point of view, selection of the industries at the third stage of development is quite crucial as it is the future growth of the industry that is relevant and not its past performance. There are a number of examples where the share prices of companies in a decline industry have been artificially hiked up in the market. This is justified on the basis of good record of its performance. But the fact of the matter is that a company in a declining industry would sooner or later feel the pinch of its features and an investor investing in companies at this stage would experience reduction in the value of his investment in due course.

Q7. What are the features that should be considered while selecting the industry?

Ans. Given below are some of the features that could be considered for a detailed investigation while selecting an industry for investment. These features broadly relate to the operational and structural aspects of the industry.

(i) State of competition in the industry : It is an important input in investment decision making. Knowing about the state of competition in a particular industry, therefore, is a must. Questions those are relevant in this context are :

– Which firm in the industry plays a leadership role and how firms compete among themselves?

– How is the competition among domestic and foreign firms both in the domestic and the foreign markets? How do the domestic firms perform there?

– Which type of products are manufactured in this industry? Are these homogenous in nature or highly differentiated?

(ii) Cost conditions and profitability : The worth of a share depends on its return and the return depends on profitability of the company. Interestingly growth is an essential variable but its mere presence does not guarantee profitability. Profitability depends upon the state of competition prevalent in the industry, cost control measure adopted by its constituent units and the growth in demand for its products. While conducting an analysis from the point of view of cost and profitability, some relevant aspects to be investigated are :

– How is the cost allocation done among various heads like raw materials, wages and overheads?

Knowledge about the distribution of costs under various heads is very essential as this gives an idea to the investors about the controllability of costs. Some industries have overhead costs much higher than others. Likewise, labour cost is another area that requires close scrutiny. This is because finally whether labour is cheap or expansive depends on the wage level and labour productivity is taken into account.

– Price of the product of the industry.

– Capacity of production-installed, used, unused etc.

– Level of capital expenditure required to maintain or increase the productive efficiency of the industry.

Profitability is another area that calls for a thorough analysis on the part of investors. However, such an analysis can being by having a bird's eye view of the situation. In this context ratio has been found quite useful. Some of the important ratios often used are :–

– Gross Profit Margin ratio

– Operation Profit Margin ratio

– Rate of Return on Equity

– Rate of Return of Total Capital

Ratios are not an end in themselves. But they do indicate possible areas for further investigation.

(iii) Technology and Research : Due to increase in competition in general, technology and research play a crucial part in the growth and survival of a particular industry. However, technology itself is subject to change; sometimes, very fast, leading to obsolescence. Thus only those industries which are updating themselves in the field of technology could have a competitive advantage over others in terms of the quality, pricing of products, etc.

The relevant questions to be probed further by the analyst in the respect could include the following :–

– What is the nature and type of technology used in the industry?

– Are there any expected changes in the technology in terms of offering new products in the market leading to increase in sales?

– What has been the relationship of capital expenditure and the sales over time? Whether more capital expenditure has led to increase in sales or not? The impact of all these factors have to be finally translated in terms of two most crucial numbers, i.e., sales and profitability – their level and expected rate of change during short, intermediate and long run.

Q8. What are the techniques of industry analysis?

Ans. Various techniques of industry analysis are the following : -

End Use and Regression Analysis : It is the process whereby the analysis or investor attempts to diagnose the factors that determine the demand for the output of the industry. This is also known as end-use or product-demand analysis. In this process, the investor hopes to uncover the factors that explain the demand. Some of the factors found to be powerful in explaining the demand for the industry are : GNP, disposable income, per capita consumption, price elasticity techniques like regression analysis and correlation have been often used. These help to identify the important factors/variables. However, one should be aware of their limitations.

Inputs Output Analysis : This analysis helps us understand demand analysis in greater detail. Input output analysis is very useful technique that reflects the flow of good and services through the economy. This analysis includes intermediate steps in the production process as the good proceed from the raw material stage through final consumption. This information is reflected in the input-output table reflects the pattern of consumption at all stages-not just at the final stage of consumption of final goods. This is done to detect any changing pattern or trends that might indicate the growth or decline of industries.

Chapter – 7

Company Level Analysis

Q1. Why is company level analysis important for investment decisions?

OR

Why is company analysis the most important part of the E-I-C- analysis?

Ans. Fundamental analysis helps the investor by providing a benchmark in terms of intrinsic value. This value is dependent upon economy, industry and company fundamentals. Out of these three, company level analysis provides a direct link between investor's action and his investment goal in operational terms. This is because an investor buys the equity share of company and not that of industry and economy. Industry and economy framework indeed provide him with proper background against which he buys the shares of a particular company. This setting is nevertheless very important, but for action to take place it is the company that provides investors actual key settings. A careful examination of the company with its quantitative and qualitative fundamentals is, therefore, very essential. As Fischer and Jordan have aptly put it, "A good economic analysis inform the investor about the property of a current stock purchase, regardless of the industry in which he might invest. If the economic outlook suggests purchase at this time, the economic analysis along with the industry analysis will aid the investor in selecting their proper industry in which to invest. Nonetheless, knowing when to invest and in which industry is not enough. It is also necessary to know which companies in which industries should be selected".

Q2. How the value of a stock can be measured?

Ans. A common valuation measure is **Book Value**, which is the networth of a company as shown in the balance sheet. Book value can be expressed on per share basis and in such a case, the book value per share is equal to net worth divided by the number of shares outstanding. The book value is derived based on certain accounting assumptions. An important assumption is related to valuation of assets. Assets are valued after deducting the depreciation value from the acquisition cost. Depreciation amount of an asset for a period is computed based on the initial estimated life of the machine. There is no guarantee that the amount provided as depreciation is equal to loss in the value of the asset and it may be either more or less than the actual loss in the value of the asset.

Another measure close to book value is **liquidation value** per share. This represents the amount of money that could be realized by breaking up the firm, selling its assets, repaying debt and then distributing remainder to the shareholders. If there is an active takeover market, the price of the stock should be at least equal to liquidation value. Otherwise, corporate raiders would find it profitable to acquire the firm and then take up liquidation.

Value of a firm can also be measured by computing the replacement cost of the asset less debt. Replacement cost can be measured if you could find out what is the current cost of putting up a similar plant. For many industries, the cost per unit of capacity (like cost of 1 million ton of cement plant) is available. If the market price is below to this replacement cost level, then firms intending to expand will find it easier to acquire the firm than putting up one more plant.

All the above measures fail to look into the earning capability of the firm by using the assets. It is quiet possible that firms can use the assets and earn superior return because of several other advantages or skills available within the firm. On the other hand, market value of the firm takes into account such future income arising out of the use of assets. The ratio of market price to replacement cost popularly called **Tobin's *q*.**

Q3. List the factors that helps in determining P/E ratio?

Ans. P/E ratio is broadly determined by:

– Dividend pay out

– Growth

– Risk free rate

– Business risk

– Financial risk

Thus, other things remaining the same,

(1) Higher would be the P/E ratio, if higher is the growth rate or dividend payout or both.

(2) Lower would be P/E ratio, if higher is

(a) Risk free rate,

(b) Business risk,

(c) Financial risk.

Q4. What are the different methods of forecasting EPS?

Ans. There are various methods employed to assess the future outlook of the revenue, expenses and earnings of the firm given the economic and industry outlook. These methods can be broadly classified into two categories, namely, traditional and modern. Under the traditional approach, the forecaster obtains the estimate of single value of the variable. While in the case of modern approach, he gets the range of values with the probability of each occurrence.

Under the traditional approach the following methods of forecasting are adopted:

– ROI approach
– Market share approach
– Independent estimates approach

ROI Approach : Under this approach, attempts are made to relate the productivity of assets with the earnings. That is, returns earned on the total investment (assets) are calculated and estimates regarding earning per share are made. Simply stated,

Return on Assets = EBIT/Assets

Return on assets (ROA) is a function of the two important variables viz., turnover of assets and margin of profit. In other words,

Return on Assets = Assets Turnover x Profit Margin

Where,

Asset Turnover = Sales/Assets

Profit Margin = EBIT/Sales

Therefore, ROA = (Sales/Assets) × (EBIT/Sales),

ROA is thus a function of (1) number of times the asset base is utilized and converted into sales (asset turnover) and (2) profits earned on the sales (Profit margin). Once an analyst or investor forecast the individual components of ratio, it is possible to forecast the ROA. ROA will be useful to forecast the EBIT. EBIT requires a minor adjustment before getting earnings per share. The adjustment is on account of debt used by the firms.

Leverage is the use of borrowed funds in the enterprise with a fixed cost. It is often said that as borrowed funds increase in relation to equity funds in the total financing mix, borrowing cost would not only increase, but increase more rapidly than the amounts borrowed. This happens because the suppliers of funds now perceive the business more risky when borrowed funds are utilized beyond a certain point. The relationship between Return on Equity (ROE), ROA and debt can be explained as follows:

Rate of Return on Equity = R + (R-I) L/E

Where, R = Return on Assets

I = Effective interest rate

L/E = Total outside liabilities/equity

If we multiply of earnings is the central theme in the company level analysis, it requires an understanding of the earnings formation process. The ROI approach provides a framework for analyzing the effects and interaction between the return a firm earns on its assets and the manner it is financed.

Once this return generating power is understood by the analyst, he can forecast the key variables in the model and substitute the forecasted values into the model and forecast Earnings after Tax (EAT).

Based on the chemistry of earnings, the analyst can further use the following equations to calculate the earnings per share :

$$EPS = \frac{[(1 - T)\{R + (R - I)L/E\}E]}{\text{Number of shares outstanding}}$$

Market share Approach : This approach emanates from the industry analysis. Once the estimate about the future prospects of the industry is completed, the analyst would then look into the firms, which are the leaders and pacesetters in the industry and would then find out the market share of the firm to be analysed. The following steps can be adopted to implement this method :–

(1) Estimate the industry's total sales

(2) Estimate the firm's share in the total sales in the industry i.e. market share.

(3) Estimate the profit margin

(4) Multiply sales by profit margin to get total earnings

(5) Divide earnings by number of shares outstanding to get EPS.

(6) Multiply EPS by P/E ratio to get market price per share

Independent Estimates Approach : Under this approach, each and every item of revenue and expense is estimated separately and summed up to arrive at the future EPS. All the three approaches are traditionally utilized by security analysts. However, these are not mutually exclusive approaches. But one important and common limitation of these approaches is that they indicate point estimate of EPS and HPY and therefore, attach 100% probability of outcome.

Under modern approaches to forecasting earnings of a company, statistical techniques are used. The following techniques are generally included in this category.

– Use of regression and correlation analyses

– Use of trend analysis

– Decision tree analysis.

Regression and Correlation Analyses : In order to find out the interrelationship of relevant variables, the techniques of regression and correlation analyses are used. When the inter-relationship covers two variables, simple regression is used and for more than two variables, multiple regression technique is used. Using this approach, security analysts may find out the interrelationship between the variables belonging to the economy, industry and the company. Major advantages in its application relate to deriving the forecasted value as well as testing the reliability of the estimates.

Trend Analysis : While using this technique, the relationship of only one variables is tested over time using the regression technique. In a way, it is the simple regression technique where the interrelationship of a particular variable is tested vis-à-vis time. That is why the name trend analysis. It is quite useful to understand the historical behavior of the variable for the purpose of the security analysis.

Decision Tree Analysis : The above two methods are considered superior to the traditional methods employed to forecast the value of earnings per share. However, an important limitation remains. Both these methods provide only point estimate of the forecast value. In order to improve decision making process, information relating to the probability of occurrence of the forecast value is quite useful. Thus a range of values of the variables with the probabilities of occurrence of each value will go a long way to improve decision by the investor. To overcome these limitations, decision tree and simulation techniques are used. Under the decision tree analysis the decision is assumed to be taken sequentially with probability of each sequence. Thus, in order to find out the probability of the final outcome, given various sequential decisions along with probabilities, the probabilities of each sequence is to be multiplied and summed up. In practice, whenever security analyst attempts to use decision tree analysis in conducting analysis of the securities, he starts with estimating the sales.

Q5. 'Evaluation of management is the main challenge in company analysis'. Comment & Explain how would you go about it.

Ans. Analyst is required to bear in mind qualitative/subjective factors. An alert analyst would be able to gather such information from the following sources :–

(1) Company's financial statements

(2) Financial Press, magazines etc.

(3) Company's officials

This information may relate to the following factors :–

(i) Availability of infrastructure

(ii) Inventory-size, value, risk

(iii) Order book position

(iv) Product risk

(v) Marketing and distribution

(vi) Components of cost-fixed and variable

(vii) Availability of raw material inputs

(viii) Cost of inputs

(ix) Quality of personnel

(x) Quality of management

(xi) Future plans

With the qualitative factors in mind, an investor/analyst can judge whether the quantitatively derived measure of value of an equity is reasonable or not and accordingly take informed risk while taking the decision to invest or disinvest shares of a company. Or all the qualitative factors, quality of management is most important. Needless to say, the assessment of quality and competence of management is perhaps most difficult. Some critical aspects of company management are ***commitment and competence, future orientation, image building, investor friendliness and government relation building.***

As far as commitment is concerned, the investors must look up the past record of management to particularly see that it did not indulge in premature diversion of funds from one company to another. The competence of the management may be viewed in terms of the composition of the board, professional qualifications and experience of the members of board and the chief executive. The future orientation of a company management can be gauged through research and development expenditure, managerial development and training expenses and unexhausted fund-raising capacity of the company. It is also important to undertake sufficient image building activities for a company. The image building activities of a management will be reflected in its community development activities and management of relations with the press and media. The investor friendliness of the management can be assessed from its dividend policies, i.e. payment of dividend in cash or kind and issue of bonus shares. Management of shareholder grievances can give fair idea about the investor friendliness of company management.

Another aspect of company management, which is particularly important in a country like India, characterized by high degree of government regulation, is its track record of managing relations with the government. Management, though most difficult to evaluate, holds the real key to the quality of equity investment decision. As part of fundamental analysis, company management must be evaluated for its commitment, competence and capacity to manage operations of the company and shareholder, community and government relations. Past track record of the management in this regard can come handy. The problem is particularly challenging where it is a new management, without having past track record. Such a situation would perhaps demand venture capitalist skills.

Chapter – 8

Technical Analysis

Q1. What is technical analysis? Differentiate between fundamental & technical analysis? **[June 2005, Q4, June 2007 Q7(f)]**

Ans. Technical Analysis is concerned with a critical study of the daily or weekly price and volume data of the Index comprising several shares, like Bombay Stock Exchange Sensitive Index (SENSEX), or of a particular Stock, like Infosys or Hindustan Lever. The objective of the technical analysis is to predict or forecast the short, intermediate and long term price movements. It uses only the data generated from the market. Such market generated data includes price, volume, number of trades, 52-week high or low price, intra-day spread, dealers buy-sell quote spread, number of advances and declines, number of Stocks hitting the new high and low, open interest, etc. Some of the basic assumptions of the technical analysis are :–

(1) Market value is determined solely by the interaction of supply and demand.
(2) Supply and demand are governed by numerous factors, both rational and irrational.
(3) Stock prices tend to move in trends, which persists for an appreciable length of time.
(4) Changes in trend are caused by shifts in demand and supply.
(5) Shifts in demand and supply can be detected through chart analysis and some chart patterns repeat themselves.

Technical analysis assumes that there is a sufficient lag between the arrival of information and its ultimate impact on the Stock prices. The analysis fails if the information never incorporated in the prices (inefficient market) or instantaneously reflected in the prices investors or analysts are able to understand the impact of information on prices and entering into the Stock.

The basic differences between technical and fundamental analysis are listed below :–

Technical Analysis	Fundamental Analysis
Focus on timing and likely price changes; Not bothered about the intrinsic value.	Focus on valuation of intrinsic value and through such value, identifying stocks which are under-priced or over-priced
Focuses on internal factors-factors that are available in the market (price, volume, etc.)	Focus on external factors – factors that are outside the market (annual reports, industry report, economic estimates, etc.
Focus is generally on near (short) term changes in the prices though intermediate and long-term forecasts are also done	Focus is on long-term expected price. Typically follows buy-hold-sell strategy once the stock is identified and investment period is defined.
Focus is more on price direction than price target or forecast	Focus is on price target; not generally bothered for short-term price changes.
Easier and faster Voluminous data.	Requires considerable time for analyzing
Simultaneously applied to many stocks	Difficult to apply for a large number of stocks unless a big analysts team is set up.

Q2. Give the basic tenets of Dow Theory?

[June 2005 Q7(a), Dec 2006 Q7(c)]

Ans. Technical Analysis evolved in 1900-1902 when Charles H. Dow presented the celebrated Dows Theory in a series of editorials in the Wall Street Journal in USA. The Classical Technical Analysis evolved gradually in the early part of the 20th century, and deals with a detailed study of price bar charts of the indices as well as the individual stocks.

Dow Theory and its Basic Tenets : To start with, the Dow's Theory put forward six basic tenets as follows :–

(1) The Averages Discount Everything : Daily prices reflect the aggregate judgment and emotions of all stock market participants. This process discounts (takes into account) everything known and predictable that can affect the demand-supply relationship of the stocks.

(2) The Market Has Three Movements : Primary movements, secondary reactions, and minor movements. The primary movement is the long range cycle that carries the entire market up or down. The secondary reactions act as a restraining force on the primary movement and tends to correct deviations from it. Secondary reactions usually last from several weeks to several months in length. The minor movements are the day-to-day fluctuations in the market. Minor movements have little analytic value because of their short duration and variation in amplitude.

3) Price Bar Charts Indicate Movements.

4) Price/Volume Relationships Provide Background.

5) Price Action Determines The Trend.

6) The Averages Must Confirm : The movement of two different market indices must confirm each other to confirm the trend.

Q3. Explain the "Elliott Wave Theory". [Dec 2007 Q7(d)]

Ans. The Elliott wave principle is a form of technical analysis that attempts to forecast trends in the financial markets and other collective activities. It is named after Ralph Nelson Elliott (1871–1948), an accountant who developed the concept in the 1930s: he proposed that market prices unfold in specific patterns, which practitioners today call Elliott waves. Elliott published his views of market behavior in the book The Wave Principle (1938), in a series of articles in Financial World magazine in 1939, and most fully in his final major work, Nature's Laws – The Secret of the Universe (1946). Elliott argued that because humans are themselves rhythmical, their activities and decisions could be predicted in rhythms, too. Critics argue that the Elliott wave principle is pseudoscientific and contradicts the efficient market hypothesis.

Q4. What are the different types of charts used by a technical analysts? [June 2005 Q7(c)]

Ans. Charting represents a key activity for the technical analyst. The two oldest and most widely used charting procedures are point-and-figure (P&F) charting and bar charting. The major features of P&F charting are that (1) it has not time dimension, (2) it disregards small changes in the stock price and (3) it requires a stock to reverse direction a predetermined number of points before a change in direction is recorded on the chart. P&F charts were used earlier because it is easier to graph manually because it considers only prices on days when there is a major change and in that process, it uses roughly about 20% of total number of prices. With good computer facility and special packages for graphing, there are only very few users of P&F charts.

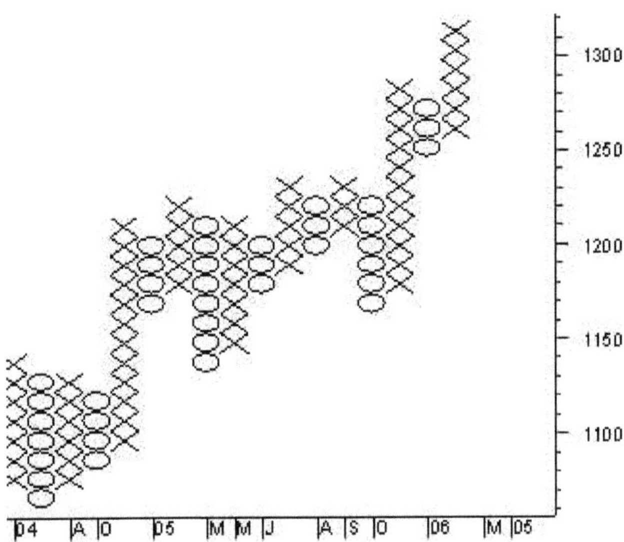

On the other hand, bar chart contain measures on both axis – price on the vertical axis and time on the horizontal axis. On the bar charts, rather than just plotting a point on the graph, the analyst plots a vertical line to represent the range of prices of the stock during the period. The length of the bar represents high and low price of the day whereas the open and close prices are shown as a small ticker on both sides of the bar.

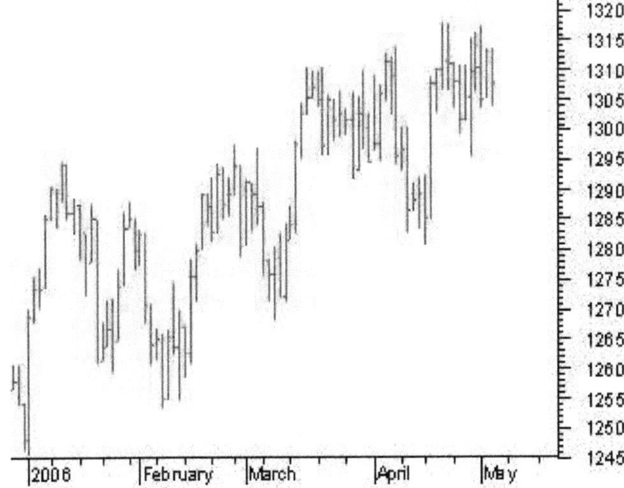

Generally, bar charts also shows at the bottom volume information for the period of which price information is depicted.

The third and most popular type of chart in recent days is candle stick charts. It uses bar chart as a basis but put a small box using open and closer ticker of the bar charts. In order to distinguish whether close is higher or lower than opening price, the body of the candle stick is colored. Normally, a black color indicates a bearish candle stick, meaning the closing price of the day is less than opening price of the day. On the other hand, a white candle indicates, bullish candle meaning closing price is higher than opening price. For the Infosys stock, the candle stick chart is shown below :

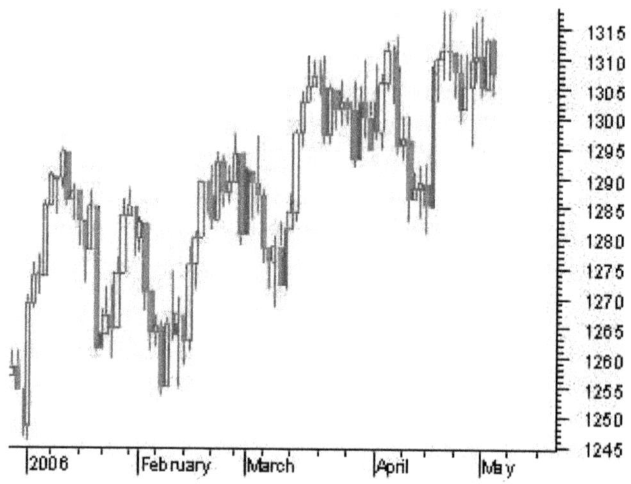

There is yet another simple charting method, where only one of the four prices (open, high, low and close) is used. It is a line chart where you can witness some continuity in the price line.

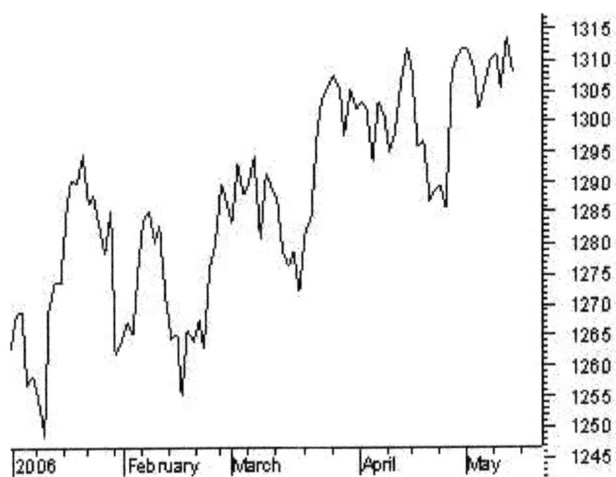

Q5. Which methods are used by technical analysts to analyze the stocks to make investment decisions?

Ans. Technical analysts broadly use two methods to analyze the stocks to find whether it is worth to buy the stock or sell the stock or hold the stock. In the first analysis, the analyst uses the price chart as it is to find trends and patterns. In the second approach, the analysts converts the market information into certain statistical figures and draw conclusion.

1) Analysis of Price Patterns and Trends : Though the time and speed of the adjustment process differ depending on the type of the information and its availability to the investors, they could be broadly classified into certain patterns and this knowledge could be used subsequently to predict the future behavior of the prices. The analysis of patterns is the first principle in the technical analysis and the success of this method of analysis of stock prices depends on the ability of the user in recognizing the patterns.

There are three basic patterns in the stock price movements. They are : uptrend, downtrend and sideways patterns.

The uptrend pattern is recognized the moment the stock form a new high (ascending top) and some times it is also preferred to wait for the formation of ascending bottom. The uptrend pattern once emerged will continue till the time a downtrend pattern is seen in the prices. The downtrend pattern is recognized once the price fails to create a new high and some times it may be preferred to wait for the information of descending bottoms. The purchase decision can be effected once the uptrend pattern is seen and stocks could be hold till the time the downward pattern is noticed. The investor can also go short in the downward pattern. The duration of these two trends for many stocks in the Indian market is fairly long and consistent investment decision on the basis of pattern recognition offers a substantial gain to the investors.

The technical analysts also usually draw lines by connecting the bottoms and tops of uptrend and downtrend respectively. These lines are used to get early warning signal for the reversal of the trend.

There are several variations in trendline pattern. Typically, analysts use more than one trendline to draw such new patterns like Head and shoulders, triangles, double tops or bottoms.

Head and shoulders : The formation is encountered when a bar chart forms a hump followed by a peak, and then another hump. A line joining the lowest points of the humps and the peaks products a resistance line which foresees a bearish market. A reversed head and shoulders formation is the opposite of this, and depicts an on coming bullish tendency.

Triangles : These are formed when the peak point of descending tops fall on a line, as well as the ascending bottoms fall on a different line, and both the lines join up at a point in the future. If the prices break out of this triangle upwards, it indicates bullishness, and if the prices break out on the downside, it indicates bearishness. The odds are that the new move will proceed in the same direction as the one prior to the triangle's formation.

Flags and Pennants : These are forms when, in the midst of a big bull run, the price chart indicates a halt and the boundaries of this consolidation form a flag (parallel lines) or pennant (lines sloping down and up to meet at a point in future). These are formed almost exactly half-way between the bottom and the top, signaling bullish conditions.

A few other important patterns like 'rounding tops and bottoms', 'triangle' and 'double' and triple tops and bottoms' are also useful in investment decision making.

Rounding tops and bottoms : Shows a gradual reversal of the trend from downtrend to uptrend or uptrend to downtrend. The pattern which looks like a *Bowl or Saucer* moves forward with higher momentum after the formation of pattern. Though a safe pattern in view of availability of sufficient time to recognize and initiate action, they are less frequent in actively traded stocks. Actively traded stocks change trend without moving sideways. However, this pattern can be seen in weekly charts and charts of small value stocks.

Double and triple tops and bottoms : Pattern is a horizontal pattern that forewarns reversal in the trend. A 'double or triple tops' pattern is formed when the uptrend in a stock is resisted at a particular level. In a normal market, this pattern shows that a group of traders who had earlier accumulated stocks at lower levels is waiting to liquidate their position once the price reaches the specific level. If the supply at that level is of small quantity and the underlying demand is sufficient, then the stock will easily break the resistance and create a new peak above the previous one. The absence of this break in the resistance level gives way to the formation of double or triple tops pattern and stock price moves downward on the formation of this pattern. The 'double or triple bottoms' pattern indicates strong demand at a particular level and the stock bottoms out at this level.

2) Analysis of Oscillators or Price Indicators : The modern technical analysis deals with indicators, such as moving averages, exponential moving averages, weighted moving averages, moving averages cross over, various types of bands around the moving averages like the bands in terms of standard deviations, Bollinger bands, etc., and the rate of change, etc. Several oscillators are also used, like stochastic, relative strength index (RSI), strength relative to a market index, moving average convergance divergence (MACD) technique. The basic difference between price trends and oscillators is, price trends are often difficult to interpret and what action has to be followed is not defined clearly. On the other hand, oscillators clearly define the investment decision rule.

Moving Average : An average is the sum of prices of a share over some weekly divided by the number of weeks. This point is market on the latest date for which a price bar has been plotted. This process is repeated for the previous dates. The points thus obtained are connected together to give the Moving Average line.

There is another type of moving average called exponential moving average. In an Exponential Moving Average, more weight is given on the most recent data and less weight is given to the older data. Moving Averages smoothen out the apparent erratic movement of share prices and highlight the underlying trend. Moving averages are fairly simple to interpret. The decision rule is :

Buy : When the price line crosses the pre-determined moving averages from bottom, buy the stock and hold it as long as the price line is above the moving average line.

Sell : When the price line crosses the pre-determined moving averages from the top, sell the stock. If short selling is allowed, take short position and hold it as long as price line is below moving averages.

Though moving averages helps investors to take such decision, one has to experiment with different moving averages to find which is suitable for the stock and do lot of mock trading before started using them in the real world. This warning is given because some of you might get tempted to invest in the stocks based on such simple tools.

b) Moving Average Convergence Divergence (MACD) Indicator : MACD is also based on moving averages and used normally for intermediate trend analysis. The MACD is the difference between a 26-day and 12-day exponential moving average. A 9-day exponential moving average, called the "signal" (or "trigger") line is plotted on top of the MACD to show buy/sell opportunities. The MACD proves most effective in wide-swinging trading markets. There are three popular ways to use the MACD : crossovers, overbought/oversold, and divergences.

Crossovers : The basic MACD trading rule is to sell when the MACD falls below its signal line. Similarly, a buy signal occurs when the MACD rises above its signal line. It is also popular to buy/sell when the MACD goes above/below zero.

Overbought/Oversold Conditions : The MACD is also useful as an overbought/oversold indicator. When the shorter moving average pulls away dramatically from the longer moving average (i.e., the MACD rises) it is likely that the security price is overextending and will soon return to more realistic levels. MACD overbought and oversold conditions exist vary from security to security.

Divergences : An indication that an end to the current trend may be near occurs when the MACD diverges from the security. A bearish divergence occurs when the MACD is making new lows while prices fail to reach new lows. A bullish divergence occurs when the MACD is making new highs while prices fail to reach new highs. Both of these divergences are most significant when they occur at relatively overbought/oversold levels.

MACD is equally efficient indicator for those who don't want to buy and sell stocks frequently. For instance, a person who follows MACD may have to buy and sell stocks around four to five times in a normal year.

Figure : a typical (negative) divergence trade using a MACD histogram. At the right-hand circle on the price chart, the price movements make a new swing high, but at the corresponding circled point on the MACD histogram, the MACD histogram is unable to exceed its previous high of 0.3307. (The histogram reached this high at the point indicated by the lower left-hand circle.) The divergence is a signal that the price is about to reverse at the new high, and as such, it is a signal for the trader to enter into a short position.
Source: Source: FXTrek Intellicharts

c) Relative strength Index : This index emphasizes market moves before they occur. When the price of a stock advances, the closing price is higher than the closing price of the previous day. When the price of the stock declines, the closing price is lower than the closing price of the previous day. However, the rise or fall of a market is not smooth. During the rising phase, the price falls several times, while during the falling phase, the price rises several times. Relative Strength Index tell us whether the net difference between the closing prices is increasing or decreasing.

RSI is computer either on 14-days or 14-week basis.

The formula for 14-week Relative Strength Index (RSI) is given below :–

RSI = 100-[100/1+RSI)

$$\text{Where RS} = \frac{\text{Average of 14 weeks up closing prices}}{\text{Average of 14 weeks down closing prices}}$$

This is a powerful indicator and pinpoints buying and selling opportunities ahead of the market. It ranges in value from 0 to 100. Values above 70 are considered to denote overbought conditions, and values below 30 are considered to denote oversold conditions.

There are several other indicators available in the market. Some of the popular indicators are listed below :

1) Accumulation/Distribution

2) Momentum

3) On Balance Volume

4) Price Patterns

5) Price ROC

6) Stochastic Oscillator

7) Volume

8) Volume Oscillator

Q6. What are the different price volume & other indicators of the market? Give their interpretation. [June 2007 Q7(e)]

Ans. Technical indicators help not only to predict individual stock price behavior but also the trend of the market. Some important Price, Volume and other indicators of market are highlighted below :

1) Price Advances vs. Declines : By comparing number of shares which advanced and those declined during a certain period of time, one may know what the market is really doing. The difference between the advances and declines is called 'breadth of market'. During a bull market if breadth declines to new lows while the stock market index makes new highs a peak in the average is suggested. The peak will be followed by major downturn in stock prices generally.

2) High-low Differential or Index can be used as a supplementary measure to 'breadth of the market' to predict market. In theory, a rising market will generally be accompanied by an expanding number of stocks attaining a new highs and a dwindling number of new lows. The reverse will hold for a bearish market.

3) The volume of short selling which refers to selling shares that are not owned, can be useful indicator of the market as well as for individual stocks. Short selling, or as it is called short interest also, can be related to average daily volume. The short interest for a period say a month, divided by average daily gives a ratio. This ratio indicates for many days of trading it would take to use up total short interest. In general when the ratio is less than 1.0, the market is considered weak or weakening. It is common to say that the market is overbought. A decline should follow sooner or later. The zone between 1.0 and 1.5 is considered a neutral indicator. Values above 1.5 indicate bullish territory with 2.0 and above highly favorable. This market is said to be 'oversold'.

4) Odd-lot trading which can be measured by constructing an odd-lot index by relating odd-lot purchase to odd-lot sales (Purchase + Sales), can indicate the direction of the market, as technicians feel that the odd lotters are inclined to do the wrong thing at critical turns in the market. Rising index indicates rising market and failing index indicates falling market which, in effect, mean selling proportionately less at or near the market peak and selling proportionately more before a rise in the market.

5) Mutual-funds Cash as a Percentage of Net Assets on a daily or weekly or monthly basis has been a popular market indicator. The theory is that a low cash ratio, say about 5% would indicate a reasonably fully invested position leaving negligible buying power indicating that the market is due for climb down. High cash ratio indicates possibilities of market climb up.

In the U.S. two confidence indicators have been quite popular with market analyst. One is Barron's ratio of higher-to-lower grade bond yield. The second is Standard and Poor's low priced and high grade common stocks. A rise in Barron's ratio indicates narrowing of the spread between high and low grade bonds which is considered indicative of the rising markets. A fall in the ratio would indicate declining markets.

The S&P confidence indicator relates low-priced (speculative) stocks to the high-grade (quality) stocks. A rise in the ratio (low priced/high grade) indicates rising market, while a fall in the ratio is indicative of declining market.

General Motors Theory is that as General Motors goes so goes the market.

Indeed, the number of indicator technicians use to predict changes in the direction of the overall market is almost limitless.

Q7. Critically evaluate the limitations of Technical analysis in Indian context? [June 2005 Q4]

Ans. The averages discount everything : This is valid even in India. The most popular depictions of averages are simple moving average (average of close, high or low price of a given period) and exponential moving averages (which extend the average over the entire record, assigning more weight to the most recent data). Moving averages of 30 days or 5 weeks depict short-term trend and moving averages of 200 days or 14 to 40 weeks depict long term trend. The crossover of two averages indicate that the trend is changing direction. For instance, if the 5-weeks moving average crosses the 14-week moving average from below to above, it indicates beginning of bullish phase, and may define buying opportunities. The reverse is true if crossing is from above to below.

The market has three movements : Primary, Secondary and Minor. Elliot Ware Theory is the most popular depiction of this principle. It states that the market moves up in five waves, i.e., five up or down, e.g., three moves up and two down, while it moves down in three to five waves. These waves are primary, secondary and tertiary superposed on each other, and it takes experience to separate the three movements. However, in India the market suffers frequent upheavals because of the frequent changes in the government policy, as well as speculative activity indulged in by brokers, and it is not unusual to see the market gain by 25% post-budget, and the individual stocks may jump up or down by 50% within a few weeks due to speculation. Hence in India it is not clear to what extent this theory applies, though some analysts persist in trying to fit the market movements to this theory.

Price bar charts indicate movement : This is true, but moving averages remove the daily or weekly fluctuations and bring out the trend more reliably.

Price/Volume relationships provide background : Unfortunately volume data are not reported in India, and the volume data of specified group shares, where in forward trading is allowed by the exchanges, is published after delay of several weeks. Since forward trading is no indicator of the actual market activity, these relationships are of little value in India.

Price action determines the trend : This is true in India as well.

The averages must confirm : This is based on the premise that if one group of activity, say manufacturing, does not trend in the direction of another group, say transportation, it indicates an oncoming change of trend of the market.

In the Indian Stock Market, it is not unusual to find that the price of a share doubled in few days, and fall back to its original value a few days later. All these malpractice leave their mark on the prices of stocks. Thus one can suspect whether the charts represent the true balance of the demand and the supply forces. Hence, it is possible that some of the technical analysis techniques suitable in other market may not be suitable in India and indicators evolved for American conditions may lead to erroneous conclusions. It is always desirable to do extensive research and experience before taking up technical analysis based investment decision.

Chapter – 9

Efficient Market Hypothesis (EMH)

Q1. Explain the EMH & three forms of market efficiency.

Ans. 'Efficient Market Hypothesis', is based on the premise that current market price is a true reflection of the value of the securities (stocks) and hence it is futile to expect that fundamental or technical analysis will yield a superior return by identifying under-priced or over-priced stocks. Under efficient market hypothesis, investors can expect a return commensurate with the risk associated with such investments.

The Efficient Market Hypothesis states that at any given time, security prices fully reflect all available information. The implications of the efficient market hypothesis are truly profound.

Under this efficient investors can not outperform the market since there are numerous knowledgeable analysts and investors who would not allow the market price to deviate from the intrinsic value due to their active buying and selling. The current market price therefore reflects the intrinsic value at all time and hence, there is no need for fundamental analysts or technical analysis. Empirically also market prices have been observed to move randomly or independently. A net outcome of all this had been a good deal of confused surroundings of the efficient market model or random walk model.

An efficient market is defined as a market where there are large numbers of rational, profit-maximizers actively competing, with each trying to predict future market values of individual securities, and where important current information is almost freely available to all participants. In an efficient market, competition among the many intelligent participants leads to a situation where, at any point in time, actual prices of individual securities already reflect the effects of information based both on events that have already occurred and on events which, as of now, the market expects to take place in the future. In other words, in an efficient market at any point in time the actual price of a security will be good estimate of its intrinsic value.

The random walk theory asserts that price movements will not follow any patterns or trends and that past price movements cannot be used to predict future price movements.

Notion of financial market efficiency is in fact akin to the concept of profit in a perfectly competitive market. Abnormal or excess profits, in such a market are competed away. In an efficient market new information is discounted as it arrives. Price instantaneously adjusts to a new and correct level. An investor cannot consistently earn abnormal profits by undertaking fundamental analysis (to identify undervalued/overvalued securities) or by studying the behavior of share prices with a view to discerning definite patterns. Isolated instance of windfall gains from the stock market does not negate the theory that markets are efficient.

Paradox of the efficient market is that it is efficient because of the organized and systematic efforts of thousand of analyst to evaluate intrinsic values. It ceases to be efficient the moment such efforts are abandoned by the investing community and analyst firms. Market prices will promptly and fully reflect what is known about the companies whose shares are traded only if investors seek superior returns and analyze information promptly and perceptively.

There are three forms of market efficiency :–

a) Weak form of efficiency : The weak form means that the current prices of stock already fully reflect all the information that is contained in the historical sequence of prices. Hence abnormal profits cannot be earned by studying the past behavior of share prices. In other words, weak form of efficiency implies that you can't make excess profits by trading on past trends.

You have to buy and sell stocks every day, and in doing so, you have to pay brokerage fees. Thus, while major patterns in stock prices should not exist, weak patterns that are too costly to arbitrage may persist. It these simple trends are arbitraged away, then the market will follow a random walk, i.e. past deviation from expected returns tell you nothing about future deviations from expected returns.

A weak-form efficient market is one in which past security prices are impounded into current prices. Since past prices are deemed public information, weak form of efficiency implies semi-strong form of efficiency and semi-strong form efficiency implies strong form efficiency.

b) Semi-Strong form of Efficiency : If the market price impounds all of the information available in annual reports, news clippings, gossip columns & so on the market is then called Semi-strong form efficient. But one has to consider certain things. Whether the information put on the Internet public? Are government files available under the freedom of information act public? There must be subtle shades of semi-strong market efficiency, but they are not typically differentiated. Each new piece of information an analyst gathers should be carefully considered with regard to whether it is already impounded in the stock price.

Semi-strong form strikes at the very heart of the analyst profession. Tests of semi-strong have dealt with the speed at which market participants react to public releases of new information. Empirical evidence generally supports the contention that the public reacts quickly to information; but there is also some evidence that the market does not always digest new information correctly.

c) Strong Form of Efficiency : In the strong form of market efficiency, the securities prices reflect all information, whether published or unpublished & even private inside information. This means that even a personal note passed between the CEO and the CFO regarding a major financial decision would suddenly impact the stock price! If so, this is called **Strong-Form-Efficiency**. Few people believe that the market is strong-form efficient, but it is nice to have this benchmark!

To test the strong form three groups of investors having potential access to private information have been examined. These are :

a) Corporate Insiders

b) Stock Exchange Specialists

c) Mutual Funds.

Q2. Describe the different tests of the weak form of EMH?

[June 2007 Q7(d)]

Ans. Tests of Weak from efficiency : Two groups of tests have been formulated by researchers to test the weak form of EMH. One approach looks for statistically significant patterns in security price changes. Another approach searches for profitable short-term trading rules.

(a) Statistical tests of independence : EMH contends that security returns over time should be independent of one another because new information comes to market in a random, independent fashion and security prices adjust rapidly to this new information. Does return of day t correlate with day t-1, t-n? Two major statistical tests have been used to verify this independence.

(i) Serial Independence (Autocorrelation) : Autocorrelation measures the significance of the positive or negative correlation in return over time. Does the rate of return on day t correlate with the rate of return on day t-1 or t-2 or t-3. If the capital market is believed to be efficient then one should expect insignificant correlation for all combinations. Randomness in stock price movements can be tested by calculating the correlation between price changes in one period and changes for the same stock in another period.

If the autocorrelation is close to zero, the price changes are said to be serially independent. This is tested for over-short periods (1 to 4 days, even 9-16 days). A very low autocorrelation provides some evidence that Indian market is also showing efficiency at weak form and hence any analysis on historical price data is of little use. One of main reasons for achieving weak form of efficiency is creating an environment for active trading and reducing the transaction cost.

(ii) Runs tests confirm efficiency : Price changes may be random most of time, but occasionally become serially correlated for varying period of time. Further serial correlation coefficients can be affected by extreme values. To overcome these problems, the run test is used. Run tests ignore the absolute values of the numbers in the series and observe only their signs. Given a series of price changes, each price change is either designated a plus (+) if it is an increase in price or a minus (-) if it is a decrease in price. The result is a set of pluses and minuses just like this -+ + + - + - + + + - + — + +. A run occurs when two consecutive price changes are the same, two or more consecutive positive or negative price changes in a different direction then, such as a negative price change is followed by a positive price change, the run ends and a new run begins.

The actual number of runs observed is compared with the number that are expected from a series of randomly generated price changes. If no significant differences are found, then price changes are random in character.

(iii) Distribution Pattern : The sum or the distribution of random occurrences will statistically conform to a normal distribution. If proportionate price changes are randomly generated events, then their distribution should be approximately normal. Studies have also been undertaken on technical trading strategies based on information other than historical prices, such as odd-lot figures, volume of short sales, advance-decline ratios, chart pattern, etc. The general conclusion is that such strategies have failed to outperform a naïve buy-and-hold strategy.

(b) Tests of Trading Rules : The statistical tests of independence were too rigid to identify the intricate price patterns examined by technical analysis. Technical analysis do not accept a set number of positive or negative price changes as a signal of a move to a new equilibrium in the market. They typically look for a general consistency in the price and volume trends over time. Such a trend might include both positive and negative changes. For this reason technical analysts felt that their trading rules were too sophisticated and complicated to be simulated by rigid statistical tests. Advocates of EMH, hypothesized that investors could not derive profit above a buy and hold policy or abnormal profits using any trading rule that depended solely on any past market information about factors such as price, volume, odd lot shares or specialist activity.

Filters can be prescribed for trading as follows : A share price is increasing and a 20 percent filter has been set. Suppose it starts declining and when it reaches a level 20 per cent below its peak, it is a sell signal. Similarly, if the share is declining in price and it reverses its trend and level, then it is a buy signal. By using such buy and sell signals, using filters ranging from 1 to 50 per cent several studies found that it was not possible to earn abnormal returns. Studies of this trading rule have a range of filters from 0.5 percent to 50 percent. The results indicated that small filters would yield above average profits before taking account of trading commissions. However some filters generate numerous trades and therefore substantial trading costs. When these trading commissions were considered all the trading profits turned to losses. Alternatively, larger filters did not yield returns above those of a simple buy and hold strategy.

Therefore most evidence from simulation of specific trading rules indicate that these trading rules have not been able to beat a buy and hold policy. These results support the weak form of EMH.

Q3. Describe the different tests of the semi-strong form of EMH?

Ans. Semi-Strong form contends that all public information is fully reflected in security prices. Public information includes company financial statements, earning and dividends, bonus announcements and macro-economic data.

The most obvious indication that the market is not always and everywhere semi-strong form efficient is that money managers frequently use public information to take positions in stocks. While there is no evidence that they beat the market on a risk-adjusted basis, it is hard to believe that an entire industry of information production and analysis is for naught. It seems likely that there is value to publicly available information, however there are probably degrees to which information really is public knowledge. What is surprising is that recent studies have shown some evidence that excess returns can be made by trading upon very public information. These tests usually take the form of "backtesting" trading strategies. That is, you play a "what-if" game with past stock prices, and pretend you followed some rule, using information available only at the time of the pretend trade. One common rule that seems to perform well historically is to *buy stocks when the dividend yield is high.* This apparently has made money in the past, even though the information about which of the stocks have high yields and which of them have low yields is widely available. Another rule that generates positive excess returns in back-tests is to buy stocks when the earnings announcement is higher than expected. This seems simple, since current announcements and even forecasts are widely available as well.

The profitability of these simple trading rules depends upon the liquidity of the stocks involved and trading costs ("frictions"). Sometimes the costs outweigh the benefits. While many investment managers explain that they pursue a strategy of buying "Value" stocks (such as low P/E firms) few of these managers have consistently superior track records.

The assumption of semi-strong form efficiency is a good first approximation for a market with as many sharp traders and with as much publicly available information as the U.S. equity market.

Fama, Fischer, Jensen and Roll examined 940 Stock Splits on the New York Stock Exchange from 1927 to 1959. Price of the Stocks was examined for a period of 29 months before the date of split and 20 months after the split. The actual act of splitting did not have any impact on the wealth of shareholders. Further, stock after a stock split did not appear to produce abnormal returns.

Q4. Describe the different tests of the strong form of EMH.

Ans. To disprove strong from EMH, one has to find an insider who has profited from inside information.

The strong form of EMH is of two types :–

a) Super-strong from which includes insiders and specialists (who possess monopolistic information)

b) Near-strong form which includes private estimates developed by (who possess information) financial analysts, portfolio managers, etc.

An insider could be the company promoter, director, executive, auditor, a lawyer, stock broker, a fund manager or even a newspaper correspondent who may be privy to a certain critical development in the company which could affect the company's share prices, before the general public come to know of the development.

The regulation has also given an illustrative list of information that may be construed upon as price sensitive information. It includes financial results (both half yearly and annual), declaration of dividends (both half yearly and annual), issue of shares by way of public, rights or bonus, any major expansion or execution of new projects, amalgamation, mergers and takeovers, taxation charges, extra-ordinary events like strikes etc.

Even studies in USA that rejected the superstrong form of EMH did not report exceedingly large returns. Insiders have been able to earn abnormal returns of the order of 4-5 per cent over a period of 8 months before transaction costs. The fact that mutual funds did not outperform randomly selected portfolio probably means that mutual fund managers compete in an efficient market with other portfolio managers of equal competence.

A simple test for Strong Form of Efficiency is based upon price changes close to an event. Acts of nature may move prices, but if private information release does not, then we know that the information is already in the stock price. For example, consider a merger between two firms. Normally, a merger or an acquisition is known about by an "inner circle" of lawyers, investment bankers and the firm managers before the public release of the information. When these insiders violate the law by trading on this private information, they may make money.

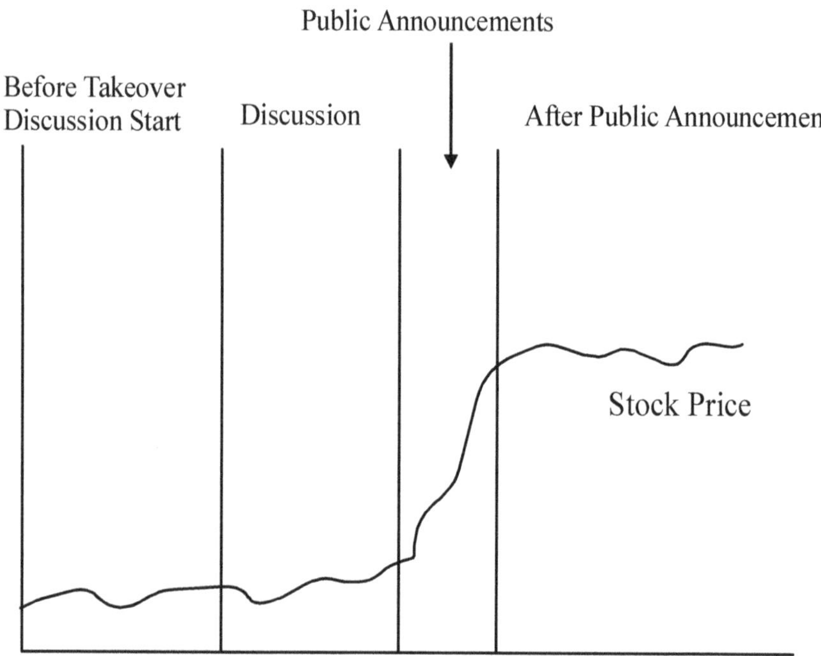

Unfortunately, stock prices typically move up before a merger, indicating that someone is acting dishonestly. The early move indicates that the market has a tendency towards strong-form of efficiency, i.e. even private information is incorporated into prices. However, the public announcement of a merger is typically met with a large price response, suggesting that the market is not strong-form efficient. Leakage, even if illegal, does occur, but it is not fully impounded in stock price.

(a) Technical Anomalies : Common techniques of technical analysis include strategies based on relative strength, moving averages, as well as support and resistance. The majority of researchers that have tested technical trading systems and the weak-form efficient and that technical analysis techniques are not likely to provide any advantage to investors who use them. However others argue that there is validity to some technical strategies.

Researchers have also uncovered numerous other **stock market anomalies** that seem to contradict the EMH. The search for anomalies is effectively the search for systems or patterns that can be used to outperform passive and/or buy-and-hold strategies. Theoretically though, once an anomaly is discovered, investors attempting to profit by exploiting the inefficiency should result its disappearance. In fact, numerous anomalies that have been documented via back-testing have subsequently disappeared or proven to be impossible to exploit because of transactions costs.

(b) Stock Market Anomalies : The stock market related anomalies include –

(i) Fundamental anomalies : Value investing is probably the most publicized anomaly of the fundamental anomalies and is frequently touted as the best strategy for investing. There is a large body of evidence documenting the fact that historically, investors mistakenly overestimate the prospects of growth companies and underestimate value companies. But a study indicates that low P/E portfolio experienced superior returns relative to the market. Over 20 different studies of market reaction to earnings announcements reported post-announcement excess returns.

(ii) Calendar Anomalies : These includes anomalies like the January effect, turn of the month effect, the Monday effect and Year ending in 5 effect.

January Effect : The January Effect is particularly intriguing because it doesn't appear to be diminishing despite being well known and publicized for nearly two decades. Theoretically an anomaly should disappear as traders attempt to take advantage of it in advance. The bottom line is that January has historically been the best month to be invested in stocks.

Many believe the January effect has moved into November and December as a result of mutual funds being required to report holdings at the end of October and from investors buying in anticipation of gains in January.

Turn of the Month Effect : Stock consistently show higher returns on the last day and first four days of the month. Returns for the turn of the months were significantly above average from 1928 through 1993 and "that the total return from the S&P 500 over this sixty-five-year period was received mostly during the turn of the month."

The Monday Effect : Monday tends to be the worst day to be invested in stocks. Several studies have shown that returns on Monday are worse than other days of the week. People are generally in better moods on Fridays and before holidays, but are generally grumpy on Mondays (in fact, suicides are more common on Monday than on any other days). Investors should however, keep in mind that the difference is small and virtually impossible to take advantages of because of trading costs.

Year ending in 5 : In its existence, the DJIA has never had a down year in any year ending in 5. Of course, this may be purely coincidental.

(c) Other Anomalies :

The size effect : Some studies have shown that small firms (capitalization or assets) tend to outperform. Others have argued that it is not size that matters, it is the attention and the number of analysts that follow the stock.

Announcement Based Effect : Price changes tend to persist after initial announcements. Stocks with positive surprises tend to drift upward, those with negative surprises tend to drift downward. Some refer to the likelihood of positive earnings surprise to be followed by several more earnings surprises as the "cockroach" theory because when you find one, there are likely to be more in hiding.

IPOs, Seasoned Equity Offerings, and Stock Buybacks : Numerous studies have concluded that Initial Public Offerings (IPOs) in aggregate underperform the market and there is also evidence that secondary offerings also underperform. Several recent studies have also documented arguably related market inefficiencies. The implication seems to be that investors may do better buying stocks of firms that are repurchasing their own stock rather than from firms that are selling or issuing more of their own stock.

Insider transactions : There have been many studies that have documented a relationship between transactions by executives and directors in their firm's stock and the stock's performance. Insider buying by more than one insider is considered by many to be a signal that the insiders believe the stock is significantly undervalued and their belief that the stock will outperform accordingly in the future. However, many researchers question whether the gains are significant and whether they will occur in the future.

Q5. What are the implications of EMH for security analysis & portfolio management or portfolio selection?

Ans. There are three reasons why security analysis remains relevant even in a generally efficient market. In an efficient but less than perfect market, there is a time lag between the arrival of information and its subsequent reflection in price. During the interval, security analysis provides an opportunity to adjust portfolios profitably. Such rewards are captured by institutional investors, who have the capacity to process large amounts of data quickly and efficiently. Competition of information, which ensures market efficiency, limits the opportunity to earn above average return. The legitimate function of security analysis is to discover information before competitors get it. Security analysis is critical to the investment process even in the case of instantaneous price response. Correct pricing of assets in an efficient market (but less than perfect) does not imply investors' indifference to the choice of assets held in a portfolio. As price of security responds to new information, reflecting change in risk and returns, portfolio adjustment takes place. Security analysis and portfolio management are complementary to an efficient capital market.

There could be two important implications of EMH for portfolio selection. These are :–

1) Even simple random selection leads to portfolio, which approximates the market very closely when 15-20 stocks are held.

2) Index Funds are an outgrowth of the increasing awareness and acknowledgement of market efficiency.

Block – 4

Portfolio Theory

Chapter – 10

Portfolio Analysis

Q1. Define 'Portfolio'. Why portfolios are necessary?

OR

Why is diversification advisable in investment decisions?

Ans. The term 'portfolio' generally means a collection or combination and in the context of investment management, it means a collection of combination of financial assets (or securities) such as shares, debentures and government securities. However, in a more wider context the term 'portfolio' may be used synonymously with the expression 'collection of assets', which can even include physical assets (gold, silver, real estate, etc.)

Portfolios are necessary because of the simple fact that securities carry differing degrees of expected risk which leads most investors to the notion of holding more than one security at a time, in an attempt to spread risks by not putting all eggs into one basket'. Diversification of one's holding is intended to reduce risk in an economy in which every assets returns are subject to some degree of uncertainty. Most investors hope that if they hold several assets, even if one goes bad, the others will provide some protection from an extreme loss.

However, there is a limitation in adding securities to reduce the risk, beyond a level, diversification fails to yield further benefit by way of reducing the risk.

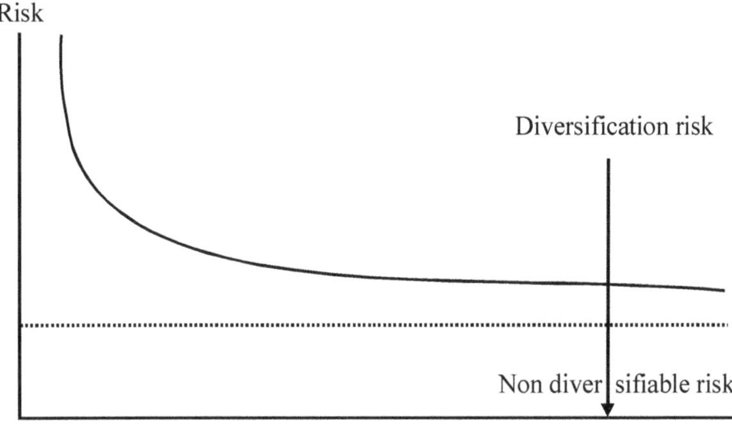

It may be noted that beyond certain portfolio size, the reduction in risk is marginal and insignificant. Several empirical studies have indicated that a portfolio comprising a few assets selected carefully for their risk-diversifying characteristics (i.e. nature and degree of variance and covariance), would be less risky than a portfolio of considerably greater size with assets being selected without regard to risk. Thus, what matters in diversification is not the number of assets per se, but right kinds.

Q2. Explain the concept of arithmetic and geometric average? Why are these returns different?

Ans. Arithmetic Average : The arithmetic average return is equal to sum of returns of 'n' period and divided by 'n'. For instance, if the stock has offered a holding period return of 11% in period 1, 12% in period 2 and 16% in period 3, then the arithmetic average return is equal to 13%. Though it is better than holding period return, this measure suffers because of its failure in considering time value of money. Another problem of this measure is differential treatment of positive and negative return. For instance if a stock price increases from Rs. 10 to Rs. 20 in period 1 and decline back to Rs. 10 in period 2, the Arithmetic average return is still positive value of 25% (period 1 return is 100% and period 2 return is 50%; The total return is 50% and hence average return is 25%)

Geometric Average : The geometric average return is based on the compound value and is also called time-weighted average return. It addresses the problem of differential treatment of positive and negative return described above. The geometric average return is computed as follows :

$$GMR = [(1 + R_1) X (1+R_2) X (1+R_3) ..... X (1+R_N)]^{1/n} - 1$$

Illustration : Five years back, you have applied and was allotted 100 shares of a company at the rate of Rs. 50 per share (Face Value Rs.10). The price at the end of each year along with annual dividend per share received from the stock are as follows :

Year	1	2	3	4	5
Dividend per share (Rs.)	1	1.5	1.5	2	2
Market Price (Rs.)	40	55	70	77	91

Find the Holding Period Return (HPR), Arithmetic Average and Geometric Average return of the stock.

HPR : [Dividend (Rs. 8) + Capital Appreciation (Rs. 41)]/Investment (Rs.50)

: 49/50 = 98% for five years or 19.60% per year.

AA Return : [R_1(-18%) + R_2 (41.25%) + R_3 (30%) + R_4 (12.86%) + R_5 (20.78%)/5

: 17.38%

Note : R_1 is equal to [(41–50)/50], R_2 is equal to [(56.5 – 40)/40], etc.

GA Return : [$(1+R_1) \times (1+R_2) \times (1+R_3) \times (1+R_4) \times (1+R_5)$ 1/5 – 1

: [(.82) × (1.41) × (1.30) × (1.13) × (1.21%)]1/5 – 1

: 15.47%

As you may observe, for the same set of data, we get different values of return. HPR is the highest and GAR is the lowest. The geometric average return measures compounds, cumulative returns over time.

Q3. How do you measure the expected return & risk of a portfolio?

[June 2007 Q4]

Ans. The return on a portfolio of asset is simply a weighted average of the return on the individual assets. The weight applied to each return is the fraction of the portfolio invested in that asset. Thus,

$$R_{(p)} = \sum_{i=1}^{n} x_i r_i$$

$R_{(p)}$ = the expected return of the portfolio

X_i = the proportion of the portfolio's initial fund invested in asset 'i'

R_i = the expected return of asset 'I', and

n = the number of assets in the portfolio.

To illustrate the application of the above formula, let us consider a portfolio of two equity shares A and B. The expected return on A is, say, 15 per cent and that on B is 20 per cent. Further assume that we have invested 40 per cent of our fund in share A and the remaining in B. Then, the expected portfolio return will be

$$0.40 \times 15 + 0.60 \times 20 = 18 \text{ per cent.}$$

It may be noted here that portfolio weight can be either positive or negative. In case of securities, the weight will be negative when investor enters into 'short sales'. Usually, the investors buy securities first and sell them later. But with a 'short sale' this process is reversed; the investors sell first the securities that they do not possess, and buy them later to cover the sales.

Assets when combined may have a greater or lesser risk than the sum of their component risk. This fact arises from the degree to which the returns of individual assets move together or interact. It is vital, therefore, to consider covariance of returns in estimating portfolio variance.

Suppose you have invested your wealth in two securities. Assume the securities prices move in opposite direction such that when one security gains, the other security incurs loss. For instance, if one security reports a gain of 10% in a period, the other one reports a loss of 5%. In the next period, the security, which lost 5% shows a gain of 12% but the other one lost 7%. Though the two securities individually has a variance, an investment of equal amount in these two securities will have a constant return of 5% during the period. In other words, the variance of the portfolio return is zero.

Thus, the portfolio risk, as measured by standard deviation, is less than the sum of component risks. The lower portfolio risk in this case is due to the fact that the returns of the select scrips have not exhibited greater tendency to move together.

The computation of the portfolio variance is based on the following formula :

$$\sigma^2_{(p)} = \sum_{i=1}^{n} \sum_{j=1}^{n} \sigma_{ij}$$

The most important element of this formula, namely, covariance. It is a statistical measure of how two random variables, such as the returns on asset 'i' and 'j', 'move together'. A negative covariance indicates a tendency for the returns to offset one another. For example, a better-than-expected return for one asset is likely to occur along with a worse-than-expected return for the other. A relatively small or zero value for the covariance indicates that there is little or no relationship between the returns for two assets.

Closely related to covariance is the statistical measure known as correlation.

The relationship is given by

$$\sigma_{ij} = \rho_{ij}\sigma_i \sigma_j$$

Where P denotes the correlation coefficient between the return on asset 'i' and that on 'j'. The correlation coefficient simply rescales the covariance to facilitate comparison with corresponding values for other pairs of random variables. The coefficient ranges from – 1 (perfect negative correlation) to + 1 (perfect positive correlation). A co-efficient of 0 indicates that returns are totally unrelated.

Suppose there are three stocks in the portfolio, then the equation to calculate risk is equal to

Stocks	Proportion of Investment	X	y	Z
		W_x	W_y	W_z
X	W_z	$W_x W_x \sigma_{xx}$	$W_x W_y \sigma_{xy}$	$W_x W_z \sigma_{xz}$
Y	W_y	$W_x W_y \sigma_{xy}$	$W_y W_y \sigma_{yy}$	$W_y W_z \sigma_{yz}$
Z	W_z	$W_= W_z \sigma_{xz}$	$W_y W_z \sigma_{yz}$	$W_z W_z \sigma_{zz}$

Scanning

In the above table $W_x W_y$ and W_z are proportions of investments made in security X, Y and Z. The variance of the security X, Y and Z appears in the diagonal cells as σ_{xx}, σ_{yy} and σ_{zz}. The covariance between the securities appears in non-diagonal cells as σ xy, σ xz and σ yz. Covariance of σ_{xy} is equal to covariance of σ_{yx}. This, if number of assets in the portfolio is three, then the portfolio variance can be expressed as follows :

$$\sigma^2_{(p)} = w_x^2\sigma_{xx} + w_y^2\sigma_{yy} + w_z^2\sigma_{zz} + 2w_x w_y \sigma_{xy} + 2w_x w_z \sigma_{xz} + 2w_y w_z \sigma_{yz}$$

The risk of the portfolio that we computed is much lower than the weighted average variance of risk of the individual securities in the portfolio. The reduction portfolio risk is mainly on account of diversification and less than perfect correlation between the stocks.

Q4. Explain the significance of correlation between securities & its impact on portfolio risk? [June 2007 Q4]

Ans. The risk of the portfolio can be reduced to zero if the correlation between the assets included in the portfolio is equal to minus 1. However, such securities are difficult to identify in the market. If two securities are perfectly correlated, then there is no diversification benefit and such combination will not reduce the risk of the portfolio. There are only very few securities in the market whose correlation is equal to minus one. What is more prevalent in the market is securities whose return are correlated between minus 1 to plus 1. Depending on the level of correlation, diversification reduces the risk of the portfolios. The relationship between the assets and its impact on portfolio risk is explained below in Fig. with the help of two securities.

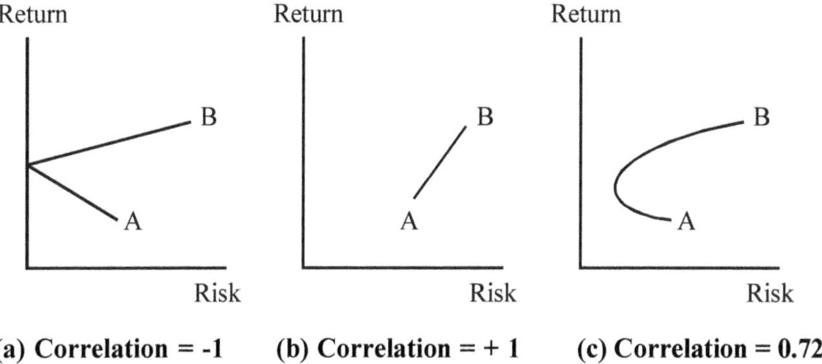

(a) Correlation = -1 **(b) Correlation = + 1** **(c) Correlation = 0.72**

Fig. (c) is more relevant for our discussion since the correlation between the securities is often less than 1 and greater than zero. In such a situation, when an investor combine such securities, the risk of the security is initially reduced but increased afterwards.

Q5. How to derive the efficient set of portfolios among the whole universe of portfolios?

Ans. If there are large number of securities in the market and if you are able to form a two-security portfolio and find the portfolio return and risk for various combinations as discussed above, then you will have a large number of graphs.

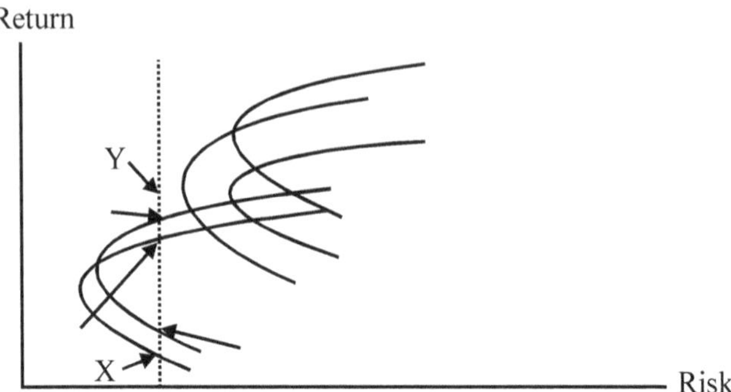

In the above Fig. we have shown six combinations. Now the issue is how to select a portfolio, which is good in terms of minimizing risk and maximizing return. Now carefully look into the above figure particularly on the dashed line. There are five portfolios offering same risk but different returns. Consider the two extreme portfolios – Portfolio X and Portfolio Y. While X offers lowest return, Y offers highest return for the same level or risk. Now, we can say all four portfolios below Y are inefficient in a sense that you would not buy such portfolio with the same risk level to earn lower return. If we eliminate all such inefficient portfolios, we will get a smooth curve, which connects the left extreme values of the curves. Such an efficient set of the portfolios are shown in fig.b.

The new curve A and B connects all left-extreme values of earlier portfolios and become efficient set of portfolio. For instance, we don't have any portfolios above this curve to show better return for a given level or risk. All portfolios below this curve of A and B are inefficient and hence no one prefer such combination of stocks. All points in the curve are efficient because it is not possible to evaluate two points in the curve and conclude one is better than the other. They are all efficient because for a higher risk, the expected return is also high. Depending on the investors risk and return expectation, they can pick up any combination. If an investor like to have low risk, then she or he will select a combination of stocks close to point A. On the other hand, if an investor likes to assumes more risk, she or he will prefer a portfolio close to point B.

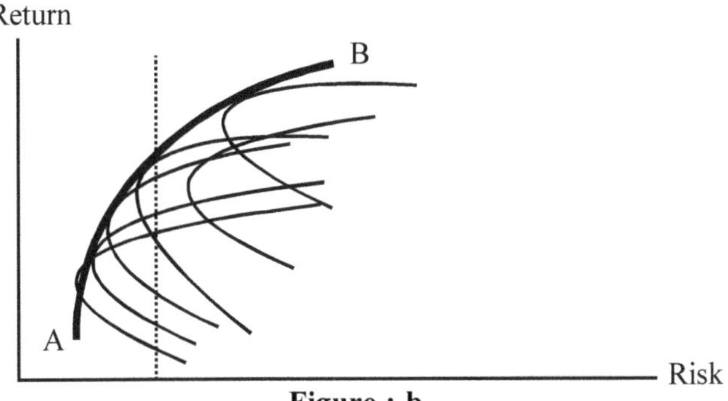

Figure : b

Q6. Write short notes on

Ans. (1) Variance Covariance Matrix : Variance-covariance matrix is a table, which symmetrically arrays the covariance between a number of random variables. Variances of the random variables lie on the diagonal of the matrix, while covariance between the random variables lie above or below the diagonal.

(2) Feasible Set : Feasible set (or opportunity set) represents the set of all portfolios that can be formed by an investors, given a population of assets.

[June 2007 Q5(a), Dec 2007 Q7(f)]

(3) Efficient Set : Efficient set (Efficient frontier) is the set of portfolios of a given population of assets which offer the maximum possible expected return for a given level of risk.

(4) Optimal Portfolio : Means the feasible portfolio that offers an investor the maximum level of satisfaction, given his or her own preference for return and risk. This portfolio is located at the point of tangency between the efficient set and an indifference curve of the investor. **[Dec 2006 Q4]**

Q7. Practical Questions

Illustration 1 : The risk and return characteristics of the two projects are shown below :

	X	Y
Expected return	12%	20%
Risk	3%	7%

An investor plans to invest 80% of its available funds in Project X and 20% in Y. The correlation coefficient between the returns of the projects is + 1.0

Find out the risk and return of the portfolio of X and Y.

Solution : The expected return of the portfolio is

Investment	Expected Return	Proportion	Weighted Return
X	12%	.8	9.6
Y	20%	.2	4.0
			13.6

The risk of the portfolio is :

$$\sigma_P^2 = \sigma_x^2\ \omega_x^2 + \sigma_y^2\ \omega_y^2 + 2\omega_x\ \omega_y\ \sigma_x\ \sigma_y\ r_{xy}$$

$= (3^2 \times .8^2) + (.2^2 \times 7^2) + 2 \times 3 \times 7 \times .8 \times .2 \times 1$

$= 14.4$

$\sigma_P = 3.8$

So, the risk and return of the portfolio are 3.8 and 13.6% respectively.

Illustration 2 : An investor is interested to construct a portfolio of two investments, S_1 and S_2. He has gathered the following information about theses investments :

	S_1	S_2
Expected	**12%**	**20%**
σ of return	**10%**	**18%**

Coefficient of correlation, r, between S_1 and S_2 =.15.

He has decided to consider only five portfolios of S_1 and S_2 as follows :

(i) All funds invested in S_1.

(ii) 50% of funds in each of S_1 and S_2.

(iii) 75% of funds in S_1 and 25% in S_2.

(iv) 25% of funds in S_1 and 75% in S_2.

(v) All funds invested in S_2.

Find out (1) Expected return under different portfolios,

(2) Risk factor associated with these portfolios,

(3) Which portfolio is best for him from the point of risk, and

(4) Which portfolio is best for him from the point of view of return.

Solution : The expected return of the portfolio is the weighted averages of the returns of the securities, the weights being the proportion of the securities, in the portfolio. The portfolio returns can be calculated as follows :

Portfolio	S_1		S_2		Expected return of Portfolio
	Prop.	Return	Prop.	Return	$\bar{r}$
1	1	.12	0	.20	.12 + 00 = 12 %
2	.50	.12	.50	.20	.06 + .10 = 16%
3	.75	.12	.25	.20	.09 + .05 = 14%
4	.25	.12	.75	.20	.03 + .15 = 18%
5	0	.12	1	.20	0 + .20 = 20%

Therefore, the expected returns from different portfolios are 12%, 16%, 14%, 18% and 20% respectively. The risk of the portfolios can be measured in terms of σ of the portfolio as follows :

$$\sigma_p = \sqrt{\sigma_1^2\ \omega_1^2 + \sigma_2^2\,\omega_2^2 + 2\omega_1\omega_2\sigma_1\sigma_2 r_{12}}$$

Portfolio	S_1	σ_1	S_2	σ_2	r_{12}	σ_P^2	σ_P	
1	1	.1	0	.18	.15	.0100	.100	= 10.0%
2	.50	.1	.50	.18	.15	.0119	.109	= 10.9%
3	.75	.1	.25	.18	.15	.0087	.094	= 9.4%
4	.25	.1	.75	.18	.15	.0198	.140	= 14.0%
5	0	.1	1	.18	.15	.0324	.180	= 18.0%

From the point of view of the return, the portfolio 5, i.e., 100% of funds invested in the security, S_2, is the best. This portfolio will earn him a return of 20%, i.e., 20% of Rs. 1,00,000 = Rs. 20,000 p.a. however, the best portfolio from the point of view of risk is one which has the least σ.The coefficient of variation, i.e., $\sigma / \bar{r}$ is also least for portfolio 3, i.e., .671 only against .833, .681, .777 and .9 for portfolios 1, 2, 4 and 5 respectively. The investor X should therefore select the portfolio 3 (i.e., 75% of funds invested in S_1 and 25% in S_2). This will give him the least risk factor of 9.4% but the return will be restricted to Rs. 12,500 only (i.e., 10% of Rs. 75,000 + 20% of Rs. 25,000).

Illustration 3 : Following information is available in respect of two securities, thin & Fat :

	Thin		Fat
Expected return	15%		20%
Standard deviation	10%		15%
Weight	50%		50%
Covariance		100	

Find out the risk and return of the portfolio. Also find out the correlation between the returns of Thin and Fat.

Solution : The expected return of the portfolio :–

$$\begin{aligned}\overline{R} &= w_T R_T + w_F R_F \\ &= .5 \times .15 + .5 \times .20 \\ &= 17.5\%\end{aligned}$$

The standard deviation of the portfolio :–

$$\begin{aligned}\sigma_P^2 &= w_T^2 \sigma_T^2 + w_F^2 \sigma_F^2 + 2\,Cov_{TF} \\ &= (.5)^2\ (10)^2 + (.5)^2\ (15)^2 + 2 \times 100 \\ &= 25 + 56.25 + 200 \\ &= 281.25 \\ \sigma_p &= 16.77\%\end{aligned}$$

Correlation between the returns : –

$$\begin{aligned}r_{TF} &= Cov_{TF} / \sigma_T\ \sigma_F \\ &= 100/(10 \times 15) \\ &= .667\end{aligned}$$

Illustration 4 : The following information is available from Mr. Z in respect of his portfolio :

	Weight	Expected Return	Standard Deviation
Security A	50%	20%	24%
B	50%	12%	16%

(i) Find out the correlation between the returns if the standard deviation of the portfolio is 20% or 18%.

(ii) Find out the standard deviation of the portfolio comprising A & B in the ratio of 25% and 75% respectively.

Solution : (i) the standard deviation of a portfolio is defined as :

$$\sigma_P^2 = w_A^2 \sigma_A^2 + w_B^2 \sigma_B^2 + 2 w_A\ w_B\ \sigma_A\ \sigma_B\ r_{AB}$$

The value of correlation, r, may be found by putting other values in this equation.

If σ_p is 20%

$$(20)^2 = (.5)^5(24)^2 + (.5)^2 + (16)^2 + 2(.5)(.5)(24)(16)(r)$$
$$400 = 144 + 64 + 192r$$
$$r = 1$$

So, the securities A & B have perfect positive correlation.

If σ_p is 18%

$$(18)^2 = (.5)^5(24)^2 + (.5)^2(16)^2 + 2(.5)(.5)(24)(16)(r)$$
$$324 = 144 + 64 + 192r$$
$$r = .604$$

(ii) Give the correlation of 1 and weights of 25% and 75%, the standard deviation of the portfolio is : –

$$\sigma_P^2 = w_A^2\sigma_A^2 + w_B^2\sigma_B^2 + 2w_A\ w_B\ \sigma_A\ \sigma_B\ r_{AB}$$
$$= (.25)^5(24)^2 + (.75)^2(16)^2 + 2(.25)(.75)(24)(16) \times 1$$
$$= 36 + 144 + 144$$
$$= 324$$
$$\sigma_p = 18\%$$

So, the standard deviation of the portfolio would be 18%.

Illustration 5 : Returns on shares of ABC Ltd. and PQR Ltd. for the past two year are as follows :

	Year 1	Year 2
ABC Ltd.	11%	17%
PQR Ltd.	20%	8%

Calculate the following :–

(a) Expected return of portfolio made up of 50 per cent of ABC Ltd. And 50 per cent of PQR Ltd.

(b) Expected return of portfolio made up of 60 per cent of ABC Ltd. and 40 per cent of PQR Ltd.

(c) Standard deviation of each stock.

(d) Covariance and coefficient of correlation between the two.

(e) Portfolio risk if both are invested in the ratio of 2 : 1

(f) Overall portfolio risk if the ratio of investment is 1: 1.

Solution : Expected rate of return of shares of ABC Ltd. :–

$$= \frac{\sum R}{n} = \frac{11+17}{2} = 14\%$$

Expected rate of return of shares of PQR Ltd. :–

$$= \frac{20+8}{2} = 14\%$$

Expected return of portfolio (50% of ABC Ltd. and 50% of PQR Ltd.) :–

$$(.5 \times 14\%) + (.5 \times 14\%) = 14\%$$

Expected return of portfolio (60% of ABC Ltd. and 40% of PQR Ltd.) :–

$$(.6 \times 14\%) + (.4 \times 14\%) = 14\%$$

Standard deviation of ABC Ltd. shares : –

$$\sigma_P = \sqrt{\frac{(11-14)^2 + (17-14)^2}{2}} = 3$$

Standard deviation of PQR Ltd. shares :–

$$\sigma_q = \sqrt{\frac{(20-14)^2 + (8-14)^2}{2}} = 6$$

Covariance between ABC Ltd. and PQR Ltd :–

$$\text{Cov.} = \frac{1}{N}\sum_{i=1}^{n}(R_A - \overline{R}_A)(R_P - \overline{R}_P)$$

$$= \frac{1}{2}\left[(11-14)(20-14) + (17-14)(8-14)\right]$$

$$= \frac{1}{2}\left[(-18) + (-18)\right]$$

$$= \frac{-36}{2} = -18$$

Coefficient of Correlation :–

$$\frac{\text{Covariance of ABC \& PQR}}{\sigma_A \ \sigma_B} = \frac{-18}{6 \times 3} = -1$$

Portfolio risk in case ABC Ltd. and PQR Ltd. are invested in the ration of 2 : 1 :–

$$\sigma = \sqrt{\omega_A^2 \sigma_A^2 + \omega_P^2 \sigma_P^2 + 2\,\omega_A \omega_p (r_{AP}\, \sigma_A\, \sigma_P)}$$

$$= \sqrt{\left(\frac{2}{3}\right)^2 \times 9 + \left(\frac{1}{3}\right)^2 \times 36 + 2 \times \frac{2}{3} \times \frac{1}{3}(-1 \times 3 \times 6)}$$

$$= \sqrt{4 + 4 - 8}$$

$$= \sqrt{0} = 0$$

Portfolio Risk in case ABC Ltd. and PQR Ltd. are invested in the ration of 1 : 1 :–

$$\sigma = \sqrt{(.5)^2 \times 9 + (.5)^2 \times 36 + 2 \times \frac{1}{2} \times \frac{1}{2}(-1 \times 3 \times 6)}$$

$$= \sqrt{\frac{9}{4} + \frac{36}{4} + (-9)}$$

$$= \sqrt{\frac{9}{4}} = 1.5$$

Chapter – 11

Portfolio Selection

Q1. Explain the method of constrained minimization problem to find out the efficient set.

Ans. An efficient set can be determined by minimising portfolio risk (i.e. return variance) for any level of expected return. The return at some level is specified and risk is minimised, we have one point (i.e. , a portfolio) on the efficient frontier. Thus, we need to solve the following constrained minimisation problem

Minimise variance $(\sigma^2_{(p)}) = \sum_{i=1}^{n} \sum_{j=1}^{n} x_i x_j \sigma_y$

Subject to the constraints :–

1) Expected return (R_P) is equal to some predetermined level R_P)

2) The sum of the portfolio weights for all assets in the portfolio must be equal to

$1; \left(\sum_{i=1} x_i = 1 \right)$

3) The portfolio weight assigned to any asset should be positive ($x_i \geq 0$, i = 1, ..., n). In other words, short sales are not allowed.

This is a quadratic programming problem because of the presence of terms like x_j^1 and x_i, x_j in the objective function.

Q2. What are the limitations of Markowitz's approach?

Ans. (1) It is easy to see that the Markowitz's approach to trace efficient set is extremely demanding in its input data needs and computation requirements. Indeed, while analysts and portfolio managers are accustomed to thinking about expected rates of return, they are much less comfortable in assessing the possible ranges of variation in their expectations, and are usually, not at all accustomed to estimating covariance of returns among assets.

(2) The problem is made more complex by the number of estimates of covariance [which is equal to (N^2-N)/2, where N is no of securities] required. For a set of 200 shares, for example, we need to compute [200 (200-1)/2] = 19,900 covariance. It is unlikely that the analysts will be able to directly estimate such a staggering number of inputs.

Q3. What are the assumptions of single index model?

Ans. The single-index model assumes that the returns of various securities are related only through common relationships with some basic underlying factor. In the words of Sharpe, this factor "may be the level of the stock market as a whole, the gross national product, some price index, or any other factor thought to be the most important single influence on the returns from securities". A casual observation of share-price movements, at least, tends to support this line of argument. There is considerable evidence that when the stock market goes down, most shares tend to decrease in price. It appears, therefore, that one reason share returns might be correlated is because of a common response to market changes as measured by the movements in, say share price index.

It is further assumed that the residuals are not correlated across shares of different companies; that is, e_i is independent of e_j for all values of i and j. This is an important assumption; it implies that the only reason shares vary together, systematically, is because of a common co-movement with the market. Thus, single-index model assumes away all other possible effects on shares' returns, such as industry effects.

Q4. Give the equation of the characteristic line.

Ans. Characteristic Line shows the linear relationship between the return on any asset and the return on the market index.

Algebraically, the characteristic line can be defined as

$$R_i = a_i + \beta_i R_m$$

Where, R_i = the return of security i

a_1 = the components of share i's return that is independent of the market's performance-a random variable;

R_m = the rate of return on market index-a random variable; and

β_i (beta) = the slope of the characteristic line that measures the expected change in R_i given a change in R_m.

It is useful to break the term R_i in two components :

1. α_i (alpha), the expected value of a_i; and
2. e_i, the random element with a mean value of zero.

In terms of graphical presentation e_i (or residuals, as they are frequently referred to) measure vertical deviations from the characteristic line. With this, equation can not be written as

$$r_i = \alpha_i + \beta_i R_m + e_i$$

where R_m and e_i (both random variables) are conveniently assumed to be not correlated with each other.

Q5. Give the important results of Single Index Model?

Ans. The following important results of single index models are :

a) expected return, $R_i = \alpha_j + \beta_i R_{m..}$

b) the variance of share's return $\sigma^2_i = \beta^2_1 \sigma^2_m + \sigma^2_{ei}$ where σ^2_m and σ^2_{ei} are variances of the distribution of R_m and e_i, respectively; and

c) covariance of returns between shares i and j, $\sigma_{ij} = \beta_i \beta_j \sigma^2_m$

It is apparent from (a) above that the expected return has two components: a unique or non-market part, α_j and market related part, $\beta_i R_m$. Even though shares have many common characteristics and, as a result, tend to move together, their numerous individual and distinguishing properties cause shares to co-move with the market at different rates. Accordingly, how sensitive a share's price is to changes in the overall market i.e. the value of its 'beta' is of great significance in determining the expected return.

Like the expected return, we can always split the variance of share's return into two parts, as shown in (b) above. The first component $\beta^2_{i2} \alpha^2_m$, is called the 'systematic risk' or 'market risk' of the investment. Since σ^2_m is the same for all shares, systematic risks will differ among different shares accordingly to the magnitudes of their 'betas', β_1. Similarly stated beta measures sensitivity of a share's price movements compared with those of the market index. Shares having betas less than 1 can be said to be 'defensive'. One per cent increase (decrease) in the market return is likely to be accompanied by a less than one per cent increase (decrease) in the shares' rate of return. The investors are thus defended to some extent against the occurrence of major down fall in the market return.

The second component of variance of share's returns, σ^2_{ei}, is known as 'residual variance' or 'unsystematic risk' or 'diversifiable risk'. If the single-index model is a valid description of the process generating shares returns, there is no need for direct estimates of the covariance. All that we need to know are the values of share betas and variance of returns on market index; the covariance between any two shares i and j can next be obtained easily by employing the relationship as noted above.

Q6. How the variance of portfolio returns is estimated?

Ans. The total risk or variance of returns on share 'i' is given by

$$\sigma^2_1 = \beta_i \sigma^2_m + \sigma^2 e_i$$

Total variance = Systematic Risk + Residual variance

This equation holds for a portfolio of shares as well. Rewriting the equation for a portfolio, we get

$$\sigma^2_1 = \beta^2_p \sigma^2_m + \sigma^2_{ep}$$

Total Portfolio variance = Portfolio Systematic Risk + Portfolio residual variance
Where the subscript 'p' denotes a portfolio
It can be further shown that

$$\beta_p = \sum_{i=1}^{n} x_i \beta_i$$

Portfolio Beta = Weighted average of individual share betas
and,

$$\sigma^2_{ep} = \sum_{i=1}^{n} x_i^2 \sigma^2_{ei}$$

Portfolio residual variance = Weighted average of individual residual variances where weights are squared.
To Illustrate the above formula of portfolio variance, let us consider the following two shares :–

Share	Beta	Residual Variance
Ashok Leyland	0.54	98.2
Grasim	1.13	62.7

Suppose, in investor is planning to put equal amounts of his investible fund in these two shares. Then we have

$$\beta_p = 0.54 \times .50 + 1.13 \times -.50 = 0.56$$

$$\sigma^2_{ep} = [98.2 \times (.5)^2] + [62.7 \times (.5)^2] = 40.2$$

If σ^2_m is equal to 81.0 per cent, the variance of the returns of the portfolio under consideration will be given by

$$\sigma^2_p = (.56)^2 \times 81.0 + 40.2 = 65.6$$

$$\sigma_p = 8.1\%$$

The portfolio's systematic risk component (β_p) has increased due to the addition of a more risky share, its non-market related risk component has declined. Given the single-index model's assumption that residuals (e ,s) of different shares are not correlated (this is already explained), it is not difficult to appreciate how a portfolio's residual variance begins to diminish as the number of shares (n) in the portfolio is increased.

Q7. Explain

(a) Lagrange Multipliers Technique (b) Corner Portfolio (c) Market Index

(d) Multi-Index Model (e) Goal Programming (f) Single Index Model

Ans. (a) Lagrange Multiplier's Technique is a technique of solving non-linear optimization problems.

(b) Corner Portfolio is an efficient portfolio with the following property: any combination of two adjacent corner portfolios will result in a portfolio that lies on the efficient set between the two corner portfolios.

(c) Market-Index (or Market Portfolio) refers to the ultimate market index, containing a common fraction of the total market value of every capital investment in the economic system.

(d) Multi-Index Model purports to explain the covariance that exist between assets on the basis of changes over time in two or more indices, such as the market, GDP, or the money supply.

(e) Goal Programming is a technique to solve optimization problem with multiple goals. When no feasible solution exists, the goal-programming model permits attaining the goals as closely as possible.

(f) Single-Index Model purports to explain the covariance, which exist between the returns on different assets on the basis of the relationship between the returns and a single index, usually the market index.

Q8. Illustrations:

Illurstration 1 : A security has a standard deviation of 2.8%. The correlation coefficient of the security with the market is 0.8 and the market standard deviation is 2.3%. The return from government securities is 12% and from the market portfolio is 18%. What is the required return on the security?

Solution : The required rate of return on the security may be found with the help of CAPM, for which β is as follows :–

$$\beta = \frac{r_{sm} \times \sigma_s}{\sigma_m}$$

$$= \frac{.8 \times 2.8}{2.3} = .974$$

$$\text{Now } R_p = I_{RF} + (R_m - I_{RF})\beta$$

$= .12 + (.18 - .12)\ .974$

$= 17.84\%$

So, the required return on security is 17.84%.

Illurstration 2 : The risk-free rate, I_{RF} is 4% and the market premium is 8.6% and β of the security is 1.3. What is the expected return of the security under CAPM? What would be the expected return if the β were to double?

Solution : With β 1.3, the risk premium for the security would be 1.3 × 8.6% = 11.18%. Now, the I_{RF} is 4%, therefore the expected return of the security would be 11.18 + 4% = 15.18%. This can also be presented as follows :–

$$R_s = I_{RF} + (R_m - I_{RF})\beta$$
$$= 4\% + (8.6\%)\ 1.3$$
$$= 15.18\%$$

If the β doubles to 2.6, then the expected return as given by the above equation would be 26.36%.

Illurstration 3 : The risk and return of the market portfolio are 12% and 19% respectively. The risk-free interest rate is 10% and unlimited lending and borrowing is possible at this rate. Comment on the efficiency of the following portfolios:

Portfolio	Expected Return	Risk (σ)
A	**24%**	**30%**
B	**22%**	**16%**
C	**17%**	**10%**

Solution : To be efficient portfolios, these must lie on the CML. In the light of the risk level given for these portfolios, their expected return should be :–

$$\text{Expected Return} = I_{RF} + (R_M - I_{RF}) \frac{\times \sigma_s}{\sigma_m}$$

$$\text{For Portfolio A} = 10\% + (19\% - 10\%) \frac{30\%}{12\%}$$
$$= 32.5\%$$

$$\text{For Portfolio B} = 10\% + (19\% - 10\%) \frac{16\%}{12\%}$$

$= 22\%$

For Portfolio C $= 10\% + (19\% - 10\%) \dfrac{10\%}{12\%}$

$= 17.5\%$

Comparison of these CML based expected returns with the given expected return of the portfolios gives an idea about the efficiency of the portfolio. Portfolio B is an efficient portfolio and its expected return (22%) is equal to CML based return. However, the other portfolios A and C are not efficient portfolios and lie below the CML.

Illurstration 4 : The riskless securities are offering a return of 8%, while return of the market portfolio is 15%. The standard deviation of the market portfolio is 2%. An investor has constructed a portfolio which has standard deviation of 1.5% and a correlation with the market return of .85. Find out the expected return of the investor.

Solution : In view of the information given, the β of the investor's portfolio can be calculated as follows :–

$$\beta = \frac{r\sigma_p}{\sigma_M} = \frac{.85 \times .015}{2} = .006375$$

Now, the expected return of the portfolio is : –

$$R_p = I_{RF} + (R_M - I_{RF})\beta = .08 + (.15 - .08).006375 = 8.04\%$$

Chapter – 12

Capital Market Theory

Q1. Distinguish between Capital Asset Pricing Model (CAPM) & portfolio theory.

Ans. The CAPM is commonly confused with portfolio theory. Portfolio theory is simply the use of statistical and mathematical programming techniques to derive optimal tradeoffs between risk and return. Under very restrictive assumptions (rarely found in financial markets), the CAPM is highly specialized subset of portfolio theory. Even so, the CAPM has become very popular as it provides a logical, common sense tradeoff between risk and return.

The major implications of the capital market theory is that the expected return of an asset will be related to a measure for that asset, known as 'beta'. The exact manner in which expected return and beta are related is specified by the Capital Asset Pricing Model or CAPM, which was developed in mid 1960s.

Q2. Define risk free asset. List out two risk free assets.

Ans. Risk-free asset is an asset, which has a certain future return. In other words, a risk-free asset is one for which there is no uncertainty regarding the future returns; that is, the investor known exactly what the value of the asset will be at the end of the holding period. Thus, variance of returns of a risk-free asset is equal to zero. A good example of such asset are short term govt. securities like t-bills.

Whether all types of government bonds are risk-free asset? It is difficult to say because long-term government bonds are exposed to certain types of risk like interest rate risk and inflation risk. For instance, if the maturity period of a government security is (say) 15 years, while the investment horizon (or the holding period) of an investor is (say) three-months, then the investor does not really know at what market price he will be able to sell the security at the end of his holding period. Any change in interest-rate structure during the holding period will influence the market price of the security. To give an idea, upward revision of interest rate will have a tendency to lower the market price, such that yield-to-maturity at market-price-based acquisition of the security of given maturity period compares well with the yield-to-maturity of new issue with similar maturity period. This is an example of what is termed as 'interest-rate-risk'. Thus, normally, the short term government securities like Treasury Bills are called risk-free securities. Can corporate debentures be treated as risk-free asset? Certainly not, because risk of default is associated with them in addition to interest rate risk and inflation risk. In fact, corporate bonds have more risk like liquidity risk. However, in relative term, they are better than equity on risk.

The co-movement of returns of risk-free asset and risky asset (or portfolio of risky assets) is always zero.

Q3. Explain the concept of risk free lending & borrowing?

Ans. Investing in a risk-free asset is frequently referred to as 'risk-free lending', since investment in such assets tantamount to giving loan directly to the government. An investor does not have to depend solely on this own wealth to decide how much to invest in assets. She/he can borrow and invest, i.e., the investor can use financial leverage. However, investor will have to pay interest on borrowed funds and such borrowing is also assumed to have same risk-free interest rate and hence deemed as "risk-free borrowing".

Q4. What would be the average rate of return & standard deviation of returns when a risk free asset is combined with a portfolio of risky assets? Also show the efficient set of portfolio with risk-free asset.

Ans. When a risk-free asset is combined with a portfolio of risky assets then the expected portfolio return (rp) is given by

$$R_p = X R_f + (1 - x) R_i \quad \text{(a)}$$

Where,

X = the proportion of the portfolio invested in a risk-free asset;
R_f = risk-free rate of return; and
R_i = expected return on risky portfolio 'i'

For risk-free asset variance and covariance terms are Zero, i.e. $\sigma_f^2 = 0$ and $\sigma_{if} = 0$; and so the standard deviation is given by :–

$$\sigma_p^2 = (1 - x)^2 \sigma_i^2$$

Or $$\sigma_p = (1 - x)\sigma_i$$

As the equations (a) and (b) are both linear, the returns-risk graph for portfolio possibilities, combining the risk-free asset and risky portfolios on Markowitz efficient frontier, is represented by a straight line. Figure a illustrates the position

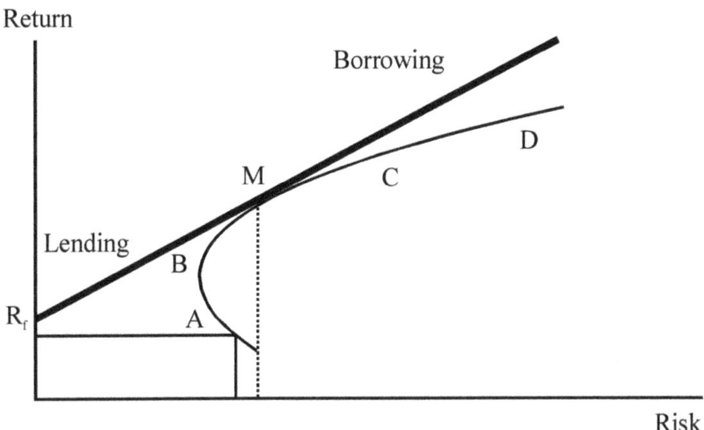

Figure : Efficient set of portfolios with risk free asset

The set of efficient portfolios market in the curve A, B, M, C and D are set of portfolios consisting of risky assets. Suppose there is a risk-free asset offering a return of Rf. Now compare an investment in the portfolio of A (consisting of risky assets) and investment in risk-free security. Investment in risk-free security offers a return higher than A but without any risk. Thus, investment in risk-free security is superior to investments in A and in that process A become inefficient portfolio. A tangent line drawn from Rf through the curve A-B-M-C-D- is now become efficient portfolio. Only one portfolio marked 'M', which consists of risky assets falls under the new efficient frontier. Such portfolio is called 'market portfolio' which consists of all risky assets. Investors can now earn any return they like on the efficient frontier by investing a part of money in M and the rest in Rf.

Q5. Show the workings with respect to expected return & risk of a leveraged portfolio with the help of an example?

Ans. In the real world, investors often purchase assets with borrowed funds. Let us assume that investors can borrow, whatever amount he wants, at a risk-free rate. In other words, we are assuming that risk-free lending and risk-free borrowing are the same. Now, suppose that an investor borrows an amount equal to 50 per cent of his original wealth of, say Rs.10000. So he has total of Rs.15,000 which he proposes to invest in portfolio M. What is the proportion of fund being invested in M? It is given by

$$1 - x = 15{,}000/10{,}000 = 1.5$$

However, the sum of proportions being invested in risk-free assets and M must still equal one, which means that

X = – 5,000/10,000 = – 0.5

The negative sign indicates borrowing, on which there will be interest payment at Rf. Thus restating equation, we have

R[= – 0.5 Rf + 1.5 Rm

Assuming that Rf = 8% and Rm = 20%, the return on the leveraged portfolio will be

= –0.5 (0.8) + 1.5 (0.20) = 0.26 and 26 per cent

which is significantly higher than Rm, the expected return of 20 per cent on risky portfolio M. Using equation, the standard deviation of returns from leveraged portfolio works out to

$$\sigma_p = (1 - (-.5))\,\sigma_m = 1.5\,\sigma_m$$

Thus, our investor could increase return along the line Rf – M – Q. Herein lies the advantage of owning a 'leveraged' portfolio. However, leveraging also involves a trade-off' the risk of a leveraged portfolio is always higher than that of tangency portfolio, M (in the instant case it is 11.5 times).

Q6. What does CML represent? What happens to the capital market line & the choice of an optimal portfolio if borrowing rate is allowed to exceed the lending rate? [June 2007 Q5(a)]

Ans. CML represents the risk premium as a result of taking on extra risk. James Tobin added the notion of leverage to Modern Portfolio Theory by incorporating into the analysis an asset, which pays a risk-free rate of return. By combining a risk-free asset with risky assets, it is possible to construct portfolios whose risk-return profiles are superior to those of portfolios on the efficient frontier. Consider the diagram below:

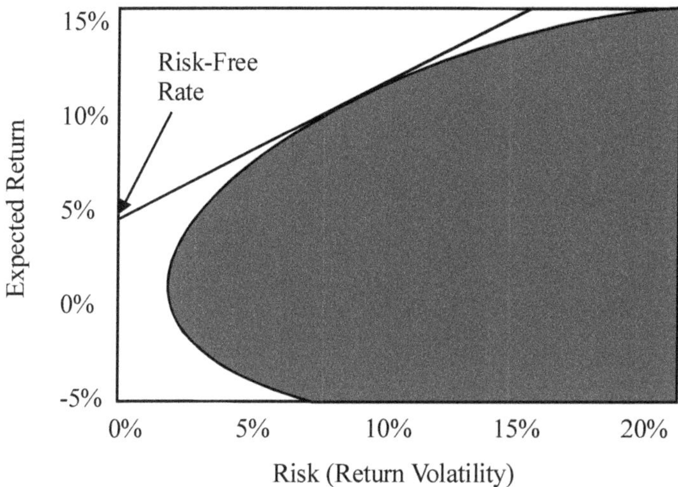

The capital market line is the tangent line to the efficient frontier that passes through the risk-free rate on the expected return axis.

The risk-free rate is assumed to be 5%, and a tangent line-called the capital market line has been drawn to the efficient frontier passing through the risk-free rate. The point of tangency corresponds to a portfolio on the efficient frontier. That portfolio is called the "super efficient" portfolio.

All types of investors, whether aggressive or conservative, will achieve their desired risk-return levels by combining market portfolio with risk-free lending or borrowing along the CML. The term $r_m - r_f / \sigma_m$, the slope of capital market line, can be thought of as the market price of risk for all efficient portfolios. It is extra return that can be gained by increasing the level of risk (standard deviation) on an efficient portfolio by one unit.

With the two terms, CML sets the expected return on an efficient portfolio as

(Price of time) + [(Price of risk) × (Amount of risk)]

When Risk-Free Rates are different : Figure below shows the modified efficient set; it consists of three distinct but connected segments $R_{fL} - M_L - M_B - B$

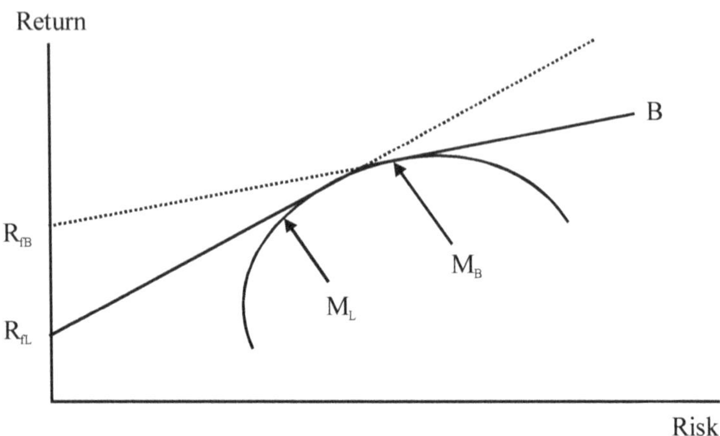

The construction of this efficient set can be explained as follows : If $R_{fL} = R_{fB}$, then the resulting efficient set will be given by the straight line from R_{fL} through M_L. On the other hand, if risk-free lending and borrowing rates are the same, but the rate is set at a higher level equal to R_{fB}, then the efficient set of portfolios will lie on the straight line from R_{fB} through M_B. We may note that M_B is at a higher level than M_L on Markowitz's efficient set, since it corresponds to a tangency point associated with higher risk-free rate, R_{fB}.

Now, since the investor cannot borrow at R_{fL}, that part of the line emanating form R_{fL} that extends past M_L is not available to the investors (shown in fig. by dotted lines) and can be removed from out consideration. Again, since the investors cannot invest in a risk-free asset that earns a rate equal to R_{fB}, that part of the line from R_{fB} and going through M_B, but lying to the left of M_B, is not available to the investors; and, hence, can be ignored. On the whole, R_{fL} - M_L - M_B - B becomes the relevant efficient set to investors who can lend at Rf_{LL} and borrow at R_{fB}.

Q7. Explain CAPM. List out its assumptions. [Dec 2007 Q4]

Ans. The CAPM model describes the relationship between risk and expected return, and serves as a model for the pricing or risky securities. CAPM says that the expected return of a security or a portfolio equals the rate on a risk-free security plus a risk premium. If this expected return does not meet or beat required return then the investment should not be undertaken.

The CAPM builds upon the Markowitz portfolio model and capital market line.

Assumptions of CAPM are : –

1) Investors evaluate portfolios by looking at expected returns and standard deviations of those portfolios over a one-period horizon.

2) Investors, when given a choice, between two otherwise identical portfolios, will choose the one with higher expected return.

3) Investors, when given a choice, between two otherwise identical portfolios, will choose the one with the lower standard deviation or risk.

4) Individual assets are infinitely divisible, meaning that an investor can buy a fraction of a share if he or she so desires.

5) There is a risk-free rate at which in investor may either lend money or borrow money.

6) Taxes and transaction costs are irrelevant.

7) All investors have the same one-period horizon.

8) The risk-free rate is the same for all investors.

9) Information is freely and instantly available to all investors.

10) Investors have homogeneous expectations, meaning that they have the same perception in regard to the expected returns, standard deviations and covariance of returns between any two assets.

Needless to say, many of these assumptions are unrealistic. But, then assumptions are necessary in building a model.

Q8. Show the relationship between CML, CAPM & SML. What are the limitations of CAPM & SML? [Dec 2006 Q7(d), Dec 2007 Q4]

Ans. Given the capital market line (CML) and the dominance of the market portfolio, the relevant risk measure for an individual risky asset is its covariance with the market portfolio (Cov_{im}), or what is known as its 'systematic risk'. When the covariance is standardized by the covariance for the market portfolio, we obtain the well-known 'beta' measure of systematic risk and a security market line (SML) that relates the expected return for an asset to its beta. Under the CAPM, the postulated relationship is such that higher an asset's beta, the higher its expected return.

It is not possible for any stock to offer a risk-return relationship below or above the CML. If it is below the CML, such stocks are known as overpriced stocks (meaning they offer, lower return for a given level of risk and there is an alternative portfolio on the line of CML, which offer higher return) and investors will start selling the stock until its return increases to the level of CML. The same applies if there is a stock above CML in terms of risk and return and investors will buy such stocks by offering higher price until its return declines to CML. In CML, one can observe only two points namely Rf and M. Since M is an efficient portfolio, we assume that the risk associated with the M is the least. Further it is also a diversified portfolio and hence one can expect no unsystematic risk.

If the stock falls on the CML line, it's return (R_s) should satisfy the following equation.

$$B_s = R_f + \beta_s (R_m - R_f)$$

$$\text{where } \beta_s = \sigma_{sm} / \sigma^2 m$$

The term B_s, representing covariance of returns between assets 's' and the market portfolio divided by return variance of market portfolio, is known as "beta co-efficient" or simply "beta" for asset. The above equation is the most often written form of the CAPM. If the beta and expected return of stocks are plotted, the line that shows the risk and return of all stocks in the market is called security market line (SML).

Security returns is directly related to beta, as the CAPM asserts. Research results suggest that the CAPM does not reflect the world well at least when tested using ex-post data. Critics have pointed out that the inadequacy of the model is due to its austerity. The market, in principle includes all stocks, a variety of other financial instruments, and even non-marketable assets such as an individual's investment in education; to which no market index like the SP 500 Index in US or Bombay Stock Exchange National Index (or any other index used to represent the market) can be a perfect proxy. And when we measure market risk using an imperfect proxy, we may obtain a quite imperfect estimate of market sensitivity. Secondly, the CAPM asserts that only a single number-market return – is required to measure risk. The actual returns depend upon a variety of anticipated and unanticipated events. Thus, while systematic factors are the major sources of risk in portfolio return, different portfolios have different sensitivities to these factors.

Q9. Elaborate APT as a pricing model.

Ans. At the core of APT is the recognition that the several systematic factors affect security returns. It is possible to see that the actual return, R, on any security or portfolio may be broken down into three constituent parts, as follows : –

$$R = e + bf + e$$

Where :

E = expected return on the security

b = security's sensitivity to change in the systematic factor

f = the actual return on the systematic factor

e = returns on the unsystematic factors.

The above equation merely states that the actual return equals the expected return, plus factor sensitivity times factor movement, plus residual risk. The APT Equation may thus be expanded to :

$$R = E + (b_1)(f_1) + (b_2)(f_2) + (b_3)(f_3) + (b_4)(f_4) + e$$

Each of the four middle terms in this equation is the product of the returns on a particular economic factor and the given stock's sensitivity to that factor. Some of the factors empirically found to be useful in measuring risk are :

- Changes in expected inflation, unanticipated changes in inflation, industrial production, default-risk premium and term structure of interest rates.
- Default risk, term structure of interest rates, inflation, long term expected growth rate of profits for the economy, and residual market risk.

Illustration 1 : The expected return of the market portfolio is 14% and the risk-free rate is 10%. The standard deviation of the market portfolio is 28% whereas the standard deviation of the portfolio of an investor is 37%. Find out the expected return of the investor as per CML.

Solution : Expected return as per CML is :–

$$R_P = I_{RF} + (R_m - I_{RF})\frac{\sigma_p}{\sigma_m}$$

$$= .10 + (.14 - .10) \times \frac{37}{28}$$

$$= 15.28\%$$

So, the expected return of the investor is 15.28%

Illustration 2 : Following information is provided in respect of a security :–

$$I_{RF} = 8\%$$

$$R_m = 16\%$$

$$\beta = .7$$

i) Find out the expected return of the security, and

ii) If the other security has an expected return of 24%, what must be its beta?

Solution : i) The expected return of the security is : –

$$R_s = I_{RF} + (R_M - I_{RF})\beta$$

$$= 0.8 + (.16 - .08)\ .7$$

$$= 13.6\%$$

ii) The β of the security : –

$$R_S = 24\%$$

$$R_M = 16\%$$

$$I_{RF} = 8\%$$

Now, β on the basis of CAPM is : –

$$.24 = 0.8 + (.16 - .08)\beta$$

$$= .08 + .08\beta$$

$$\beta = .16 + .08$$

$$= 2$$

Illustration 3 : Following information is available in respect of a security:

β of the security	**0.8**
Rate of return on market portfolio	**15%**
Risk-free interest	**7%**

Find out the expected rate of return of the security. Also find out the β of the security which has an expected return of 20%.

Solution :

Risk-free rate, $I_{RF} = 7\%$

Market Return, $R_M = 15\%$

$$\beta = .8$$

$$R_S = I_{RF} + (R_M - I_{RF})\beta$$

$$= .07 + (.15 - .07).8$$

$$= 13.4\%$$

β of a security which has return of 20%

$$R_S = 20\%$$

$$R_S = I_{RF} + (R_M - I_{RF})\beta$$

$$.20 = .07 + (.15 - .07)\beta$$

$$\beta = 1.625$$

Chapter – 13

Portfolio Revision

Q1. Define Portfolio Revision? Distinguish between 'active' and 'passive' strategies of portfolio revision?

OR

Why portfolio revision is necessary? [Dec 2006 Q6]

Ans. Portfolio revision involves changing the existing mix of securities. The objective of portfolio revision is similar to the objective of portfolio selection i.e., maximizing the return for a given level of risk or minimizing the risk for a given level of return. It calls for reallocation of funds between bond and stock market through economic analysis, reallocation of funds among different industries through industry analysis and finally selling and buying of stocks within the industry through company analysis.

In the context of portfolio management the need for revision is even more because the financial markets are continually changing. Thus the need for portfolio revision might simply arise because market witnessed some significant changes since the creation of portfolio. Further, the need for portfolio revision may arise because of some investor-related factors such as (i) availability of additional wealth, (ii) change in the risk attitude and the utility function of the investor, (iii) change in the investment goals of the investors and (iv) the need to liquidate a part of the portfolio to provide funds for some alternative uses. The other valid reasons for portfolio revision such as short-term price fluctuations in the market do also exist. There are thus numerous factors, which may be broadly called market related and investor related.

Active strategy of portfolio revision involves a process similar to portfolio analysis and selection which is based on an analysis of fundamental factors covering economy, industries and companies as well as technical factors. As against this, under passive strategy some kind of formula plans are followed for revision.

Active revision strategy seeks 'beating the market by anticipating' or reacting to the perceived events or information. Passive revision strategy, on the other hand, seeks 'performing as the market'. The followers of active revision strategy are found among believers in the "market inefficiency" whereas passive revision strategy is the choice of believers in the 'market efficiency'. However, some of the formula strategies are on the premise of market inefficiency. The frequency of trading transactions, as is obvious, will be more under active revision strategy than under passive revision strategy and so will be the time, money and resources required for implementing active revision strategy than for passive revision strategy. In other words, active and passive revision strategies differ in terms of purpose, process and cost involved. On the face of it, active revision strategy might appear quite appealing but in actual practice, there exist a number of constraints in undertaking portfolio revision itself.

Q2. What are the common constraints in portfolio revision?

Ans. There are number of constraints in portfolio revision, in general, and active portfolio revision, in particular.

Transaction Cost : Buying and selling of securities involve transaction cost including brokers' fee. Frequent buying and selling for portfolio revision may push up transaction costs beyond gainful limits.

Taxes : In most of the countries, capital gains are taxed at concessional rates. But for any income to qualify as capital gains, it should be earned after lapse of a certain period. To qualify such concessional rate of 10% tax, investors today need to wait for one year after the purchase. The minimum period required to qualify for long-term capital gain is one year for financial assets. Frequent selling for portfolio revision may mean foregoing capital gains tax concession. Higher the tax differential (between rates of tax for income and capital gains), higher the constraint. Even for tax switches, which means that one stock is sold to establish a tax loss and a comparable security is purchased to replace it in the investor's portfolio, one must wait for a minimum period after selling a stock and before repurchasing it, to be able to declare the gain or loss. If the stock is repurchased before the minimum fixed period, it is considered a wash sale, and no gain or loss can be claimed for tax purpose.

Statutory Stipulations : In many countries including India, statutory stipulations have been made as to the percentage of investible funds that can be invested by investment companies/mutual funds in the shares/debentures of a company or industry. In such a situation, the initiative to revise portfolio is most likely to get stifled under the burden of various stipulations. Government owned investment companies and mutual funds are quite often called upon to support sagging markets (albeit counters) or cool down heated markets, which puts limit on the active portfolio revision by these companies.

No Single Formula : Portfolio revision is not exact science. The entire process if fairly cumbersome and time-consuming.

Q3. Give the assumptions & limitations of formula plans & critically evaluate the different formula plans available for investors?

[Dec 2006 Q6, Dec 2007 Q6]

Ans. Mechanical portfolio revision techniques have been developed to ease the problem of whether and when to revise to achieve the benefits of buying stocks when price are low and selling stocks when prices are high. These techniques are referred to as formula plans. There are three popular formula plans namely, Constant-Dollar-Value Plan, Constant Ratio Plan and Variable Ratio Plan.

The formula plans are based on the following assumptions :–

1) The stock prices move up and down in cycles.

2) The stock prices and the high grade bond prices move in the opposite directions.

3) The investors cannot or are not inclined to forecast direction of the next fluctuation in stock prices which may be due to lack of skill and resources or their belief in market efficiency or both.

The use of formula plans call for the investor to divide his investment funds into two portfolios, one aggressive and the other conservative or defensive. The aggressive portfolio usually consists of stocks while conservative portfolio consists of bonds. The formula plans specify pre-designated rules for the transfer of funds from the aggressive into the conservative and vice-versa such that it automatically causes the investor to sell stocks when their prices are rising and buy stocks when their prices are falling.

Constant-Dollar-Value Plan : The Constant-Dollar-Value Plan (CDVP) asserts that the dollar value (or Rupee Value in Indian Context) of the stock portion of the portfolio will remain constant. This, in operational terms, would mean that as the value of the stocks rises, the investor must automatically sell some of the shares to keep the value of his aggressive portfolio constant. If, on the other hand, the prices of the stocks fall, the investor must buy additional stocks to keep the value of aggressive portfolio constant. By specifying that the aggressive portfolio will remain constant in dollar value, the plan implies that the remainder of the total fund will be invested in the conservative fund. The investor must choose pre-determined action points, also called revaluation points, very carefully. The action points can have significant effect on the returns of the investor. Action points placed at every change or too close would cause excessive transaction costs that reduce return and the action points placed too far apart may cause the loss of opportunity to profit from fluctuations that take place between them.

Assume an investor has Rs.20,000 and she divides the investment in two equal parts of Rs.10,000 each. The first part was invested in bonds and the second one was invested in equity shares. She watches price movements of stocks and bonds regularly and decides to sell the shares if the equity portfolio wealth appreciated more than 20% of initial investment of Rs.10,000 (i.e. Rs.12,000) and invest the sale proceeds in bonds. Similarly, if the equity portfolio depreciates by 20% of initial wealth of Rs.10,000 (i.e. Rs.8,000), she will transfer Rs. 2,000 from bonds (by selling bonds) to equity and by buying equity so that the equity part will be brought back to Rs.10,000. In other words, the action point is when the equity portfolio appreciates or depreciates by 20%.

The constant-ratio plan specifies that the value of aggressive portfolio to the value of the conservative portfolio will be held constant at the pre-determined ratio. This plan automatically forces the investor to sell stocks as their prices, rise, in order to keep the ratio of the value of their aggressive portfolio to the value of the conservative portfolio constant.

Likewise, the investor is forced to transfer funds from conservative portfolio to aggressive portfolio as the price of stocks fall. For example, the starting point and other information are the same as in the previous example. The desired ratio is 1:1. The initial fund of Rs.20,000 is thus divided into equal portfolios of Rs.10,000 each. The action points are pre-determined at $\pm$.10 from the desired ratio of 1.00.

The constant-ratio plan calls for more transactions than the constant-dollar-value plan did, but the actions triggered by this plan are less aggressive. This plan yielded an increase in total value at the end of the cycle compared with the total value yielded under constant-dollar-value plan. It did, however, outperform the buy-and-hold strategy.

Variable-ratio plan is more flexible variation of constant ratio plan. Under the variable ratio plan, it is provided that if the value of aggressive portfolio changes by certain percentage or more, the initial ratio between the aggressive portfolio and conservative portfolio will be allowed to change as per the pre-determined schedule. Some variations of this plan provide for the ratios to vary according to economic or market indices rather than the value of the aggressive portfolio. Still others use moving average of indicators. In order to illustrate the working of variable ratio plan let us continue with the previous example with the following modifications:

The variable-ratio plan states that if the value of the aggressive portfolio rises by 20 per cent or more from the present price of Rs.25, the appropriate ratio of the aggressive portfolio will be 3:7 instead of the initial ratio of 1:1. Likewise, if the value of the aggressive portfolio decreases by 20 percent or more from the present price of Rs.25, the appropriate percentage of aggressive portfolio to conservative portfolio will be 7.3

The revaluation actions/transactions undertaken are also fewer under this plan compared to other two plans. Variable ratio plan may thus be more profitable compared to constant-dollar-value plan and the constant-ratio plan. But, as is obvious, variable ratio plan demands more forecasting than the other formula plans. The variable ratio plan requires forecasting of the range of fluctuations both above and below the initial price (or say median price) to establish the varying ratios at different levels of portfolio values.

Indeed, none of the formula plans are a royal road to riches, First, as an effort to provide mechanical rules for portfolio revision, they make no provision for what securities should be selected for investment. Second formula plans by their nature are inflexibility makes it difficult to know if and when to adjust the plan to new conditions emerging in the investment environment. Finally, in the absence of much faith in the market efficiency, particularly in the development of stock markets, there may not be many followers of formula plans for portfolio revision.

Q4. Write short notes on
(a) Dollar (or rupee) cost Averaging (b) Share Averaging

Ans. (a) Under this method, an investor will invest a constant amount every period (say monthly) in single or group of stocks or invest in index funds. In that process, if the stock price is low, the investor would be in a position to buy more stocks (or more units in the case of mutual funds investments) and if the prices are high, then the investor will purchase less number of stocks or units. Since the amount invested is same irrespective of the market conditions, this technique is referred to as Dollar or Rupee cost averaging. Over a period of time (after couple of bull and bear markets), one can expect the average cost of holding per share will be considerably less than the current market price. Note that one has to wait for minimum period to see the impact of such plans.

(b) Share Averaging : Under this method, the investor will buy the same quantity of stock every period (say month) irrespective of the market price. That is when the market is bullish, the investor will invest more money and when the market is bearish, she or he will invest less money. In that process, it automatically allows the investors to save more in bonds when the market is not doing well and invest more in stocks when the market is doing well.

Q5. Compare and contrast the dollar (or rupee) cost averaging and share averaging.

Ans. When the market prices are volatile, the constant dollar or rupee cost averaging is better than share averaging. On the other hand, if the market is on the uptrend for a long period of time, share averaging will yield better returns. Further share averaging may demand more investment if the prices have gone up too high. In dollar cost averaging, the amount is held constant and one can plan for such periodic investment in portfolio of stocks. Depending on the investors' willingness to invest money and availability of money and also their forecast on the future, they can choose one of the two methods.

Block – 5

Institutional and Managed Portfolios

Chapter – 14

Performance Evaluation of Managed Portfolio

Q1. Differentiate between the performance measurement & performance evaluation of an investment portfolio?

Ans. Performance measurement is just an accounting function, which attempts to reconcile the end of period with the beginning period values. Performance evaluation on the other hand addresses the issues of whether :–

– The past performance was superior or inferior

– Such performance was due to skill or luck

– Future performance will be similar or not

Portfolio performance is generally evaluated over a time interval of at least four years, with returns for a number of sub-periods within the interval-like monthly or quarterly, so that there is fairly adequate number of observations for statistical evaluation. The calculation of portfolio return is fairly simple when there are no deposits or withdrawals of money from a portfolio during a time period. In that case, the market value of the portfolio in the beginning and at the end of the period are determined for computing the portfolio return. The three steps involved in the computation of the return are illustrated in Table.

Step 1 : Portfolio Value-Beginning

Shares	No. of Shares	Market Price	Portfolio Value Beginning
A	50	100	5,000
B	100	70	7,000
C	200	40	8,000
D	500	60	30,000
Total (V_0)			**50,0000**

Step 1 : Portfolio Value-Ending

Shares	No. of Shares	Market Price	Portfolio Value Beginning
EA	50	200	10,000
FB	100	40	4,000
GC	200	110	22,000
HD	500	80	40,000
Total (V_1)			**76,0000**

Step 3 :

Portfolio Return : = (V1-V0) / V0
= (76,000 - 50,000) / 50,000
= 52%

Performance measurement becomes difficult when a client adds or withdrawals money from the portfolio. The per cent in the market value of the portfolio as computed above may not be an accurate measurement of the portfolio's return in that case. For example, if the beginning value of the portfolio is Rs. 50,000 in cash in nearly November, the value at the end of the year would be Rs. 1,00,000. The portfolio return in this case will be

$$\frac{1,00,000 - 50,000}{50,000} = 100\%$$

However, the entire return was not due to the investment manager. A more accurate measure would be :–

$$\frac{(1,00,000 - 30,000) - 50,000}{50,000} = 40\%$$

Q2. Explain the difference between dollar or value weighted rate of return & time-weighted rate of return? [Dec 2007 Q5(a)]

Ans. It is also called as the internal rate of return. The interest rate that equates the initial contribution and the cash flows that occur during the period with the ending value of the fund is the dollar-weighted rate of return. Note, we don't need to make any adjustment for Rupee investment since the dollar actually means value.

For example, a portfolio has market value of Rs. 100 lakhs. In the middle of the quarter, the client deposits Rs. 5 lakhs and at the end of the quarter the value of the portfolio is Rs. 103 lakhs. The dollar-weighted return would be calculated by solving the following equation for r

$$100 = \frac{-5}{(1+r)} + \frac{103}{(1+r)^2}$$

r = -.98% which is a semi-quarterly rate of return.

This can be converted into quarterly return with the help of the following equation.

$$[1 + (-0.0098]^2 - 1 = -1.95\% \text{ per quarter.}$$

The time-weighted rate of return is the weighted average of the internal rates of return for the sub-periods between the cash flows and it is weighted by the length of the sub-periods. In the other words, the geometric (compounded) return measured on the basis of periodic market valuations of assets is time-weighted return. The equation for time-weighted rate of return for 4 sub-periods is

$$\text{Annual Return} = [(1+r_1)(1+r_2)(1+r_3)(1+r_4)]^{1/4} - 1$$

Let us now make a quick comparison of Dollar-Weighted and Time-Weighted Returns. A portfolio of Rs.50 lakhs declines to Rs. 25 lakhs in the middle of the quarter at which point, the client deposits Rs. 25 lakhs with the portfolio management firm. Note before the investment of additional investment, the investor lost 50% of the return. At the end of the quarter, the portfolio has a market value of Rs. 100 lakhs. Now the investor during the second period has gained 100% return. The semi-quarterly dollar-weighted return for this portfolio would be :

$$50 = \frac{-25}{(1+r)} + \frac{100}{(1+r)^2}$$

r = 18.6%

Quarterly dollar-weighted return = $(1.186)^2 - 1$ = 40.66%. However, its quarterly time-weighted return would be $[(1 - 0.5)(1 + 1)]^{1/2} - 1 = 0$ per cent. There is a lot of difference in returns. Each rupee lost half its value in the first half and the remaining half doubled in value in the second half. Thus assuming that a rupee at the beginning was worth a rupee at the end of the quarter, a time-weighted return is a more accurate measure than the dollar-weighted return. A dollar-weighted return is strongly influenced by the size and the timing of the cash flows (that is deposits or withdrawals) over which the investment manager has no control.

Q3. How can the performance of a mutual fund be evaluated?

Ans. The performance of a mutual fund can be evaluated by using the beginning and the end period net asset values as follows :

$$R_p = \frac{(NAV_t - NAV_{t-1}) + D_t + C_t}{NAV_{t-1}}$$

The one period rate of return for a mutual fund (R_p) is defined as the change in net asset value (NAV) plus its cash disbursement (D) and capital gains disbursements (C). Net asset values of the fund are adjusted for bonus and rights.

Q4. Discuss the sharpe, treynor & Jensens measures of portfolio returns?

OR

How to measure the risk-adjusted returns?

Ans. Risk-adjusted return given an idea of whether the return earned is commensurate with the risk incurred.

It is a measure of how much risk a fund or portfolio assumed to earn its returns. This is usually expressed as a number or a rating. The performance of a fund should be assessed in terms of return per unit of risk. ***Two well-known measures of risk adjusted return are used for the purpose, one is the Sharpe ratio and the other is the Treynor ratio.***

Sharpe Ratio : Sharpe ratio is the ratio developed by Bill Sharpe and is calculated by subtracting the risk free rate from the rate of return for a portfolio and dividing it by the standard deviation of the portfolio returns. It tell us whether the returns of the portfolio were because of smart investment decisions or by excess risk.

Sharpe ratio = (Portfolio return - risk free return)/Portfolio Standard Deviation

Or

$$[r_p - r_f] / \sigma_p$$

i.e., realized return on the portfolio (r) in excess of risk-free rate (r_f) divided by the standard deviation of the portfolio (σ_p).

For example, let's assume that we look at a one-year period of time where an index fund returned 11% and Treasury bills earned 6%. If the standard deviation of the index fund was 20%, then the Sharpe ratio is computed as follows :

Sharpe ratio = [11– 6] / 0.20 = 25

Treynor Ratio (Reward to Variability ratio) : Treynor Ratio measures the returns earned in excess of those that could have been earned on a riskless investment, per unit of market risk assumed. This ratio is similar to Sharpe Ratio except it uses beta instead standard deviation. It is the ratio of a fund's average excess return to the fund's beta.

T = Return of Portfolio – Return of Risk Free Investment/Beta of Portfolio

Or

$$[r_p - r_f]/\beta_p$$

i.e. realised portfolio return (r_p) in excess of risk-free rate (r_f) divided by the beta of the portfolio (β_P).

The absolute risk adjusted return is the Treynor ratio + the risk free rate.

For instance, assume two portfolios A and B. The respective returns are 12% and 14% with a beta of 0.7 and 1.2 respectively. If the Risk Free Rate = 9%, then the Treynor's ratio is computed as follows :

T (A) = [12 – 9] / 0.7 = 4.25

Risk adjusted rate of return of Portfolio A = 4.25 + 9 = 13.25%

T (B) = [14 – 9] / 1.2 = 4.17

Risk adjusted rate of return of Portfolio B = 4.17 + 9 = 13.17%

Both these measures provide a way of ranking the relative performance of various portfolios on a risk-adjusted basis. For investors whose portfolio is a predominant representation in a particular asset class, the total variability of return as measured by standard deviation is the relevant risk measure.

The ranking on both these measures will be identical when both the funds are well diversified. A poorly diversified fund will rank lower according to the Sharpe measure than the Treynor ratio. The less diversified fund will have greater risk when using standard deviation is used.

Differential Return (Jensen Measure) : Jensen's measure is an absolute measure of performance, adjusted for risk. This measure assesses the portfolio manager's predictive ability. The objective is to calculate the return that should be expected for the fund, given the risk level and comparing it with the actual return realised over the period.

The model used is ;

$$R_{jt} - R_{ft} = a_i + \beta_i (R_{mt} - R_{ft}) + e$$

The variables are expressed in terms of return and risk.

R_{jt} = Average return on portfolio for period t

R_{ft} = Risk-free rate of interest for period t

a_i = Intercept that measures the forecasting ability of portfolio manager

β_i = A measure of systematic risk

R_{mt} = Average return on the market portfolio

e = Error term

In both Sharpe and Treynor models, it is assumed that the intercept is at the origin. In the Jensen model, the intercept can be at any point, including the origin.

If the intercept is a_1 and has a positive value, it indicates that the superior return has been earned due to superior management skills. On the other hand if the intercept is zero, it indicates neutral performance. This manager has done as well as an unmanaged randomly selected portfolio with a buy-and-hold strategy. If the intercept is negative, then the managed portfolio did not do as well as an unmanaged portfolio of equal systematic risk.

Jensen's measure is illustrated below :

Actual Returns and Risk

	R_{ft}	R_{jt}	R_{mt}	Beta
Fund A	5	12	15	0.50
Fund B	5	20	15	1.50
Fund C	5	14	15	1.10

From Jensen's equation, the return on the portfolio (assuming c = 0 and the intercept (a_i) is at the origin) is :

$$R_{jt} = R_{ft} + \beta_1 (R_{mt} - R_{ft})$$

Fund A

$R_{jt} = 5 + 0.5 (15 - 5) = 10$

$a = 12 - 10 = 2\%$ (Excess Positive Return)

Fund B

$= 5 + 1.5 (15 - 5) = 20$

$a = 20 - 20 = 0\%$ (Neutral Performance)

Fund C

$= 5 + 1.10 (15 - 5) = 16$

$a = 14 - 16 = -2\%$ (Negative Return)

Jensen measure not only calculates the differential between actual and expected earnings, but also enables an analyst to determine whether the differential return could have occurred by chance or whether it is significantly different from zero in a statistical sense.

The R^2 for regression of the fund returns with the market returns indicates the degree of diversification of the fund. Higher the R^2, the more the fund is correlated with the market index; and less the unsystematic risk, the better diversified is the fund.

Q5. What are the problems associated with risk adjusted.

Ans. The problems of using the risk-adjusted performance measures are:

- **Use of Market Surrogate:** All measures other than reward to variability ratio requires the identification of a market portfolio. Whatever Surrogate is used for market portfolio it can be criticized as being inadequate. By making slight changes in the surrogate, performance ranking can vary.
- **Choice of Risk-Free Rate:** The choice of a risk-free rate has to be appropriate. If the risk-free rate is too low, then the benchmark portfolio based on it may give too high a return, making it difficult for the portfolio to show superior performance against the benchmark.
- **Validity of CAPM:** reward to volatility measure and differential return measure involves data, using the Capital Asset Pricing Model. But CAPM may not be the correct asset-pricing model in all circumstances. Other asset pricing models are being developed where the risk would incorporate many other factors apart from market related risk.

Q6. What are benchmark folios? How are they used to evaluate the performance of a portfolio manager? [June 2007 Q6]

Ans. Benchmark portfolio is a tool for the meaningful evaluation of the performance of a portfolio manager. The more the benchmark reflects the manager's stated style, the more accurately the performance of the manager's skill can be assessed. Specialised benchmarks are called 'normal portfolios'. They are especially constructed by mutual consent of the client and the manager to reflect the client's need and the manager's style.

Rather than using a market index like the Bombay Stock Exchange's Sensitive Index or the Economic Times Index, a benchmark portfolio would use a portfolio with predominantly value-oriented shares for a value manager, growth-oriented shares for a growth manager and small capitalization shares for a small-cap (size) manager. It is quite possible for an investment manager to perform better than the benchmark, though the benchmark may itself underperform in relation to a market index.

The process of constructing a benchmark portfolio involves :–

a) Defining the universe of stock to be used for the benchmark portfolio, and

b) Defining the weightage of the stocks in the universe.

An investment manager's month-end portfolio can be examined for the last five years to get an idea of the average exposure of the manager to various factors (industry, capitalisation, P/E etc.) The more stable the exposure and the investment style, the easier it should be to build benchmarks with appropriate weights.

Performance attribution analysis, is a means of evaluating an investment manager's performance, the return and the sources of return relative to a benchmark portfolio. This analysis looks to an investment manager's total 'excess' return, or 'Active Management Return' (AMR) relative to its benchmark over the given period. It also looks at the components of AMR stock selection, industry selection and market timing.

The benchmark portfolio return is a 'buy-and-hold' return on a predetermined portfolio tailored to a manager's style. The cumulative excess return or cumulative AMR is the difference between actual portfolio and the benchmark return over the evaluation period.

Q7. How does a portfolio manager ensure greater returns than the normal average returns?

Ans. Portfolio Managers need a clear and relevant method of attributing returns to various activities that comprises the investment management process viz. *investment policy or risk taking, market timing and stock selection.*

The most important decision as part of investment strategy is asset allocation. For that portion of the portfolio that the portfolio manager allocates to equities (or if the fund is equity based fund), he should strive to buy shares in excellent businesses at prices that make business sense. Search for opportunities that offer the highest predictable annual compounding rate of return possible, where the risk is reasonable in light of the potential reward.

Further, he should make long-term investments in the common stock of great business at prices that make economic sense given the business's intrinsic value. Moreover he should make only those investments where he is able to do so at fair or bargain prices. The price he pays determines the rate of return.

Example : A mutual fund scheme has offered a return to 15% during a period when the market index (like Sensex or Nifty) reported a return of 8%. The risk-free rate during the period was 6%. The standard deviation of returns of the market index and the portfolio are 12% and 10% respectively. The beta of the portfolio is 0.75. The scheme has reported an excess return of 9% (15% -6%) over and above the risk-free return and we need to find out the sources of such excess returns with the help of information given.

Since the beta of the stock is 0.75, the expected return of the fund as per CAPM is

$$E(R) = R_f + \text{eta}\,(R_m - R_f) = 6\% + 0.75\,(8\% - 6\%) = 7.5\%$$

Against this expected return 7.5%, the fund has offered a return of 15%. The difference of 7.50% can be attributed to selectivity or ability of the fund managers in selecting the stocks. The balance 7.5% represents the premium for risk.

To earn excess return, portfolio managers bear additional risk. By using the Capital Market Line (CML) we can determine the return commensurate with risk as measured by the standard deviation of return. The normal return for Fund A, using total risk would be :

$$R_f + [(R_m - Rr_f) (\sigma_p / \sigma_m)$$

$$\text{i.e. } 6\% + [8\% - 6\%) (10\% / 12\%)] = 7.67\%$$

The difference between this normal return of 7.67% and the expected normal return computed earlier (7.50%) is 0.17. This additional expected return is on account of diversification risk.

The fund offered a return to 15% against the expected return of 7.50% and the excess return is attributed to selectivity. However, selectivity increases diversification risk, which was quantified as 0.17%. If we remove the compensation required for bearing diversification risk, the net return attributed to selectivity is 7.33%.

The overall performance of a Fund can be thus decomposed into (i) due to selectivity and (ii) due to risk taking.

Portfolio Managers can also achieve superior performance by picking up high beta stocks during a market upswing and moving out of equities and into cash in declining markets. To study market timing ability, one could calculate the quarterly returns for a Fund and for the market index like Bombay Stock Exchange's National Index of a 5 year period and plot them on a scatter diagram. Then a characteristic line can be fitted.

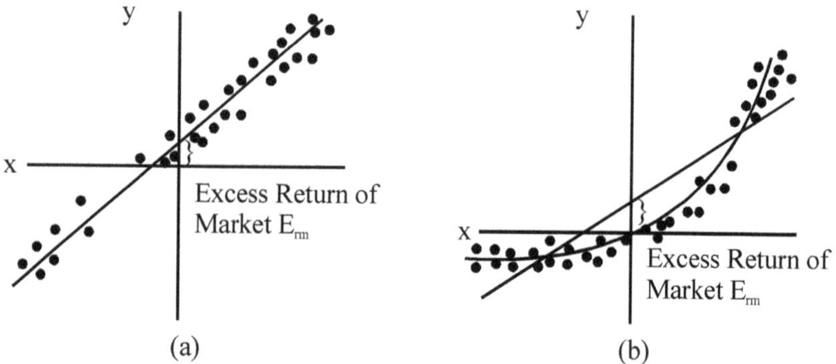

Figures gives the excess return of the fund on the Y-axis and the excess return of the market index on the X-axis. Both figures reveal positive ex-post alphas. The scatter diagram in Figure (a) shows that all the point cluster close to the regression line indicating that the relationship between portfolio excess return and market excess return is linear. The average beta of the portfolio is fairly constant or the beta of the portfolio was roughly the same at all times. Since alpha is positive, it appears that the excess return is due to his stock selection abilities.

In Figure (b), the points in the middle lie below the regress line and those at the ends lie above the regression line. This suggests that the portfolio consisted of high beta securities when market return was high and low beta securities when the market return was low.

000lationship, we can fit a curve to the points plotted by adding a quadratic term to the simple linear relationship.

$r_p = a + b_{rm} + cr^2_m$ where

r^2_m = return on the market index squared

r_p = return on the fund (portfolio),

a, b, c = values to be estimated by regression analysis.

The Figure indicates that the curve becomes steeper as one moves to the right of the diagram. The Fund movements are implied on the upside and *vice-vera.* This implies that the Fund manager was anticipating market changes correctly and that the superior performance of the Fund manager was anticipating market changes correctly and that the superior performance of the fund can be attributed to skill in timing.

Illustration 1: NAV of an equity scheme of a mutual fund was Rs. 12.50 in the beginning of a year. The mutual fund has distributed a dividend of Rs. 1.30 per unit during the year and has an NAV of Rs. 12.80 at the end of the year. Find out the percentage return of the mutual fund.

Solution : Return of a mutual fund may be found as follows :–

$$\text{Return} = \frac{\text{Rs. } 1.30 + (\text{Rs. } 12.80 - 12.50)}{\text{Rs. } 12.50} \times 100$$

$$= \frac{\text{Rs. } 1.30 + \text{Re. } 0.30)}{\text{Rs. } 12.50} \times 100$$

$$= 12.80\%$$

Illustration 2 : A mutual fund has an NAV of Rs. 20.10 in the beginning of the month. It distributed a return of Re. 0.04 and capital gains of Re 0.10 during the month. The NAV at the end of the month was same at Rs. 20.10. Find out the monthly rate of return.

Solution :

$$\text{Return} = \frac{\text{Re. } 0.04 + \text{Re. } 0.10}{\text{Rs. } 20.10} \times 100$$

$$= .7\%$$

Chapter – 15

Investment Companies

Q1. Explain the concept of 'investment companies'? Why is there a need for investment companies?

Ans. Funds, which specialize in investments on behalf of their Investors are called Investment Companies. An investment company is a pool of funds belonging to many individuals that is used to acquire a collection of individual investments such as stocks, bonds and other publicly traded securities. While some of the investment companies offer these services indirectly, others offer such services directly. *Investment companies, which offer direct services, often called as mutual funds.*

Investment companies typically offer some service not directly related to investing the money in securities but the amount collected against such services are invested in securities and income earned out of that are shared with the customers of service. To give an example, suppose if you have taken a life insurance policy from Life Insurance Corporation of India or any other newly formed private sector insurance company, you are actually getting an insurance product or service. Insurance policies invariably have two components namely risk cover and savings. Such insurance companies in addition to protecting the family of policyholders in the event of loss of policyholders' life also offer a return on the savings part in the form of bonus. In order to reward the policy holder with such return, insurance companies invest money in securities of different types. Another example is pension funds, which also collect regularly some amount from the subscribers and reward the subscribers by providing pension for the subscribers as well as her/his family. Specialised Pension Funds are yet to take off in India but LIC, UTI and ITI-Pioneer Mutual Fund have already floated pension funds schemes. Many mutual funds and private life insurance companies are in the process of bringing such schemes to investors. In contrast with investment companies, the mutual funds are not offering any other services other than investment services to investors. Mutual funds collect money from investors and simply invest the amount in securities as per the scheme. At the end of the scheme or periodically, the return earned from the scheme is distributed to the holders of mutual funds units after deducting management fees.

Q2. Discuss the role of insurance companies? Write short note on Life Insurance Corporation of India & General Insurance Companies?

Ans. Insurance industry is one of the several industries, which was earlier under the monopoly of the government, opened up for competition. Today, in addition to Life Insurance Corporation of India and General Insurance Corporation of India and its Associates, there are large number of private players like HDFC Standard Life, ICICI-Prudential, etc. have entered into the market.

The LIC of India was established by an Act of Parliament in 1956. The corporation central office is located in Mumbai and there are seven zonal offices one each at Mumbai, Kolkata, Delhi, Kanpur and Chennai.

Some of the objectives that the Corporation pursues are listed below:–

– Spread Life Insurance much more widely and in particular to the rural areas and to the socially and economically backward classes with a view to reaching all insurable persons in the country and providing them adequate financial cover against death at a reasonable cost.

– Maximize mobilization of people's savings by making insurance-linked savings adequately attractive.

– Deploy the funds to the best advantage of the investors as well as the community as a whole, keeping in view national priorities and obligations of attractive return.

– Act as trustees of the insured public in their individual and collective capacities.

– Meet the various life insurance needs of the community that would arise in the changing social and economic environment.

During the last five decades, the Corporation has grown huge in size in terms of collecting the savings and also investing the same in the market.

LIC offers a number of plans, which can be broadly classified as plans for individuals, group scheme and pension plans. The various schemes offered by LIC are :

(a) Plans for Individuals

Whole life schemes

Term assurance plan

Capital market linked plans

Joint life plan

(b) Group Schemes

Group Term Insurance Schemes

Group Gratuity Scheme

Group Superannuation Scheme

Group Leave Encashment Scheme

(c) Pension Plans

New Jeevan Akshay I

New Jeevan Dhara I
New Jeevan Suraksha I

Some of the reasons on why should an individual has to take insurance policy are listed below :

Protection : Savings through life insurance guarantee full protection against risk of death or the saver. In life insurance, on death, the full sum assured is payable (with bonuses wherever applicable) whereas in other savings schemes, only the amount saved (with interest) is payable.

Aid to thrift : Life insurance encourages 'thrift'. Long term saving can be made in a relatively 'painless' manner because of the 'easy installment' facility built into the scheme (method of paying premium either monthly, quarterly, half yearly or yearly)

Liquidity : Loans can be raised on the sole security of a policy, which has acquired loan value. Besides, a life insurance policy is also generally accepted as security for even a commercial loan.

Tax Relief : Tax relief in Income Tax and Wealth Tax is available for amounts paid by way of premium of life insurance subject to Income Tax rates in force. Assesses can avail themselves of provisions in the law for tax relief. In such cases the assured in effect pays a lower premium for his insurance than she/he would have to pay otherwise.

Money when you need it : A suitable insurance plan or a combination of different plans can be taken out to meet specific needs that are likely to arise in future, such as children's education, start-in-life or marriage provision or even periodical needs for cash over a stretch of time. Alternatively, policy moneys can be so arranged to be made available at the time of one's retirement from service to be used for any specific purpose, such as for the purchase of a house or for other investments. Subject to certain conditions, loans are granted to policyholders for house building or for purchase of flats.

General Insurance Companies : Unlike Life Insurance, there is no saving under general insurance. Policyholders take the policy and get an insurance cover for their machine, office, house, health, etc. Though no income is distributed back to policyholders, the general insurance companies are major investors in the market.

Q3. What are the different types of pension plans? Give the names & benefits of some pension plans in India?

Ans. A pension plan is an agreement to provide income to participants upon their retirement. These funds are mostly tax deductible and investment income of the fund is also not taxed. Distributions from the fund whether to the employer or employee are taxed as ordinary income. There are two types of pension plans.

(a) Defined Contribution : Contribution rules are usually specified as a predetermined fraction of salary through that fraction need not be constant and can be changed over the course of employee's career. Pension benefits are not specified other than at retirement the employee applies that the total accumulated value of contributions and earnings on those contributions to purchase an annuity. The employee often has a choice over both the level of contribution and the way the account is invested.

(b) Defined benefit : The benefit formula typically takes into account years of service of the employer and levels of wages or salary. The employer or an insurance company hired by the sponsor guarantees the benefits and thus absorbs the investment risk. The obligation of the plan sponsor to pay the promised benefits is like a long-term liability of the employer.

The name of some pension plans in India are :–

(a) Jeevan Akshay-I of LIC of India

Salient Features :

Minimum age at entry	:	40 Last Birthday
Maximum age at entry	:	79 Last Birthday
Minimum Purchase Price	:	Rs.25,000/-
Minimum Annuity Installment	:	Rs.250/-

(b) New Jeevan Suraksha-I/New Jeevan Dhara-I

Benefits :–

(a) On investing : The Notional Cash option together with Reversionary Bonuses and Final additional Bonuses (if any) with or without 25% commutation will be compulsorily converted into annuity having following options :–

– Annuity for life.

– Annuity for life with guaranteed period of 5, 10, 15, 20 years.

– Joint life and last survivor annuity to the annuitant and his/her spouse under which annuity payable to the spouse on death of the purchaser will be 50% of that payable to the annuitant.

– Life annuity with return of purchase price.

– Life annuity with annuities increasing at a simple rate of 3% per annum.

(b) During Deferment : A term rider option will be available. On the death of the policy holder who has opted for the term Assurance rider (provided the policy is in-force), the Term Assurance Sum Assured along with all premiums (excluding term Assurance premium and extra premium if any) paid up to the date of death accumulated at the rate of 5% p.a. compounding or at such rates as decided by the Corporation from time to time will be paid to the nominee. When the policy is not in-force, only return of premiums with interest as stated above will be available.

(c) Paid up, Guaranteed and Special Surrender Value :–

– **For Annual Premium Plans :** The Guaranteed Surrender Value will be equal to 90% of all premiums paid excluding the first year premium, all Term Assurance premium and extra premium (if any). This will be allowed after at least two full years premiums have been paid and will be available after two full years have been completed from the date of commencement. However, the policy can not be surrendered after the annuity vests.

– **For Single Premium Plan :** The Guaranteed Surrender Value will be 90% of the single premium paid. Surrender will be allowed 2 years after the commencement of the policy.

– **Special Surrender Value :** For Annual premium policy this will be available at least two years after date of commencement and during deferment period if at least two full years' premium have been paid.

(d) Non-forfeiture regulations : If, after at least two full years premiums are paid in respect of this policy, any subsequent premium be not duly paid, the policy shall not be wholly void, but the amount of Notional Cash Option shall be reduced to such a sum as shall bear same ratio to the original, as the number of premiums actually paid shall bear to the total number of premiums originally stipulated for in the policy. The policy so reduced will thereafter be free from all liabilities for payment of the within mentioned premiums but shall not be entitled to participate in future profits. The existing vested Bonus additions will attach to the reduced paid up policy and this will determine the reduced annuity payable on vesting. The option of commutation of 25% pension will also be available on the vesting age.

C) Pioneer ITI Mutual Fund – Pension Scheme :–

Fund Suitability : For investors seeking tax rebate plus the returns and safety of fixed income investments as well as those saving for retirement. Ideal for a time horizon of 3 years plus.

Highlights :–

– Tax rebate of 20% for the investments upto Rs.60,000 under Sec 88 (xiiic)
– Premature withdrawal after 3 years at a nominal charge on the NAV
– Choice of 2 plans – Dividend Scheme & Growth Scheme
– Convenience of investing amounts as low as Rs.500
– Income tax benefits under Sec.48 & 112.

Chapter – 16

Mutual Funds

Q1. Discuss briefly the concept of Mutual Fund and advantages of investing in mutual funds? [June 2005 Q5(a)]

Ans. A Mutual Fund is a trust that pools the savings of a number of investors, who share a common financial goal. Mutual funds make investments in the stock and debt markets on behalf of investors joining the scheme and thus offers two special services namely expertise in investments and diversification. A small investor with a surplus funds of say Rs.10,000 per year may not be in a position to get such expert advice of diversification without mutual funds. Investors thus not only share a common financial goal but also share the cost associated with expert advice and diversification. Some of the objects that mutual funds pursue on behalf of their investors are attractive yields, capital appreciation, holding the safety and liquidity as prime parameters.

Thus a Mutual Fund is the most suitable investment for the common man as it offers an opportunity to invest in a diversified, professionally managed basket of securities at a relatively low cost.

The flow chart below describes broadly the working of a mutual fund.

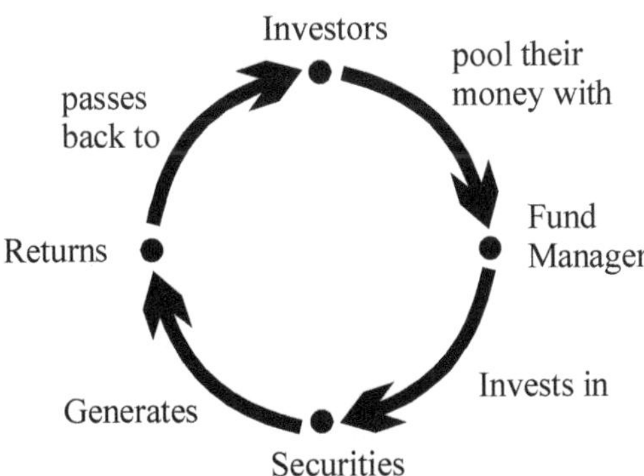

Figure : Mutual Fund Operation Flow Chart

By investing in various Mutual Fund Schemes, small investors or middle income investors seek the following advantages compared to other types of investments :–

(i) Professional Management : No impulsive decision making regarding purchase or sale of share/securities, since the funds are managed by expert, professional fund managers who have access to latest and detailed information regarding the stock market and individual scrips.

(ii) Diversification : Investment variety and spread in different industries.

(iii) Convenient Administration : Freedom from paper work

(iv) Return Potential : Even the smallest dividend or capital gain gets reinvested, thus enhancing the effective return.

(v) Low Costs

(vi) Liquidity : Liquidity through buy back arrangements of the mutual fund or listing on some stock exchanges after a certain lock-in period.

(vii) Transparency

(viii) Flexibility

(ix) Choice of schemes

(x) Tax benefits : Tax benefits on invested amounts/returns of dividend/ capital gains

(xi) Well regulated

(xii) Capital appreciation : Without having to watch the upward or downward performance curves of different scripts.

Q2. Describe how the mutual funds are organized?

OR

Discuss the role of the Registers, Transfer Agents, Custodian & Fund Manager in a mutual fund.

Ans. A Mutual Fund can be constituted either as a corporate entity or as a trust. In India, Unit Trust of India (UTI) was set up as a corporation under an Act of Parliament in 1964. SEBI regulation on Mutual Funds requires a mutual fund be constituted in the form of a trust. The instrument of trust shall be in the form of a deed, duly registered under the provision of the Indian Registration Act, 1908 (16 of 1908) executed by the sponsor in favour of the trustees named in such an instrument. While Mutual Funds registered as trust floats schemes and collects money, the actual investment is made by a different entity called Asset Management Company (AMC). AMC is typically constituted as a company registered under Companies Act, 1956.

Mutual Funds are to be sponsored by an individual or group of individuals or companies. Sponsors also appoint Trustees who will manage the mutual funds. Sponsors or Trustees also appoint AMC and enter into an agreement with them for the management of funds. In practice, sponsors also promote an AMC for the mutual funds. Transfer Agent maintains the records of unit holders and make changes when investors buy or sell Units. Custodian keeps the securities purchased by the fund.

Asset Management Companies : As per guidelines, AMC shall be authorized for business by SEBI on the basis of certain criteria and the Memorandum and Articles of Association of the AMC would have to be approved by SEBI. Accordingly, no company can register as an AMC under the Companies Act 1956 without the Memorandum and Articles of Association being approved by SEBI.

Transfer Agents : The major responsibilities include :–

i) Receiving and processing the application form of investors

ii) Issuing of Unit/Share Certificates on behalf of Mutual Fund

iii) Maintain detailed records of Unit holders transactions

iv) Purchasing, selling, transferring and redeeming the Unit/Share Certificates.

v) Issuing of income/dividend Warrants, Cheques etc.

vi) Creating security interest on Units/Certificates for allowing loans against them

Advertiser : Major responsibilities of an advertiser include :–

i) Helping mutual funds organizers to prepare a media plan for marketing the fund

ii) Issuing/buying the space in the space in newspapers and other electronic media for advertising the various features of a fund.

iii) Arranging for hoardings at public places

Advisor/Manager : It is generally a corporate entity who does the following jobs :–

i) Professional advice on the Fund's investments.

ii) Advice on Asset Management Services.

Trustee : Trustees provide the overall management services and charge management fee.

Custodian : A custodian, which is again a corporate body does the following functions :–

i) Holds securities

ii) Receives and delivers securities whenever investors sells and buys Units.

iii) Collects income/interest/dividends on the securities.

iv) Holds and process cash

Besides the above, other players who are involved in the Mutual Fund activities are as under :–

i) Fund Administrator;

ii) Fund Accounting Services;

iii) Legal Advisors;

iv) Fund Officers;

v) Underwriters/Distributors;

vi) Legal Advisors

Q3. How the mutual funds can be classified according (a) to structure (b) to investment objective?

Ans. Mutual funds could be classified in many ways based on structure, objectives of investment, pattern of investments and returns, etc.

Based on structure, mutual funds could be classified as :–

1) Open – Ended Schemes

2) Close – Ended Schemes

3) Interval Schemes

Based on the investment objective, the classification could be :

a) Growth Funds

b) Income Funds

c) Balanced Schemes

d) Money Market Schemes

e) Other Special Schemes

Open-Ended Funds : Under open-ended scheme, the mutual fund will announce daily purchase and sale price of the Units of the scheme. An open-ended funds is one that is available for subscription all through the year. These do not have a fixed maturity. Investors can conveniently buy and sell Units at Net Asset Value ("NAV") related prices. The key feature of open-ended schemes is liquidity.

Close-Ended Funds : Under close-ended schemes, there is no repurchase facility. However, the Units are listed in the stock market and investors can sell and buy Units like any other securities in the market. The scheme has a specific life (say 10 years or 5 years) and the end of the period, the mutual fund sells securities bought under the scheme and disburses the proceeds to Unit holders. In close-ended funds, no fresh Units are created after the original offer of the scheme expires. The Shares/Units of these funds are not redeemable at their NAV during their life as are in the case of open-ended funds. The Shares of such funds are traded in the secondary market on stock exchanges at market price that may be above or below their NAV.

Interval Funds : Interval funds combine the features of open-ended and close-ended schemes. They are open for sale of redemption during pre-determined intervals at NAV related prices.

The classification of Mutual funds on the basis of investment objectives are :

Growth Funds : The aim of growth funds is to provide capital appreciation over the medium to long-term. Such schemes normally invest a majority of their corpus in equities. Growth schemes are ideal for investors having a long-term outlook seeking growth over a period of time.

Income Funds : The aim of income funds is to provide regular and steady income to investors. Such schemes generally invest in fixed income securities such as bonds, corporate, debentures and Government securities. Income funds are ideal for capital stability and regular income.

Balanced Funds : The aim of balanced funds is to provide both growth and regular income. Such schemes periodically distribute a part of their earning and invest both in equities and fixed income securities in the proportion indicated in their offer documents. In a rising stock market, the NAV of these schemes may not normally keep pace, or fall equally when the market falls. These are ideal for investors looking for a combination of income and moderate growth.

Money Market Funds : The aim of money market funds is to provide easy liquidity, preservation of capital and moderate income. These schemes generally invest in safer short-term instruments such as treasury bills, certificates of deposit, commercial paper and inter-bank call money. Returns on these schemes may fluctuate depending upon the interest rates prevailing in the market.

Load Funds : A load fund is one that charges a commission for entry or exit. That is, each time you buy or sell Units in the fund, a commission will be payable. Typically entry and exit range from 1% to 2%.

No-Load Funds : A No-Load Funds is one that does not charge a commission for entry or exit. The advantage of a no load fund is that the entire corpus is put to work.

Tax Saving Schemes : These schemes offer tax rebates to the investors under specific provisions of the Indian Income Tax laws as the Government offers tax incentives for investment in specified avenues. Investments made in Equity Linked Saving Schemes (ELSS) and Pension Schemes are allowed as deduction u/s88 of the Income Tax Act, 1961.

Special Schemes :

Industry Specific-Schemes : Industry Specific Schemes invest only in the industries specified in the offer document. The investment of these funds is limited to specific industries like InfoTech, FMCG, Pharmaceuticals etc.

Index Schemes : Index Funds attempt to replicate the performance of a particular index such as the BSE Sensex or the NSE 50.

Sectoral Schemes : Sectoral Funds are those, which invest exclusively in a specified industry (like Pharma fund or IT fund) or a group of industries or various segments such as 'A' Group shares or initial public offerings.

Q4. Discuss the Mutual Fund investment process?

Ans. Creation of a Portfolio : The portfolio of a mutual fund depends on the objectives of each scheme/fund floated by a mutual fund. For example, the objective of an income-oriented scheme is to provide regular monthly income to its shareholders. The portfolio of such a fund should consist of fixed income bearing securities so that the fund can achieve its objective. It has been learnt from Indian experience that the portfolio of such a fund consists of mainly the following securities :–

Non Convertible Debentures (NCD's) – 75 to 90%.

Call Money – 10 to 25%

The fund manager of a mutual fund is the person responsible for buying these securities in such a way that the fund is able to achieve its objectives. A fund manager tries to create a well diversified portfolio of securities so that unsystematic risk is reduced significantly and returns expected on individual securities and on portfolio is directly related to 'market risk' or systematic risk. While buying these securities, the fund manager takes into consideration the following norms for each kind of security.

Non-convertible debentures : –

(i) Asset Cover or Security Cover : A company must maintain a minimum asset cover. This cover is calculated on the basis of secured borrowings and debentures charged to fixed assets, whereby fixed assets should be in general more than one time of the total such existing borrowings and debentures secured by equitable mortgage on fixed assets. The movable fixed assets are generally excluded from the calculations.

(ii) Interest Cover : PBIDT (profit before interest, depreciation and taxes) should be around two times the existing interest liability plus the interest liability on the proposed debentures so as to protect the payment of interest on the debentures. This cover is to be calculated on the basis of the average of the proceeding three years profit figures.

(iii) Company must have paid dividend for the last three or minimum two preceding years.

(iv) Networth of the company should be around Rs. One Crore.

Small variations in the above norms are accepted provided the company is otherwise very sound and the rate of return is higher than normal.

Equity Shares (Common Norms for Primary as well as Secondary Market) :–

Management : First and foremost emphasis is placed on quality of management because unless the management is efficient and professional even a good project can fail.

Industry : The industry in general should be growth oriented, expanding and modernizing, etc. Mutual Funds avoid seasonal and declining industries.

Government Policy : A fund manager constantly studies the economic and fiscal policies of the government and analyses their impact on the companies.

Analytical Studies : A fund manager studies the full details of the past performance of companies including turnover, profitability, earnings, track record and financial strength. He also compares it with the industry in which the company falls. He studies the expansion, diversification and other plans or the companies to assess their future outlook and potential.

Market Study : Fund managers also assess the standing of the company, its general reputation, its market share and the competition it is likely to face.

Studies on Industries : A mutual fund undertakes the studies of the industries to find out the outlook as well as the problems and faced by the industries and in turn the units in the said industries.

Besides studying the above fundamental factors, for both primary and secondary market operations, a fund manager uses the following additional tools to decide the timing for entering into secondary market operations. However, this is not a rigid formula.

(a) 'PE' Ratio (Price Earning Ratio)

(i) Average 'PE' ratio for the industry.

(ii) Average 'PE' ratio of the company based on the last three years.

(iii) Earnings per share of last year x Average 'PE' ratio of the company.

(b) High and Low Price : A fund manager is also aware that the market fluctuates as a normal pattern 3-4 times in a year and these movements are watched for proper opportunities. For this purpose, a chart showing the trends in price movements for the previous year is prepared.

(c) Book Value : A mutual fund calculates the book value (less revaluation reserves) and compares it with the market price. If the market price is twice or thrice the book value, the share is over priced and if the market price is less or equal, the share is called under priced.

Constant review and revision of investment requires :–

(i) Continuous monitoring of the quality of management of the companies in which investment has already been made.

(ii) Continuous financial analysis and trend analysis of the companies' balance sheets/profit & loss accounts to choose sound companies and off-load investment made in companies where the performance is lacking.

(iii) Continuous analysis of the securities market trends.

Whereas a Funds Manager takes into consideration all fundamental and technical analyses while making initial purchase of securities, continuous monitoring jobs are done generally by a research cell of the mutual funds in India. Measurement of risk involved in the expected rate of return is very essential before diversification of any portfolio can be undertaken by a mutual fund. A research executive measures the risk by taking variance and standard deviation of return. A large variation around the average would indicate great uncertainty regarding the expected return.

Q5. Give the restrictions on the investment by mutual funds imposed by SEBI.

Ans. To protect general investors' interest the Securities and Exchange Board of India has placed certain restrictions on the investment by mutual funds in India as follows :–

(1) No individual scheme of the Mutual Fund should invest more than 5 per cent of its corpus in any one company's shares.

(2) No Mutual Fund under all its schemes should own more than 5 per cent of any company's paid up capital carrying voting rights.

(3) No Mutual Fund under all its schemes taken together should invest more than 10 per cent of its funds in the shares or debentures or other securities of a single company.

(4) No Mutual Fund under its schemes taken together should invest more than 15 per cent of its funds in shares and debentures of any specific industry (such as cotton textiles, tea, tyres etc.) except where a scheme has been floated for investments in one or more specified industries.

(5) Privately placed debentures, securitized debt and other unquoted debt instruments holdings shall not exceed 10 per cent in case of growth funds and 40 per cent in case of income funds.

Q6. Systems & Control are as important as creation of portfolio of securities in managing a portfolio by a mutual fund. Comment.

Ans. For managing a portfolio, it is not only the creation, re-creation and regrouping of various securities which is important for achieving the desired rate of return, but various kinds of systems and controls are needed. A Mutual Fund generally provides the desired controls through its accounting and custodian system.

Accounting System : As accounting system must clearly disclose :–

(i) The policy in respect of recognition of revenue and income from investment.

(ii) The policies relating to valuation of investments.

(iii) The aggregate carrying value and market value of non performing assets under each type of investment.

(iv) Provision to be made for depreciation/loss in the value of non performing investment

(v) Per unit Net Asset Value (NAV) at various intervals and at the end of the accounting year.

Custodian System : A custodian system should provide/ensure :–

(i) Timely receipt and delivery of cash and securities;

(ii) Delivery of securities only upon receipt of payment and payment only upon receipt of securities;

(iii) Timely resolution of discrepancies and failures;

(iv) Segregation of assets by the custodian and regular inventory verification;

(v) Regular reconciliation of assets to accounting records;

(vi) Securities are properly registered;

(vii) Proper nomination and record of declared dividend and other corporate actions.

All the above accounting policies and custodian system if pursued by Mutual

Funds help them to maintain a clear picture of all investment and their performance in a portfolio.

Q7. Write short notes on (a) Bond Rating, (b) Exchange Privilege, (c) Junk Bond, (d) Short Selling, (e) Systematic Withdrawal Plan, (f) Asset Allocation Fund

Ans. (a) Bond Rating : System of evaluating the probability of whether a bond issuer will default. Various firms analyze the financial stability of both corporate and government bond issuers. Ratings range from AAA or Aaa (extremely unlikely to default) to D (currently in default). Bonds rated BBB or below are not considered to be of investment grade. Mutual funds generally restrict their bond purchases to issues of certain quality ratings, which are specified in their prospectuses.

(b) Exchange Privilege (or switching privilege) : The right to transfer investments from one fund into another, generally within the same fund group, at nominal cost.

(c) Junk Bond : A speculative bond rates BB or below. "Junk Bonds" are generally issued by corporations of questionable financial strength or without proven track records. They tend to be more volatile and higher yielding than bonds with superior quality ratings. "Junk bond funds" emphasize diversified investments in these low-rated, high-yielding debt issues.

(d) Short Selling : The sale of a security which is not owned by the seller. The "short-seller" borrows stock for delivery to the buyer, and must eventually purchase the security for return to the lender.

(e) Systematic Withdrawal Plans : Many mutual funds offer withdrawal programs whereby shareholders receive payments from their investments. These payments are usually drawn from the fund's dividend income and capital gain distributions, if any, and from principal only when necessary.

(f) Asset Allocation Fund : A fund that spreads its portfolio among a wide variety of investments, including domestic and foreign stocks and bonds, government securities, gold bullion and real estate stocks. This gives small investors far more diversification than they could get allocating money on their own. Some of these funds keep the proportions allocated between different sectors relatively constant, while others alter the mix as market conditions change.

Question Papers

MS-44 : Security Analysis and Portfolio Management
June, 2005

Note: Attempt any **five** questions. All questions carry equal marks. Present value tables are to be provided if asked for.

Q1. "No Investment Decisions are made without calculating risk." Do you agree? As an Investment Manager of a firm, discuss the various steps involved in the investment decision making process.

Q2. (a) What are the various methods of floating the new issue? Discuss the roles played by the Underwriter and the Bankers to the issue.

(b) Vamsi is considering the purchase of a bond currently selling at Rs. 878.50. The bond has four years to maturity, face value of Rs. 1,000 and 8% coupon rate. The next annual interest payment is due after one year from today. The required rate of return is 10%.
(i) Calculate the intrinsic value (present value) of the bond. Should Vamsi buy the bond?
(ii) Calculate the yield to maturity of the bond.

Q3. Explain fully the role played by the SEBI in the securities market as a regulator and as a developer of the capital market.

Q4. What are the major criticisms of the technical analysis? Do the technical analysis and the fundamental analysis give complementary information about securities for making informal decisions? Explain.

Q5. (a) Discuss the Markowitz Theory of Portfolio Selection. How does Markowitz Theory help in planning an investor's portfolio?

(b) An aggressive Mutual Fund promises an expected rate of return of 18% with a standard deviation of 22%. On the other hand, a conservative mutual fund promises an expected rate of return of 16% and fluctuations of 13%.
(i) In which of the funds would you like to invest?
(ii) Would you like to invest in both the funds?
(iii) If you can borrow money from your provident fund at an opportunity cost of 15%, in which fund would you invest your money?

Q6. Explain the concept of 'Mutual Fund'. What factors should be considered before selecting a Mutual Fund? Discuss the present state of the Mutual Funds in India and outline the risks involved in investing in Mutual Funds?

Q7. Write short notes on any *four* of the following:
(a) Dow theory
(b) Odd lot trading
(c) Point and Figure charts
(d) Serial bond
(e) Superfluous Diversification
(f) Market Risk

MS-44 : Security Analysis and Portfolio Management
December, 2005

Note: Attempt any **five** questions. All questions carry equal marks. Present value tables are to be provided if asked for.

Q1. "Investment is well designed and carefully planned speculation." Comment. Critically examine the recent trends in the Indian capital market.

Q2(a) What is listing? Why do companies get their shares listed on the stock exchange? Explain the pre-requisites for the listing of shares in India.

(b) Vamsi is considering the purchase of a bond currently selling at Rs. 878.50. The bond has four years to maturity, face value of Rs. 1,000 and 8% coupon rate. The next annual interest payment is due after one year from today. The required rate of return is 10%.

(i) Calculate the intrinsic value of the bond. Should Vamsi buy the bond?

(ii) Calculate the yield to maturity of the bond.

Q3. Explain in detail the role played by the Securities and Exchange Board of India in the securities market as a regulator as well as developer of the capital market.

Q4. Briefly explain Technical Analysis and Fundamental Analysis. What are the basic premises of Technical Analysis? How is it different from Fundamental Analysis?

Q5. (a) How is the Arbitrage Pricing Theory (APT) consistent with the Capital Asset Pricing Model (CAPM)?

(b) Ganga and Yamuna are the two mutual funds. Ganga has a sample mean of success of 0.14, whereas Yamuna has a sample mean of success of 0.16. Yamuna has the beta at 2.0. The beta of Ganga is one-half of the beta of Yamuna. The standard deviations of Yamuna and Gang are 13% and 17% respectively. The mean return for market index is 0.10, while the risk-free rate of return is 6%.

(i) Compute the Jensen's index for each of the funds. What does it indicate?

(ii) Compute the Treynor's index for the funds and interpret the result. Compare the results of Treynor's and Jensen's indices.

(iii) Compute the Sharpe's index for the funds and the market.

Q6. Explain the concept the Mutual Funds. Describe the various types of schemes introduced by Mutual Funds in India. Under what circumstances, can the registration of a mutual fund be terminated?

Q7. Write short notes on any four of the following:

(a) Principle of Dominance

(b) Separation Theorem

(c) Residual Analysis

(d) Factor Sensitivity

(e) Aggressive stock and Defensive stock

(f) Dow theory

MS-44 : Security Analysis and Portfolio Management
December, 2006

Note: Attempt any **five** questions. All questions carry equal marks. Present value and annuity tables are to be provided, if asked for.

Q1. (a) Explain the concept of risk. Discuss the various factors that affect risk in investment in securities.
(b) What is the role of the New Issue Market? Discuss the mechanisms of floating shares in the new issue market in India.

Q2. (a) Explain the process of Technical analysis. How is it useful to investors?
(b) A company paid a dividend of Rs. 3.70 in the previous year. The dividends are expected to grow perpetually in future at a rate of 8 per cent. Find out the share's price today if the market capitalizes dividend at 12 per cent.

Q3. What are the objectives of industry analysis? How does industry analysis help investment decisions?

Q4. What is an optimal portfolio? How is an optimal portfolio determined when lending and borrowing opportunities exist?

Q5. (a) What is portfolio evaluation? How do you carry out the portfolio performance evaluation?
(b) The following three portfolios provide the particulars given below:

Portfolio	Rate of return	σ	Correlation coefficient
A	18	27	0.8
B	14	18	0.6
C	15	08	0.9
Market	13	12	—

Risk free rate of interest is 9 percent.
(i) Rank these portfolios using Sharpe's and Treynor's methods.
(ii) Compare both the indices.

Q6. What do you understand by Portfolio Revision? Explain the various Formula Plans that are available to an investor for portfolio revision.

Q7. Write short notes on any *four* of the following:
(a) BOLT
(b) Factor Sensitivity
(c) Dow Theory
(d) Odd Lot Theory
(e) Security Market Line
(f) Warrant

MS-44: Security Analysis and Portfolio Management
June, 2007

Note : Attempt any **five** questions. All questions carry equal marks. Present value and annuity tables are to be provided, if asked for.

Q1. (a) Define Risk. What are different types of risks? Explain the methods of risks handling.
Refer to Unit-1, Q.No.-4 and Unit-2, Q.No.-5

(b) Explain briefly the functions of the Stock Market in India. Critically evaluate the role of SEBI as stock market developer and regulator.
Refer to Unit-4, Q.No.-4 and Unit-5, Q.No.-4

Q2. (a) Define Industry Analysis and bring out its relevance for selecting equity shares for investment.
Refer to Unit-6, Q.No.-5

(b) Prashanth has bought the Everest company stock that has paid Rs. 3.00 per share as dividend during the last financial year. He anticipates two situations – either a 5 per cent decline in the dividend or 5% growth in the dividend in the next year. His anticipated rate of return is 20%. You are required to calculate the price under both the situations.

Ans. Dividend paid during the last financial year = Rs. 3 per share ($D_t - 1$)
Anticipated rate of return (k) = 20%

I situation: If there is a 5% decline in dividend

$$\text{Price}_t = \frac{3(1-0.05)}{[0.20-(-0.05)]}$$

= Rs. 11.4

II situation: If there is a 5% increase in dividend

$$\text{Price}_t = \frac{3(1+0.05)}{[0.20-0.05]}$$

= Rs. 21

Q3. Why should an investor include non-security forms of investment in his portfolio? Outline the various investment avenues in the Indian Money Market.

Ans. An investor should include non-security forms of investments such as gold, silver, metal, real estate, antiques such as art pieces because even if the price of securities goes down then the investor should have other asset with which he can hedge his portfolio. For e.g., the prices of the real estate seldom go down in India. So, if the SENSEX or Nifty goes down and in turn, the prices of security goes down even then the prices of real estate would go up.

Various investment avenues in Indian Money Market: Money Market (MM) is a market for short term financial assets of maturity period less than one year. The financial assets being dealt with in MM are close substitute for money. Short term financial assets may be constructed as any financial assets which can be quickly converted into cash at a low transaction cost. Usually, the MM financial instruments have no loss in value. MM is a market for lending and borrowing of short term funds and liquidity. In MM, the excess funds of savers are employed for a short period to meet the requirements of those who have short term deficit of funds and thereby the MM earnings an equilibrium in demand and supply of short term funds.

Various instruments available for investment in money market are :–

1. Treasury Bills: A treasury bill is a promissory note issued by the government to meet its temporary financial requirement. It has provided the same purpose as the ways and means for meeting temporary deficit of the Govt. and has also been used to pay old loans or to convert loans. A special feature of t-bill is that it is issued at a discount to face value and is repayable at par on maturity with no payments made before maturity.

2. Call Money: It is the core segment of the Indian money market and is dominated by the commercial banks. Banks are the borrowers of call funds and banks and financial institutions are also lenders for call funds. Since banks have to meet their CRR requirements from their Net Time and Demand Liabilities (NTDL), they borrow call funds if there is any shortfall.

3. Commercial Paper (CP): Since the need for short term funds by the corporate is enormous. Corporates sometimes directly approach public for it rather than going to the banks. There is a definite advantage in terms of savings of cost while issuing CP say if a loan or a cash credit costs a borrower 10% interest, the same would not be more than 7-7.5% in case of a CP. However, the paper can be issued only by companies with good credit rating and having substantial tangible assets. Another big advantage associated with CP is that it can be issued at short notice and in smaller sizes.

4. Certificate of Deposit (CD): It is a receipt given to a depositor by a bank for making a deposit with it. However, it is different from a fixed deposit in the sense that it is freely transferable and the rate of interest is not fixed and is usually determined through negotiations between the banker and the investor. Today, the main investor in the CD's are the banks and the financial institutions.

5. Commercial Bills: For the business that is done on credit the main line of finances is the commercial bill. The market for commercial bill is often called the discount market as the bill is usually discounted by banks. Banks have the option of rediscounting them with RBI.

Q4. What is the risk of a Portfolio? Under what conditions can the portfolio risk be minimized?

Refer to Unit-10, Q.No.-3 and Q.No.-4

5. (a) What is efficient frontier? Explain about the capital market line and choice of an optimal portfolio, if borrowing rate is allowed to exceed the lending rate.

Refer to Unit-10, Q.No.-6(3) and Unit-12, Q.No.-6

(b) A security pays a dividend of Rs. 3.85 and currently sells at Rs 83. The security is expected to sell at Rs. 90 at the end of the year. The security has a beta of 1.15. The risk free rate is 5 per cent and the expected return on market index is 12 per cent. Assess whether the security is correctly priced.

Ans. Current Price = Rs. 83

Dividend = Rs. 3.85

Expected Price = Rs. 90

Expected Return of Security= $\frac{[90 + 3.85 - 83]}{83} \times 100$

= 13.0790

Beta of Security (F) = 1.15

Risk Free Rate (R_f) = 5%

Expect Market Return (R_m) = 12%

So, Return of security as per CAPM,

$$R_s = R_f + \beta(R_m - R_f)$$

= 5% + 1.15 (12% - 5%)

= 13.05%

Since, the return on security as per CAPM is more than the expected return of security. So the security is not correctly priced, the security is underpriced.

Q6. What are benchmark portfolios? How are they used to evaluate the performance of a portfolio manager? Discuss with suitable examples.
Refer to Unit-14, Q.No.-5

Q7. Write short notes on any *four* of the following:
(a) Agency Cost
Refer to Unit-2, Q.No.-14

(b) Dow Theory
Refer to Unit-8, Q.No.-2

(c) E.I.C. Approach
Refer to Unit-6, Q.No.-2

(d) Filter Test
Refer to Unit-9, Q.No.-2

(e) Market Breadth Index
Refer to Unit-8, Q.No.-6

(f) Technical Analysis
Refer to Unit-8, Q.No.-1

MS-44: Security Analysis and Portfolio Management
December, 2007

Note : Attempt any **five** questions. All questions carry equal marks. Present value and annuity tables are to be provided, if asked for.

Q1. "The institutional investors have emerged as the most important group of investors in corporate securities." Discuss this statement fully. Also identify the different categories of institutional operating in the Indian securities market.

Ans. An important feature of the development of stock market in India in the last 15 years has been the growing participation of Institutional Investors, both foreign institutional investors and the Indian mutual funds combined together, the total assets under their management amounts to almost 18% of the entire market capitalization.

The Indian stock market has come of age and has substantially aligned itself with the international order. Over the last fifteen years the following developments have made the Indian stock markets almost on par with the global markets :–

- Screen based trading systems replaced the conventional open outcry system of trading and everyone acclaims the contribution of the screen based trading in developing the culture of equity investing.
- The replacement of the fourteen-day account period settlement system give way to rolling settlements on T+2 basis has brought down the settlement risk substantially.
- Dematerialization of securities
- Demutualization of exchanges
- Derivatives trading

Infact, today we have one of the most modern securities Market among all the countries in the world. Along with these changes the market has also witnessed a growing trend of 'institutionalization' that may be considered as a consequence of globalization. More precisely the growing might of the institutional investors entities whose primary purpose is to invest their own assets or those entrusted to them by others and the most common among them are the mutual funds and portfolio investors. Today, giant institutions control huge sums of money which they move continuously. In European and Japanese markets, institutions dominate virtually all trading. In the US, retail investors still remain active participants.

An important feature of the development of stock market in India in the last 15 years has been the growing participation of Institutional Investors, both foreign institutional investors and the Indian mutual funds (since the pension funds are still restricted to fully participate in the stock market otherwise pension funds are big investors all world over). With the accelerating trends of reforms Indian stock market will witness more and more of institutionalization and the increasing size of money under the control, this set of investors will play a major role in Indian equity markets. The importance of institutional investors particularly foreign investors is very much evident as one of the routine reasons offered by market Pundits whenever the market rises it is attributed to foreign investors' money, no wonder we see headlines like "FIIs Fuel Rally" etc., in the business press. This is not unusual with India alone as most developed economies of today might have seen a similar trend in the past. The increasing role of institutional investors has brought both quantitative and qualitative developments in the stock market viz., expansion of securities business, increased depth and breadth of the market, and above all their dominant investment philosophy of emphasizing the fundamentals has rendered efficient pricing of the stocks.

Institutional investors are organizations which pool large sums of money and invest those sums in companies. They include banks, insurance companies, retirement or pension funds, hedge funds and mutual funds. Their role in the economy is to act as highly specialized investors on behalf of others. For instance, an ordinary person will have a pension from his employer. The employer gives that person's pension contributions to a fund. The fund will buy shares in a company, or some other financial product. Funds are useful because they will hold a broad portfolio of investments in many companies. This spreads risk, so if one company fails, it will be only a small part of the whole fund's investment. Institutional investors will have a lot of influence in the management of corporations because they will be entitled to exercise the voting rights in a company. They can engage in active role in corporate governance. Furthermore, because institutional investors have the freedom to buy and sell shares, they can play a large part in which companies stay solvent, and which go under. Influencing the conduct of listed companies, and providing them with capital are all part of the job of investment management.

India has witnessed over a decade of FIIs portfolio flows and with each passing year, these flows have gained in their significance and have played a key role in the overall Indian economy. Investments by foreign institutional investors are typically synonymous with portfolio investments in India, with more than three months left in the current calendar year FIIs have invested a net of $10.47 billion in Indian equities, just $0.23 billion short of record high ($10.7 billion) they clocked in the whole calendar year 2005.

Classified on the basis of category, long-term institutional investors like foreign pension funds continued to show interest in Indian securities markets. Moreover, many foreign governmental agencies showed interest in the Indian capital market and many of them got registered as FIIs. Other categories of FIIs registered belonged to traditional institutions like mutual funds, investment trusts, managers of such funds, banks etc. The total number of sub-accounts registered with SEBI also increased from 1,889 as on March 31, 2005 to 2,488 by end-March 2006.

Q2. (a) What are the objectives and functions of SEBI? Explain the role of SEBI in a stock exchange.

Ans.

Securities and Exchange Board of India (SEBI) was first established in the year 1988 as a non-statutory body for regulating the securities market. It became an autonomous body in 1992 and more powers were given through an ordinance. Since then it regulates the market through its independent powers.

Objectives of SEBI : As an important entity in the market it works with following objectives :–

1. It tries to develop the securities market.
2. Promotes Investors Interest.
3. Makes rules and regulations for the securities market.

Functions of SEBI : Find below SEBI's important functions : –

1. Regulates Capital Market
2. Checks Trading of securities.
3. Checks the malpractices in securities market.
4. It enhances investor's knowledge on market by providing education.
5. It regulates the stockbrokers and sub-brokers.
6. To promote Research and Investigation

Role of SEBI : Since its inception SEBI has been working targeting the securities and is attending to the fulfillment of its objectives with commendable zeal and dexterity. The improvements in the securities markets like capitalization requirements, margining, establishment of clearing corporations etc. reduced the risk of credit and also reduced the market.

SEBI has introduced the comprehensive regulatory measures, prescribed registration norms, the eligibility criteria, the code of obligations and the code of conduct for different intermediaries like, bankers to issue, merchant bankers, brokers and sub-brokers, registrars, portfolio managers, credit rating agencies, underwriters and others. It has framed bye-laws, risk identification and risk management systems for Clearing houses of stock exchanges, surveillance system etc. which has made dealing in securities both safe and transparent to the end investor.

Another significant event is the approval of trading in stock indices (like S&P CNX Nifty & Sensex) in 2000. A market Index is a convenient and effective product because of the following reasons :–

- It acts as a barometer for market behavior;
- It is used to benchmark portfolio performance;
- It is used in derivative instruments like index futures and index options;
- It can be used for passive fund management as in case of Index Funds.

Two broad approaches of SEBI is to integrate the securities market at the national level, and also to diversify the trading products, so that there is an increase in number of traders including banks, financial institutions, insurance companies, mutual funds, primary dealers etc. to transact through the Exchanges. In this context the introduction of derivatives trading through Indian Stock Exchanges permitted by SEBI in 2000 AD is a real landmark.

SEBI appointed the **L.C. Gupta Committee** in 1998 to recommend the regulatory framework for derivatives trading and suggest bye-laws for Regulation and Control of Trading and Settlement of Derivatives Contracts. The Board of SEBI in its meeting held on May 11, 1998 accepted the recommendations of the committee and approved the phased introduction of derivatives trading in India beginning with Stock Index Futures. The Board also approved the "Suggestive Bye-laws" as recommended by the Dr LC Gupta Committee for Regulation and Control of Trading and Settlement of Derivatives Contracts.

(b) Assuming that the firm pays tax at 50% rate, compute the after-tax cost of capital in the following cases :

(i) A 9-5% preference share sold at par.

Ans. The after tax cost of the preference share will be 9.5%

(ii) A perpetual bond sold at par, coupon rate of interest being 11-50 per cent.

Ans. The after tax cost of bond is

kd (I – T) = 0.115(1-0.5)

= 0.0575

= 5.75%

(iii) A ten-year 7 per cent, Rs. 100 bond sold at Rs. 94.

Ans. The after tax of bound is (Using approximation method) :–

$$= \frac{(I-T)[INT + \frac{1}{n}(f - B_0)]}{\frac{1}{2}[f + B_0]}$$

$$= \frac{(1-0.5)[7+\frac{1}{10}(100-94)]}{\frac{1}{2}(100+94)} = 3.91\ \%$$

(iv) A preference share sold at Rs. 110 in five years.

Ans. $100 = \sum_{t=1}^{5} \frac{9}{(1-k_p)^t} + \frac{110}{(1+k_p)^5}$

By trial & error, use find kp = 0.106 or 10.6%

(v) An equity share selling at a current market price of Rs. 24 and paying a current dividend of Rs. 1.75 per share which is expected to grow at a rate of 7 per cent.

Ans. $k_e = \frac{Divi}{Po} + g$

$$= \left[\frac{1.75(1+0.07)}{24} + 0.07\right] \times 100 = 14.80\%$$

Q3. What is Industry analysis? Bring out its relevance to the security analyst.

Ans: Industry Level Analysis : Industry level analysis focuses on a particular industry rather than on the broader economy. In this analysis, the main parameters to be looked at are the composition of the industry, its criticality vis-à-vis the national economy, its position along the industrial life cycle, entry and exit barriers. All these factors have a bearing upon the performance of the company.

Industry is a combination or group of units whose end products and services are similar. Having a common market, the participants in the industry group face similar problems and opportunities. To the extent that an industry loses or gains from certain happenings, the performance of the participants is sure to be similarly impacted. These happenings may be technological changes, shifts in consumer preferences, availability of substitutes etc. These changes also drive the life cycle of the industry.

The industry life cycle or the industry growth cycle can be divided into three major stages-pioneering stage, expansion stage and stagnation stage. The pioneering stage is related to sunrise status of the industry. It is the stage when technological development takes places. The products have been newly introduced in the market and they gain ready acceptance. The pioneering units in the industry make extraordinary profits and thus attract competition. As competition increases profitability in the industry comes under strain and less efficient firms are forced out of the market. At the end of the pioneering stage, selected leading companies remain in the industry.

In the expansion stage of the growth cycle the demand for the products increases but at a lower rate. There is less volatility in prices and production. Capital is easily available in plenty for these units. Due to retention of profits, internal accruals increase.

At the stagnation stage, the growth rate initially slows down, then stagnates and ultimately turns negative. There is no product innovation. External capital is hard to come by. Even the internal capital takes flight. This stage of the industry is most valuable during times of slow down in national economy.

A **sample of industry level analysis is given hereunder :–**

Watches: time to tap the potential

Source: Sowmya Krishnan - Business Line

Dynamic market conditions, cut throat competition, presence of multiple brands, low growth rates, high manufacturing costs and low capacity utilization - this is how the dial of the Indian watch industry looks today.

Low and middle end drives growth

The total demand for watchers in India is estimated to be above 25 million pieces every year, out of which the organized sector supplies around 11 million. As only one-fourth of the population owns a watch, there is huge untapped potential. How much of this will actually turn into demand depends entirely on the creative capabilities of the players.

Industry sources peg the growth rate for the industry at a modest 5 per cent and see the mid price segment as the high growth category.

Both Titan and Timex, the two major Indian manufacturers, are concentrating on the mid-price segment, that is, in the Rs. 1,000 - 5,000 range, though around 70 per cent of all watches sold cost less than Rs. 1,000. As Mr. Kapil Kapoor, Managing Director, Timex Watches, puts it, "though the growth in the watch market has come down to around 3.5 per cent, there has been considerable growth in the premium and middle-end segments due to the entry of internal brands".

Mr Bijou Kurien, Chief Operating officer, Watches division, Titan Industries Explains, "With the availability of so many brands prices at the premium end, the perception of an expensive watch has changed. People do not mind paying a higher price for a watch."

Untapped rural potential

Most organized players are eyeing the urban population. For 730 million rural Indians, there are only 90 million watches. Effectively, about 80 per cent of the untapped potential is in rural India.

Only HMT has a present in this segment. Its hand-wound or non-automatic, watches are still popular in the rural areas. None of the other brands has been able to penetrate this market. Titan did try, but could not make break through. It is now interested in acquiring a 74 per cent stake in HMT. If this happens, Titan would get access to an established rural market access.

While both Timex and Maxima have stuck to the urban market, Titan is trying to expand into rural India. But it may take a while for the market to add volumes for the watch-markers.

Cut-throat competition

Low growth rates and availability of a variety of brands have intensified competition. Each player clearly targets products at different segments and at different price points in order to corner a larger piece of the cake.

Of the 25 million watches sold in India, 18-19 million are sold in the sub Rs. 1,000 category. This category traditionally grew at 0 per cent and was dominated by the unorganized sector.

But over the last couple of years, the organized players are making their presence felt in a big ways.

Titan introduced' Sonata' in this category. Priced between Rs. 300 and Rs. 750, it was huge success contributing around 30 per cent of the Titan's watch sales in 2001. HMT, which has most of its products in this range, took a heavy beating losing market share to the emerging brand 'Maxima' and to some extent to 'Sonata'.

HMT's market share stands at 14 per cent while Timex gained 18-22 per cent. Timex repositioned its branch ad "America's No. 1 watch" with a thrust on technology, which helped it gain market share.

With Maxima targeting the mass segment with its separate collections for kids, youth and the steel collection priced in the Rs. 450-1,500 range, it is making its presence felt across segments where Titan has strong hold.

Trying different hands

A watch is now looked at as personal accessory, an extension of a person's lifestyle. The design of the dial and the strap influence a buyer's choice rather than just the function. Also, a whole new range of technologically superior watches has also entered the market.

With the emergence of this trend, the players have clearly segmented their consumer base targeting niche markets with different products. While Titan introduced 'Dash' targeted at children, Maxima launched 'Lil Dolphin' for the same segment.

Another niche segment caters to the technology savvy consumers, with brands such as 'EcoDrive' from Citizen, 'Cognoscenti' from Timex and 'Edge' from Titan.

There is also the fashion segment, where each player has a collection for men and women. For instance, Titan has 'Fast track', and Raga, Regalia and Royale in the stylish segment. International brands, such as Swatch and Espirity also have a presence. While most foreign brands have their products targeted at one niche segment, either fashion or function or style domestic players have different products targeted at different segments.

The stress is on constant innovation in style, design and products that would keep the interest alive in the various segments. This is a challenge every player is facing to keep up its market share.

Strengths in distribution network

For the domestic players, distribution network and presence across wide geographical areas are major advantages.

With the emergence of many retail chains the trend is slowly shifting towards the 'Shop-in-shop' concept. Customers now want to look at the variety on offer and then decide for themselves.

This has prompted the players to make their products available at retailing outlets and super markets, apart from dedicated retail outlets.

Imported watches too are slowly catching up to set up exclusive showrooms, though in very small numbers. Their geographical presence is restricted to the metros.

To that extent, established players, such as Titan and Timex have an advantage.

After-sales service is an other area where established players are trying to create a barrier and protect themselves from foreign brands.

The significance of industry analysis can be established by considering the performance of other industries too in a similar fashion. The analysis indicates the value to investors in selecting certain industries while avoiding others. The analysis also establishes the need for investors to continue analyzing industries by showing the inconsistency of industry performance over consecutive yearly periods.

Industry analysis usually involves several steps. As a first step, industries are analyzed in terms of their stage in the life cycle. The idea is to assess the general health and current position of the industry. This may be followed by an Assessment of the position of the industry in relation to the business cycle and macroeconomic conditions; an analysis of the competitive structure prevailing in the industry and a study of the impact of changes in government policy on the industry.

The most important of the characteristics that are to be evaluated in an industry analysis can be enumerated as given below : –

1. Past sales and earnings performance.
2. Permanence of the industry.
3. The attitude of the government towards the industry.

4. Labor conditions within the industry.
5. The competitive conditions as reflected by the existence of the entry barriers.
6. The stock prices of the firms in the industry relative to their earnings.

Q4. Discuss the CAPM and its application in portfolio selection. Explain the relationship between SML, CML and Characteristic Line.

Ans. Capital Asset Pricing Model : The CAPM developed by William F Sharpe, John Linter and Jan Mossin establishes a linear relationship between the required rate of return of a security and its beta. Beta, as we know is the non-diversifiable risk in a portfolio. A portfolio's standard deviation is a good indicator of its risk. Thus if adding a stock to a portfolio increases its standard deviation, the stock adds to the risk of the portfolio. This risk is the un-diversified risk that can not be eliminated. Beta measures the relative risk associated with any individual portfolio as measured in relation to the risk of the market portfolio.

$$\text{BETA} = \frac{\text{Non Diversifiable Risk of Asset or Portfolio}}{\text{Risk of Market Portfolio}}$$

Thus Beta is a measure of the non-diversifiable or systematic risk of an asset relative to that of the market portfolio. A beta of 1 indicates an asset of average risk. If beta is more than 1, then the stock is riskier than the market. On the other hand, if beta is less than one, market is riskier.

Mathematically, the equation of CAPM is given as under :–

$$Rs\ (s) = Rf + b\ (Rm\text{-}Rf)$$

Where Rs = Expected return on the security
Rf = Risk Free return
Rm = Return from the market portfolio
B = Beta

The CAPM is based on a list of critical assumptions : –

- Investors are risk averse and use the expected rate of return and standard deviation of return as appropriate measures of risk and return for their portfolio.
- Investors make their investments decisions based on a single period horizon which is the immediate next time period.
- Transaction costs are either absent or so low that these can be ignored.
- Assets can be bought and sold in any desired unit.
- The investor is limited by his wealth and the price of the asset only.
- Taxes do not affect the choice of buying assets.
- All individuals assume that they can buy the assets at the going market price and they all agree on the nature of the return and risk associated with each investment.

In the CAPM, the expected rate of return is equal to the required rate of return because the market is in equilibrium. The risk-less rate can be earned by investing in instruments like treasury bills. In addition to the risk free rate, investors also expect a premium over and above the risk free rate to compensate them for investing in risky assets since they are risk averse. Thus the required rate of return for the investors becomes equal to the sum of Risk-free rate and the risk premium.

The risk premium can be calculated as the product of Beta and market risk premium, i.e. difference between expected rate of return and risk-free rate of return.

Securities market line : The SML essentially graphs the results from the capital asset pricing model (CAPM) formula. The *x*-axis represents the risk (beta), and the *y*-axis represents the expected return. The market risk premium is determined from the slope of the SML.

The Security Market Line

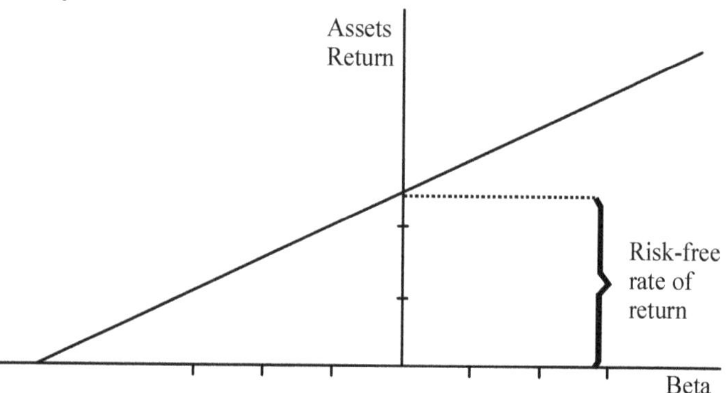

The relationship between β and required return is plotted on the securities *market line* (SML) which shows expected return as a function of β. The intercept is the nominal risk-free rate available for the market, while the slope is $E(R_m - R_f)$. The securities market line can be regarded as representing a single-factor model of the asset price, where Beta is exposure to changes in value of the Market. The equation of the SML is thus :

$$E(R_i) - Rf = \beta\ [E(Rm) - Rf]$$

It is a useful tool in determining if an asset being considered for a portfolio offers a reasonable expected return for risk. Individual securities are plotted on the SML graph. If the security's risk versus expected return is plotted above the SML, it is undervalued since the investor can expect a greater return for the inherent risk. And a security plotted below the SML is overvalued since the investor would be accepting less return for the amount of risk assumed A line used in the capital asset pricing model to illustrate the rates of return for efficient portfolios depending on the risk-free rate of return and the level of risk (standard deviation) for a particular portfolio.

The formula for CAPM is **Ks = Krf + B (Km - Krf).**

Let's assume that the risk free rate is 5%, and the overall stock market will produce a rate of return of 12.5% next year. You see that GullyBaba Company has a beta of 1.7

A graph of this situation, will look like as given below :–

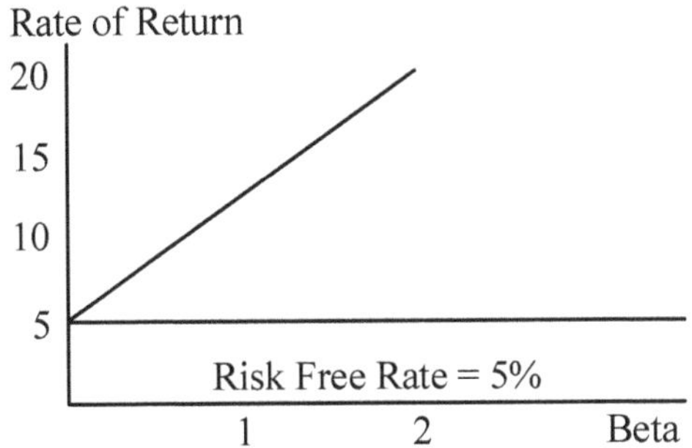

- On the horizontal axis are the betas of all companies in the market
- On the vertical axis are the required rates of return, as a percentage

The red line is the Security Market Line : The SML graphs the relationship between risk and return. The securities market line is a straight line. It touches the efficient frontier and passes though the risk free rate of return. The SML lies above the efficient frontier, except at the one point where it touches. This shows that the availability of a risk free asset improves the returns available for a any given level of risk and vice-versa.

The capital market line (CML) is a kind of graph, originating from the capital asset pricing model (CAPM). The CAPM is used to confirm a theoretically-suited necessary rate of return on an asset when it is about to be added to an existing and well-performing portfolio.

The CML is used to determine the rate of return for certain efficient portfolios. This analysis is dependent upon the risk-free rate of return and the amount of risk involved in a particular portfolio. The Sharpe ratio, through certain calculations, represents the proportion of risk and extra return that a portfolio provides. The portfolio which has the highest Sharpe ratio is known as the market portfolio. Every portfolio included in the market portfolio is optimized for a certain amount of risk. The amount of risk related to the particular asset is considered with importance.

According to the CAPM, the market portfolio represents the efficient frontier. The efficient frontier can be defined as an ingathering of portfolios. The market portfolio, when combined with the risk-free asset, is capable of producing a higher return than the efficient frontier. The combination of the market portfolio and the risk-free asset gives birth to the CML.

Experts tend to prefer CML over the efficient frontier because the CML considers the addition of a risk-free asset in the portfolio.

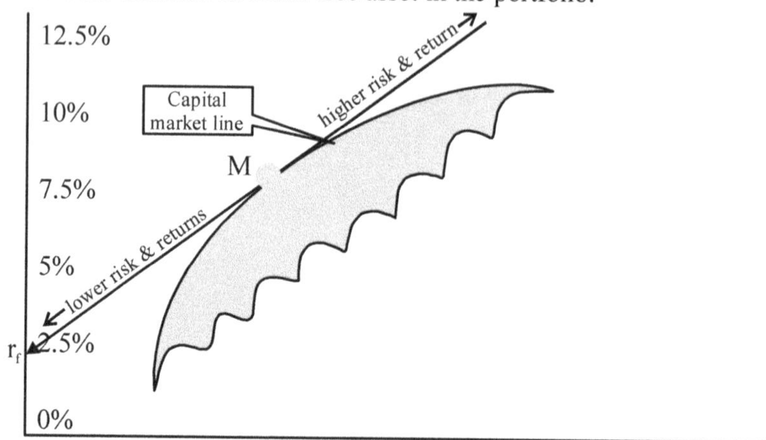

M= the entire market

r = return

σ=standard deviation, or risk

r_f=risk free rate

Capital market line is used to evaluate portfolio performance. Any point below any other point on the line will deliver lower returns but the same risk, and is therefore not ideal.

Capital market line is referred to as a measure employed to evaluate portfolio performance. Capital market line or CML is a graph employed in asset pricing models to depict rates of return in a market portfolio. Capital market line describes rates of return for efficient portfolios that are dependent on level of risk and risk free rate of return for a specific portfolio. CML originates from the assumption that all investors will possess market portfolio. Quantum of risk is positively correlated to the expected return

Capital market line is believed to be a better measure than efficient frontier as it takes into consideration risk-free asset in a portfolio. All points on the CML have better risk-return profiles when compared to any portfolio located on efficient frontier.

Characteristic line : Characteristic line is a line defined by utilizing regression analysis that sums up a specific security's or portfolios systematic risk and rate of return. The rate of return is subject to characteristic line's slope and standard deviation of returns of the specific asset. Slope of the characteristic line is typified by asset's beta. The slope ascertains risk-return trade-off. Greater risk is matched by greater returns.

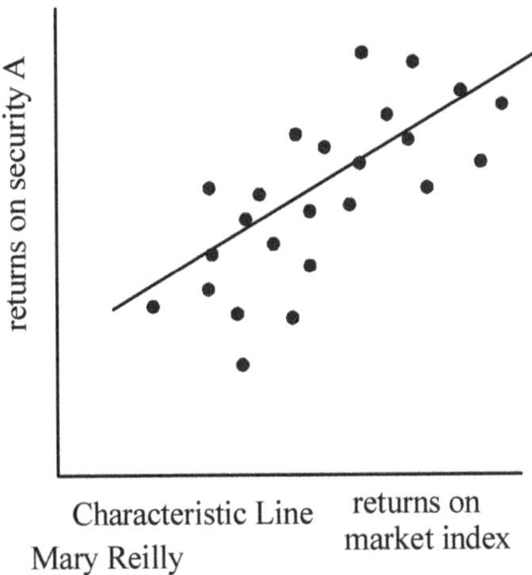

Characteristic Line
Mary Reilly

A straight line on a graph that shows the relationship over time between returns on a stock and returns on the market. The line is used to illustrate a stock's alpha (the vertical intercept) and beta (the line's slope) and to show the difference between systematic and unsystematic risk.

Characteristic Line leads to CAPM

- The characteristic regression line of an asset explains the asset's systematic variability of returns in terms of market forces that affect all assets simultaneously
- The portion of total risk not explained by characteristic line is called unsystematic risk
- Assets with high degrees systematic risk must be priced to yield high returns in order to induce investors to accept high degrees of risk that are undiversifiable in the market
- CAPM illustrates positive relationship between systematic risk and return on an asset

Differences between CML and SML

- Capital market line measures risk by standard deviation, or total risk
- Security market line measures risk by beta to find the security's risk contribution to portfolio M
- CML graphs only defines efficient portfolios
- SML graphs efficient and non-efficient portfolios
- CML eliminates diversifiable risk for portfolios
- SML includes all portfolios that lie on or below the CML, but only as a part of M, and the relevant risk is the security's contribution to M's risk
- Firm specific risk is irrelevant to each, but for different reasons

Differences between the SML and Security Characteristic Line

- SML graphs required return against betas of many securities
- Security Characteristic Line measures security returns against the market portfolio's returns
- The SML has a slope the Expected rate less the risk-free rate, and an intercept of the risk-free rate
- The SCL is used to determine how a security return correlates to a market index return and it can be used to estimate beta, the slope of the SCL
- The SML is used to estimate the required return for a security relative to its risk measured by beta
- The beta value for the SML comes from the slope estimate of the SCL

Relationship Between the SML and the Characteristic Line (In Equilibrium)

- **Characteristic Line :–**

$$r_{j,t} = A_j + \beta_j r_{M,t} + \varepsilon_{j,t}$$

$$E(r_j) = A_j + \beta_j E(r_M)$$

Security Market Line (SML) :–

$$E(r_j) = r_F + [E(r_M) - r_F]\beta_j$$

Rearranging:

$$E(r_j) = r_F(1-\beta_j) + \beta_j E(r_M)$$

Note: In equilibrium $A_j = r_F(1-\beta_j)$

Q5. (a) What is portfolio performance evaluation? Explain the various methods of portfolio performance evaluation.

Ans. Portfolio Performance Evaluation provides a selective review of the methods for measuring portfolio performance and the evidence on the performance of professionally managed investment portfolios.

Methods of portfolio performance evaluation.

Treynor Measure

Jack L. Treynor was the first to provide investors with a composite measure of portfolio performance that also included risk. Treynor's objective was to find a performance measure that could apply to all investors, regardless of their personal risk preferences. He suggested that there were really two components of risk: the risk produced by fluctuations in the market and the risk arising from the fluctuations of individual securities.

This measure was developed by Jack Treynor in 1965.

Treynor (helped developed CAPM) argues that, using the characteristic line, one can determine the relationship between a security and the market. Deviations from the characteristic line (unique returns) should cancel out if you have a fully diversified portfolio.

Treynor's Composite Performance Measure: He was interested in a performance measure that would apply to ALL investors regardless of their risk preferences. He argued that investors would prefer a CML with a higher slope (as it would place them on a higher utility curve). The slope of this portfolio possibility line is:

$$T_1 = \frac{R - R_f}{\beta_1}$$

Treynor introduced the concept of the security market line, which defines the relationship between portfolio returns and market rates of returns, whereby the slope of the line measures the relative volatility between the portfolio and the market (as represented by beta). The beta coefficient is simply the volatility measure of a stock, portfolio or the market itself. The greater the line's slope, the better the risk-return tradeoff

The Treynor measure, also known as the reward to volatility ratio, can be easily defined as:

(Portfolio Return – Risk-Free Rate) / Beta

The numerator identifies the risk premium and the denominator corresponds with the risk of the portfolio. The resulting value represents the portfolio's return per unit risk. To better understand how this works, suppose that the 10-year annual return for the S&P 500 (market portfolio) is 10%, while the average annual return on Treasury bills (a good proxy for the risk free rate) is 5%. Then assume you are evaluating three distinct portfolio managers with the following 10-year results :

Managers	Average Annual Return	Beta
Manager A	10%	0.90
Manager B	14%	1.03
Manager C	15%	1.20

Now, you can compute the Treynor value for each : –

T(market) = (.10 – .05)/1 = .05

T(manager A) = (.10 – .05)/0.90 = .056

T(manager B) = (.14 –.05)/1.03 = .087

T(manager C) = (.15 – .05)/1.20 = .083

The higher the Treynor measure, the better the portfolio. If you had been evaluating the portfolio manager (or portfolio) on performance alone, you may have inadvertently identified manager C as having yielded the best results. However, when considering the risks that each manager took to attain their respective returns, Manager B demonstrated the better outcome. In this case, all three managers performed better than the aggregate market.

Because this measure only uses systematic risk, it assumes that the investor already has an adequately diversified portfolio and, therefore, unsystematic risk (also known as diversifiable risk) is not considered. As a result, this performance measure should really only be used by investors who hold diversified portfolios.

Sharpe Ratio : Sharpe ratio is almost identical to the Treynor measure, except that the risk measure is the standard deviation of the portfolio instead of considering only the systematic risk, as represented by beta. Conceived by Bill Sharpe, this measure closely follows his work on the capital asset pricing model (CAPM) and by extension uses total risk to compare portfolios to the capital market line.

The Sharpe ratio can be easily defined as: –

(Portfolio Return – Risk-Free Rate) / Standard Deviation

Using the Treynor example from above, and assuming that the S&P 500 had a standard deviation of 18% over a 10-year period, let's determine the Sharpe ratios for the following portfolio managers :

Manager	Annual Return	Portfolio Standard Deviation
Manager X	14%	0.11
Manager Y	17%	0.20
Manager Z	19%	0.27

S(market) = (.10–.05)/.18 = .278

S(manager X) = (.14–.05)/.11 = .818

S(manager Y) = (.17–.05)/.20 = .600

S(manager Z) = (.19–.05)/.27 = .519

Once again, we find that the best portfolio is not necessarily the one with the highest return. Instead, it's the one with the most superior risk-adjusted return, or in this case the fund headed by manager X.

Unlike the Treynor measure, the Sharpe ratio evaluates the portfolio manager on the basis of both rate of return and diversification (as it considers total portfolio risk as measured by standard deviation in its denominator). Therefore, the Sharpe ratio is more appropriate for well diversified portfolios, because it more accurately takes into account the risks of the portfolio.

Jensen Measure : Like the previous performance measures discussed, the Jensen measure is also based on CAPM. Named after its creator, Michael C. Jensen, the Jensen measure calculates the excess return that a portfolio generates over its expected return. This measure is also known as alpha.

The Jensen ratio measures how much of the portfolio's rate of return is attributable to the manager's ability to deliver above-average returns, adjusted for market risk. The higher the ratio, the better the risk-adjusted returns. A portfolio with a consistently positive excess return will have a positive alpha, while a portfolio with a consistently negative excess return will have a negative alpha.

The formula is broken down as follows :–

Jensen's Alpha = Portfolio Return – Benchmark Portfolio Return

Where: Benchmark Return (CAPM) = Risk Free Rate of Return + Beta (Return of Market – Risk-Free Rate of Return)

So, if we once again assume a risk-free rate of 5% and a market return of 10%, what is the alpha for the following funds?

Manager	Average Annual Return	Beta
Manager D	11%	0.90
Manager E	15%	1.10
Manager F	15%	1.20

First, we calculate the portfolio's expected return :–

ER(D)= .05 + 0.90 (.10 – .05) = .0950 or 9.5% return

ER(E)= .05 + 1.10 (.10 – .05) = .1050 or 10.50% return

ER(F)= .05 + 1.20 (.10 – .05) = .1100 or 11% return

Then, we calculate the portfolio's alpha by subtracting the expected return of the portfolio from the actual return :–

Alpha D = 11%- 9.5% = 2.5%

Alpha E = 15%- 10.5% = 4.5%

Alpha F = 15%- 11% = 4.0%

Which manager did best? Manager E did best because, although manager F had the same annual return, it was expected that manager E would yield a lower return because the portfolio's beta was significantly lower than that of portfolio F.

(b) (i) Prashanth's Holdings Ltd. an investment company has invested in equity shares of a blue chip company its

Risk free return (Rf) = 9%

Expected total return (Rm) = 16%

Market sensitivity index (Bi) = 0.8

Calculate the expected rate of return on the investment made in the security.

Ans. E(R) = Rf + b (Rm-Rf)

where E(R) = Expected return on the security

Rf = Risk Free return

Rm = Return from the market portfolio

B = Beta

E(R) = 9% + 0.8(16% – 9%) = 14.6%

(ii) GVK Company's current market price of a share is Rs. 3.50. If the capitalization rate is 9 per cent, what is the dividend growth rate?

Ans. Ans: MP = Rs.46, D= Rs.3.50 Ke= 9%

Ke = D/MP + Growth rate (g)

9% = 3.50/46 +g

g = 1.39%

Q6. Discuss the various Formula Plans that are available to an investor for portfolio revision.

Ans. The buying and/or selling of securities according to a predetermined formula. This approach to investment decisions is intended to eliminate the investor's emotions and instead to follow a mechanical set of rules. A huge number of formula plans have been developed over the years.

Formula plans are mechanical methods of portfolio management that try to take advantage of price changes in securities that result from cyclical price movements. Formula plans, part of a conservative strategy, are designed primarily for investors who do not wish to take excessive risk but wish to quickly and favorably adjust their portfolio in response to cyclical security price changes.

The dollar cost averaging plan involves investing a fixed dollar amount in a security at fixed intervals. This is a passive buy-and- hold strategy in which a periodic dollar investment is held constant. If the share price increases, fewer shares are purchased. When the share price declines, more shares are purchased. The hoped-for outcome is growth in the value of the selected security.

A constant-dollar plan uses a two-part portfolio. The speculative portion is invested in securities having high promise of capital gain. The conservative portion consists of low-risk investments such as bonds or money market accounts. If the speculative portion of the portfolio rises a certain percentage or amount in value, the constant dollar plan uses its profits to increase the conservative portion. If the speculative portion declines in value by a specified percentage or amount, funds are transferred to it from the conservative portion.

The constant-ratio plan establishes a desired fixed ratio of the speculative to the conservative portion of the portfolio. An individual rebalances the portfolio whenever the actual ratio differs from the desired ratio by a predetermined amount. With this plan, an investor must decide what is the appropriate target ratio of the two portions of the portfolio and how far from the target ratio the actual ratio should be permitted to stray before one rebalances the portfolio. Since one expects the speculative portion of the portfolio to increase in value more rapidly than the conservative portion, this strategy should function much like the constant dollar plan.

The variable-ratio plan is a more aggressive strategy. The target ratio between the speculative portion and the conservative portion of the portfolio is varied by the investor and depends on the expected movement in value of the speculative securities. If the investor feels the market movement will be generally upward, he or she increases the proportion in speculative vehicles. If the feeling is bearish – a downward market – the proportion in conservative vehicles is increased. This strategy is not only the most aggressive but also requires more effort by the investor.

Q7. Write short notes on any four of the following:

(a) Speculation

Ans. Speculation (in a financial context) is the assumption of the risk of loss, in return for the uncertain possibility of a reward. Only if one may safely say that a particular position involves no risk may one say, strictly speaking, that such a position represents an "investment." Financial speculation involves the buying, holding, selling, and short-selling of stocks, bonds, commodities, currencies, collectibles, real estate, derivatives, or any valuable financial instrument to profit from fluctuations in its price as opposed to buying it for use or for income via methods such as dividends or interest. Speculation represents one of four market roles in Western financial markets, distinct from hedging, long- or short-term investing, and arbitrage.

(b) OTCEI

Ans. OTCEI was incorporated in 1990 as a Section 25 company under the Companies Act 1956 and is recognized as a stock exchange under Section 4 of the Securities Contracts Regulation Act, 1956. The Exchange was set up to aid enterprising promoters in raising finance for new projects in a cost effective manner and to provide investors with a transparent & efficient mode of trading. Modelled along the lines of the NASDAQ market of USA, OTCEI introduced many novel concepts to the Indian capital markets such as screen-based nationwide trading, sponsorship of companies, market making and scripless trading.

OTCEI...

-is the first screen based nationwide stock exchange in India

-is the first exchange to introduce Market Making in India

-is the first exchange to introduce Sponsorship of companies in India

-is the only exchange to allow listing of companies with paid-up below Rs.3 crores

-is the only exchange to allow companies with less than 3 year track record to tap capital market

-has shifted trading from counter receipts to share certificates

-has introduced Weekly Settlement Cycle
-allows short selling
-allows demat trading through NSDL
-has tied-up with NSCCL for Clearing

(c) Zero Coupon Bonds

Ans. A zero-coupon bond (also called a discount bond or deep discount bond) is a bond bought at a price lower than its face value, with the face value repaid at the time of maturity. It does not make periodic interest payments, or so-called "coupons," hence the term zero-coupon bond. Investors earn return from the compounded interest all paid at maturity plus the difference between the discounted price of the bond and its par (or redemption) value. Examples of zero-coupon bonds include U.S. Treasury bills, U.S. savings bonds, long-term zero-coupon bonds and any type of coupon bond that has been stripped of its coupons.

A zero coupon bond would mean a bond in which no benefit is received or receivable before the maturity or redemption.

In contrast, an investor who has a regular bond receives income from coupon payments, which are usually made semi-annually. The investor also receives the principal or face value of the investment when the bond matures.

Some zero coupon bonds are inflation indexed, so the amount of money that will be paid to the bond holder is calculated to have a set amount of purchasing power rather than a set amount of money, but the majority of zero coupon bonds pay a set amount of money known as the face value of the bond.

Zero coupon bonds may be long or short term investments. Long-term zero coupon maturity dates typically start at ten to fifteen years. The bonds can be held until maturity or sold on secondary bond markets. Short-term zero coupon bonds generally have maturities of less than one year and are called bills. The U.S. Treasury bill market is the most active and liquid debt market in the world.

(d) Elliott Wave Theory

Ans. Elliott Wave Theory interprets market actions in terms of recurrent price structures obedient to the Fibonacci sequence. Basically, Market cycles are composed of two major types of Wave : Impulse Wave and Corrective Wave. For every impulse wave, it can be sub-divided into 5 - wave structure (1-2-3-4-5), while for corrective wave, it can be sub-divided into 3 - wave structures (a-b-c).

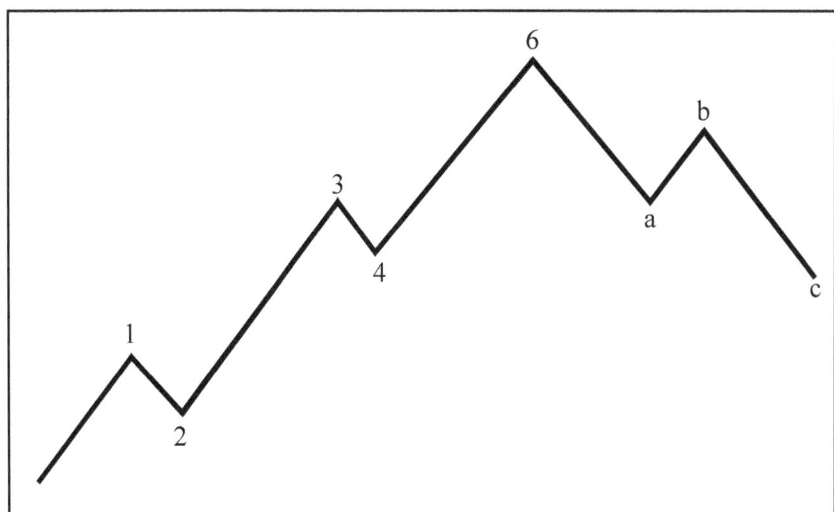

The Elliott wave principle is a form of technical analysis that attempts to forecast trends in the financial markets and other collective activities. It is named after Ralph Nelson Elliott (1871-1948), an accountant who developed the concept in the 1930s: he proposed that market prices unfold in specific patterns, which practitioners today call Elliott waves. Inspired by the Dow Theory and by observations found throughout nature, Elliott concluded that the movement of the stock market could be predicted by observing and identifying a repetitive pattern of waves. In fact, Elliott believed that all of man's activities, not just the stock market, were influenced by these identifiable series of waves.

Elliott based part his work on the Dow Theory, which also defines price movement in terms of waves, but Elliott discovered the fractal nature of market action. Thus Elliott was able to analyze markets in greater depth, identifying the specific characteristics of wave patterns and making detailed market predictions based on the patterns he had identified.

(e) Odd Lot Theory

Ans. A technical analysis theory based on using odd-lot trading behavior as a contrary indicator. This theory assumes that odd lots are traded primarily by small investors, who usually have less experience than institutional investors. Historical theory that the Odd Lot investor-the small personal investor who trades in less than 100-share quantities-is usually guilty of bad timing and that profits can be made by acting contrary to odd-lot trading patterns. Heavy odd-lot buying in a rising market is interpreted by proponents of this theory as a sign of technical weakness and the signal of a market reversal. Conversely, an increase of odd-lot selling in a declining market is seen as a sign of technical strength and a signal to buy. In fact, analyses of odd-lot trading over the years fail to bear out the theory with any real degree of consistency, and it has fallen into disfavor in recent years. It is also a fact that odd-lot customers generally, who tend to buy market leaders, have fared rather well in the upward market that has prevailed over the last fifty years or so.

(f) Efficient Frontier

Ans.

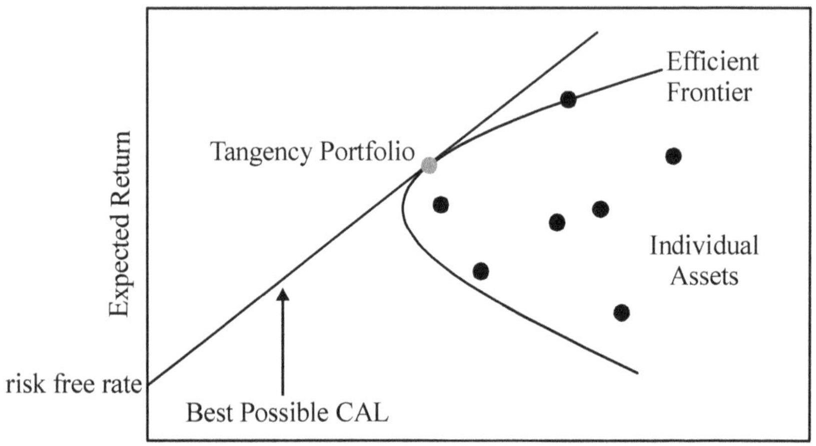

Efficient Frontier. The hyperbola is sometimes referred to as the 'Markowitz Bullet'

Every possible asset combination can be plotted in risk-return space, and the collection of all such possible portfolios defines a region in this space. The line along the upper edge of this region is known as the efficient frontier (sometimes "the Markowitz frontier"). Combinations along this line represent portfolios (explicitly excluding the risk-free alternative) for which there is lowest risk for a given level of return. Conversely, for a given amount of risk, the portfolio lying on the efficient frontier represents the combination offering the best possible return. Mathematically the Efficient Frontier is the intersection of the Set of Portfolios with Minimum Variance (MVS) and the Set of Portfolios with Maximum Return.

The efficient frontier will be convex – this is because the risk-return characteristics of a portfolio change in a non-linear fashion as its component weightings are changed. (As described above, portfolio risk is a function of the correlation of the component assets, and thus changes in a non-linear fashion as the weighting of component assets changes.) The efficient frontier is a parabola (hyperbola) when expected return is plotted against variance (standard deviation).

The region above the frontier is unachievable by holding risky assets alone. No portfolios can be constructed corresponding to the points in this region. Points below the frontier are suboptimal. A rational investor will hold a portfolio only on the frontier.

MS – 44 : Security Analysis and Portfolio Management
June, 2008

Note: Attempt any **five** questions. All questions carry equal marks. Present value and annuity tables are to be provided, if asked for.

Q1. "The investment environment has undergone sea-change in India since 1991." Explain.

Ans. Since 1991 India has undergone a sea change in its outlook toward foreign investment and global collaboration. India is committed to implementing fully economic reforms, encouraging investment and technology flows, and actively promoting and facilitating greater private sector participation in all sectors of the economy.

In 1991, a series of policy measures were announced to liberalise the FDI environment in the country. As a result, India today has one of the most attractive FDI policies in the South Asian region.

The following are some of the significant transformations which have taken place in the Indian financial and investment environment since 1991.

• Now more choices exist for the companies incorporated in India towards capital structure, financial instruments, pricing of financial instruments etc.

• Financial institution and banks have become extremely careful in lending because of their resource crunch and non-performing loans.

• More opportunities now exist for the private sector to substantially increase their investments both domestic and oversees. Further new areas like oil and gas, power, banking, insurance, telecommunication, airline, mutual funds etc. have been opened and widened for the private sector.

•The size of financial markets has grown significantly. Further, now the financial markets are more sophisticated and integrated.

• Foreign direct investment has been increased substantially and now there exists more scope for foreign institutional investors in portfolio investment.

• Interest rates are now market driven and thus have become more volatile. Exchange rates are now more unpredictable. Volatility in stock prices has increased substantially.

• Institutional investors have become more assertive and are now participating actively in corporate management to oversee that the companies focus on the creation of value for shareholders.

• Owing to deregulation, globalization and liberalization, competition among the firms has substantially increased and there has been enormous increase in business risk.

In the wake of these transformations, challenges for the finance managers have increased substantially. They have to be more careful and scientific while arriving at different financial decisions. The areas in which finance professionals have to be extremely careful in arriving at the financial decisions include: risk management, portfolio management, corporate valuation, capital structure, treasury management, value creation, corporate restructuring, asset-liability management, performance management, performance linked compensation plans, capital budgeting, working capital management etc.

The investment Environment comprises of three elements listed below:–

- Financial instruments
- Financial Institutions
- Financial markets

Several financial instruments are available in the Indian money market. These are government securities, or G-sec, preference shares, commercial papers, equity shares, certificate of deposits, call money market and industrial securities. These are discussed below.

India Financial market is one of the oldest in the world and is considered to be the fastest growing and best among all the markets of the emerging economies.

The history of Indian capital markets dates back 200 years toward the end of the 18th century when India was under the rule of the East India Company. The development of the capital market in India concentrated around Mumbai where no less than 200 to 250 securities brokers were active during the second half of the 19th century. The **financial market in India** today is more developed than many other sectors because it was organized long before with the securities exchanges of Mumbai, Ahmedabad and Kolkata were established as early as the 19th century. By the early 1960s the total number of securities exchanges in India rose to eight, including Mumbai, Ahmedabad and Kolkata apart from Madras, Kanpur, Delhi, Bangalore and Pune. Today there are 21 regional securities exchanges in India in addition to the centralized NSE (National Stock Exchange) and OTCEI (Over the Counter Exchange of India).

However the stock markets in India remained stagnant due to stringent controls on the market economy that allowed only a handful of monopolies to dominate their respective sectors. The corporate sector wasn't allowed into many industry segments, which were dominated by the state controlled public sector resulting in stagnation of the economy right up to the early 1990s. Thereafter when the Indian economy began 'liberalizing' and the controls began to be dismantled or eased out, the securities markets witnessed a flurry of IPOs that were launched. This resulted in many new companies across different industry segments to come up with newer products and services.

A remarkable feature of the growth of the Indian economy in recent years has been the role played by its securities markets in assisting and fuelling that growth with money rose within the economy. This was in marked contrast to the initial phase of growth in many of the fast growing economies of East Asia that witnessed huge doses of FDI (Foreign Direct Investment) spurring growth in their initial days of market decontrol. During this phase in India much of the organized sector has been affected by high growth as the financial markets played an all-inclusive role in sustaining financial resource mobilization. Many PSUs (Public Sector Undertakings) that decided to offload part of their equity were also helped by the well-organized securities market in India.

The launch of the NSE (National Stock Exchange) and the OTCEI (Over the Counter Exchange of India) during the mid 1990s by the government of India was meant to usher in an easier and more transparent form of trading in securities. The NSE was conceived as the market for trading in the securities of companies from the large-scale sector and the OTCEI for those from the small-scale sector. While the NSE has not just done well to grow and evolve into the virtual 'backbone' of capital markets in India the OTCEI struggled and is yet to show any sign of growth and development. The integration of IT into the capital market infrastructure has been particularly smooth in India due to the country's world class IT industry. This has pushed up the operational efficiency of the Indian stock market to global standards and as a result the country has been able to capitalize on its high growth and attract foreign capital like never before.

The regulating authority for capital markets in India is the SEBI (Securities and Exchange Board of India). SEBI came into prominence in the 1990s after the capital markets experienced some turbulence. It had to take drastic measures to plug many loopholes that were exploited by certain market forces to advance their vested interests. After this initial phase of struggle SEBI has grown in strength as the regulator of India's capital markets and as one of the country's most important institutions.

Financial Intermediaries

Financial intermediaries are banking and non-banking institutions which transfer funds from economic agents with surplus funds (surplus units) to economic agents (deficit units) that would like to utilize those funds. FIs are basically two types: Bank Financial Intermediaries, BFIs (Central banks and Commercial banks) and Non-Bank Financial Intermediaries, NBFIs (insurance companies, mutual trust funds, investment companies, pensions funds, discount houses and bureaux de change).

Financial intermediaries can be : –

- Banks;
- Building Societies;
- Credit Unions;
- Financial adviser or broker;
- Insurance Companies;
- Life Insurance Companies;
- Mutual Funds; or
- Pension Funds.

The borrower who borrows money from the **Financial Intermediaries**/ Institutions pays higher amount of interest than that received by the actual lender and the difference between the Interest paid and Interest earned is the Financial Intermediaries/Institutions profit.

Financial Intermediaries are broadly classified into two major categories:

1) Fee-based or Advisory Financial Intermediaries

2) Asset Based **Financial Intermediaries.**

Fee Based/Advisory **Financial Intermediaries**: These Financial Intermediaries/ Institutions offer advisory financial services and charge a fee accordingly for the services rendered.

Their services include : –

i. Issue Management

ii. Underwriting

iii. Portfolio Management

iv. Corporate Counseling

v. Stock Broking

vi. Syndicated Credit

vii. Arranging Foreign Collaboration Services

viii. Mergers and Acquisitions

ix. Debenture Trusteeship

x. Capital Restructuring

ASSET-BASED **Financial Intermediaries :** These Financial Intermediaries/ Institutions finance the specific requirements of their clientele. The required infra-structure, in the form of required asset or finance is provided for rent or interest respectively. Such companies earn their incomes from the interest spread, namely the difference between interest paid and interest earned.

The financial institutions may be regulated by various regulatory authorities, or may be required to disclose the qualifications of the person to potential clients. In addition, regulatory authorities may impose specific standards of conduct requirements on financial intermediaries when providing services to investors.

India was a latecomer to economic reforms, embarking on the process in earnest only in 1991, in the wake of an exceptionally severe balance of payments crisis. The need for a policy shift had become evident much earlier, as many countries in east Asia achieved high growth and poverty reduction through policies which emphasized greater export orientation and encouragement of the private sector. India took some steps in this direction in the 1980s, but it was not until 1991 that the government signaled a systemic shift to a more open economy with greater reliance upon market forces, a larger role for the private sector including foreign investment, and a restructuring of the role of government.

Q2. (a) "Stock exchanges provide the linkage between the savings in the household sector and the investments in the corporate sector." Discuss this statement and describe the steps involved in the investment process.

Ans. Savings mobilisation and promotion of investment arc functions of the stock and capital markets, which are a part of the organised financial system in India. The objective of all economic activity is to promote the well being and standard of living of the people, which depends on the income and distribution of income in terms of real goods and services in the economy.

All public companies are anxious to obtain permission from reputed exchanges for securing quotations of their shares and the management of a company is anxious to inform the investing public that the shares of the company will be quoted on the stock exchange".

The stock exchange is really an essential pillar of the private sector corporate economy. It discharges three essential functions:

First, the stock exchange provides a market place for purchase and sale of securities viz. shares, bonds, debentures etc. It, therefore, ensures the free transferability of securities which is the essential basis for the joint stock enterprise system.

Secondly, the stock exchange provides the linkage between the savings in the household sector and the investment in the corporate economy. It mobilizes savings, channelises them as securities into these enterprises which are favoured by the investors on the basis of such criteria as future growth prospects, good returns and appreciation of capital.

Thirdly, by providing a market quotation of the prices of shares and bonds- a sort of collective judgment simultaneously reached by many buyers and sellers in the market- the stock exchange serves the role of a barometer, not only of the state of health of individual companies, but also of the nation's economy as a whole.

(b) A chemical company paid a dividend of Rs. 2.35 per share of Rs. 10 each, during the current year. Forecasts suggest that earnings and dividends of the company are likely to grow at the rate of 7 percent over the next five years and at the rate of 5 percent thereafter. Investors have traditionally required a rate of return of 18 percent on these shares. What is the present value of the stock?

Ans. Present value of the share $= \frac{2.35(1.07)}{1.18} + \frac{2.35(1.07)^2}{(1.18)^2} + \frac{2.35(1.07)^3}{(1.18)^3}$

$$+ \frac{2.35(1.07)^4}{(1.18)^4} + \frac{2.35(1.07)^5}{(1.18)^5} + \frac{2.35(1.07)^5(1.05)}{(1.18)^5(0.18-0.05)}$$

$=$ Rs. 20.47

Q3. What is Security Analysis? How is fundamental analysis useful for identifying the potential securities? Explain.

Ans. Security Analysis is an examination and evaluation of the various factors affecting the value of a security.

Assumptions of Fundamental Analysis

• More often than not, the stock price does not reflect the real value of the stock itself. Market gyration and investors emotion will drive the price volatility. This result to either the stock price is overvalued or undervalued at that particular time.

• In the long run, the stock price will reflect its fundamental value. This can be months, years or even decades. Nobody knows exactly when the market will reflect the stock's true value, but its future prospect and potential growth is the best indication.

Fundamental analysis is a technique used to identify stocks that are 'undervalued' by the market, that is, they are selling at a price that is lower than the stock's intrinsic value at the time. Fundamental analysts assume that buyers will be attracted by the stock's 'cheap' price, and will collectively purchase the stock in sufficient numbers to cause its price to rise.

It has the ability to predict long-term economic, demographic, technological and consumer trends as well. And once you bought this stock at discounted price, you will on the right track to wealth.

Fundamental analysis is also used to identify so-called 'growth' stocks - stocks that have the potential to increase in value over time due to increasing earnings. BHP was, for a long time, an excellent growth stock in Australia. IBM was a classic growth stock in the United States.

To determine whether a stock is undervalued, or is a growth stock, a fundamental analyst examines numerous company statistics and other factors such as the effectiveness of the management, in order to make an assessment of the intrinsic value of the company. The relative value of the company to others in its industry, and the prevailing economic conditions, are also considered.

The company statistics examined include :–

• Liquidity patterns, such as current assets to current liabilities.

• Working capital management efficiency, such as an analysis of the value of stock held by the company, measured in days.

• Financial structures, such as the amount of gearing, balance sheet strength, and the company's debt structure.

• Profitability ratios, such as rate of return, return on assets, and the gearing of the company's earnings.

• Market performance ratios, such as dividends per share, dividend cover, dividend yield, earnings per share, discounted cash flow, the price-to-sales ratio and the price/earnings ratio.

• And many others.

Fundamental analysts obtain the data they require from company reports, announcements, financial Internet sites and from company web sites.

Q4. What is meant by 'Arbitrage Pricing Theory (APT)?' Compare and contrast CAPM and APT. Which of the two is a better model for pricing risky assets and why?

Ans. The APT is motivated by the empirical failure of the CAPM. The CAPM has only one factor (Excess return of market portfolio) to explain the excess return of the asset. The systematic risk of an asset is then given by the correlation with this factor. But in reality returns are affected by many different macroeconomic factors other than the market portfolio like

-Surprises in Inflation.

-Surprises in GNP.

-Surprises default risk premiums for bonds (measures investors confidence)

-Surprises in shifts in yield curve (where \surprise" means \realized minus expected" have been shown to have predictive power for excess returns.)

Difference in Methodology

-CAPM is an equilibrium model and derived from individual portfolio optimization.

-APT is a statistical model which tries to capture sources of systematic risk. Relation between sources determined by no Arbitrage condition.

Difference in Application

-APT difficult to identify appropriate factors.

-CAPM difficult to find good proxy for market returns.
-APT shows sensitivity to different sources. Important for hedging in portfolio information.
-CAPM is simpler to communicate, since everybody agrees upon.
-CAPM model is better for pricing risky assets. APT is an improved version of the CAPM, but why do we still use CAPM as well? Because, in practise, APT does not work better than CAPM. That happens because of estimation error. APT does not tell us how many factors we should use and it does not tell us what the factors are.
-The CAPM is more simple-minded model but we can estimate B_i and R_M a lot more precisely, so the required return is reasonably accurate. The APT may be more advanced conceptually, but this is cancelled out by the greater estimation error. In practise, the required return we come up with is not more accurate than the CAPM.
-The CAPM is simpler to understand, easier to use. The APT is more difficult to understand much harder to use. APT is rarely used for computing required return, but it has useful applications in investment management.

Q5. (a) "Portfolio Evaluation provides a feedback mechanism for improving the entire portfolio management process." Discuss.

Ans. The objective of constructing a portfolio and revising it periodically is to earn maximum returns with minimum risk. Portfolio evaluation is the process which is concerned with assessing the performance of the portfolio over a selected period of time in terms of return and risk. This involves quantitative measurement of actual return realised and the risk born by the portfolio over the period of investment. These have to be compared with objective norms to assess the relative performance of the portfolio. Alternative measures of performance evaluation have been developed for use by investors and portfolio managers.

Portfolio evaluation is useful in yet another way. It provides a mechanism for identifying weaknesses in the investment process and for improving these deficient areas. It provides a feedback mechanism for improving the entire portfolio management process.

The portfolio management process is an ongoing process. It starts with security analyis, proceeds to portfolio construction and continues with portfolio revision and evaluation. The evaluation provides the necessary feedback for designing a better portfolio next time. Superior performance is achieved through continual refinement of portfolio management skills.

Also Refer Unit 14, Q1 and Q3.

(b) (i) Mr. Vamsi is considering an investment in the stock of GPK Corporation. He expects GPK Corporation to earn a return of 14 percent in the next year. GPK's beta is 1.2, Rf is 6 percent and market return is 13 percent.

(1) Should Mr. Vamsi invest in the GPK Corporation?

(2) What should Mr. Vamsi do if beta is 1.1? Assume that other values have not changed.

(1) $E_I = E_F + (E_M - E_F)\beta i$ $\quad \beta i = Covim / Vm = \sigma im / \sigma^2 m$

β is quantity of risk; it is the covariance between returns on the risky asset, I, and the market portfolio,M, divided by the variance of the market portfolio.

If we show how to derive the CAPM equation in a simple way:
M:Market portfolio, E_F:Riske free rate, I:Risky asset

$E_I = 6\% + (13\% - 6\%)\ 1.2$

$E_I = 14.40\%$

So, Mr. Vamsi should buy the stock as his required return is less than expected return.

(2) $E_I = R_F + (R_M - R_F)\ \beta_i$

$E_I = 6\% + (13\% - 6\%)\ 1.1$

$E_I = 13.70\%$

Mr. Vamsi should not invest

(ii) An investor expects a dividend of Rs. 4 per share for each of 10 years and a selling price of Rs. 70 at the end of 10 years. Calculate the present value of share if his required rate of return is 10 percent.

Ans. Present value of share $= \dfrac{4\left[(1+0.10)^{10} - 1\right]}{(1+0.10)^{10}(0.10)}$

$+ \dfrac{70}{(1.10)^{10}}$

$= 24.59 + 26.99$

$=$ Rs. 51.58

Q6. "Formula plans are good because they aid the investor in overcoming his emotional involvement with timing of purchase and sale of stock." Discuss.

Ans. Formula plan : The buying and/or selling of securities according to a predetermined formula. This approach to investment decisions is intended to eliminate the investor's emotions and instead to follow a mechanical set of rules. A huge number of formula plans have been developed over the years.

Formula plans are mechanical methods of portfolio management that try to take advantage of price changes in securities that result from cyclical price movements. Formula plans, part of a conservative strategy, are designed primarily for investors who do not wish to take excessive risk but wish to quickly and favorably adjust their portfolio in response to cyclical security price changes

The dollar cost averaging plan involves investing a fixed dollar amount in a security at fixed intervals. This is a passive buy-and- hold strategy in which a periodic dollar investment is held constant. If the share price increases, fewer shares are purchased. When the share price declines, more shares are purchased. The hoped-for outcome is growth in the value of the selected security.

A constant-dollar plan uses a two-part portfolio. The speculative portion is invested in securities having high promise of capital gain. The conservative portion consists of low-risk investments such as bonds or money market accounts. If the speculative portion of the portfolio rises a certain percentage or amount in value, the constant dollar plan uses its profits to increase the conservative portion. If the speculative portion declines in value by a specified percentage or amount, funds are transferred to it from the conservative portion.

The constant-ratio plan establishes a desired fixed ratio of the speculative to the conservative portion of the portfolio. An individual rebalances the portfolio whenever the actual ratio differs from the desired ratio by a predetermined amount. With this plan, an investor must decide what is the appropriate target ratio of the two portions of the portfolio and how far from the target ratio the actual ratio should be permitted to stray before one rebalances the portfolio. Since one expects the speculative portion of the portfolio to increase in value more rapidly than the conservative portion, this strategy should function much like the constant dollar plan.

The variable-ratio plan is a more aggressive strategy. The target ratio between the speculative portion and the conservative portion of the portfolio is varied by the investor and depends on the expected movement in value of the speculative securities. If the investor feels the market movement will be generally upward, he or she increases the proportion in speculative vehicles. If the feeling is bearish – a downward market – the proportion in conservative vehicles is increased. This strategy is not only the most aggressive but also requires more effort by the investor.

Q7. Write short notes on any *four* of the following :

(a) Risk and Uncertainty

Ans. (a) The two are closely associated with one another, but are not identical. Uncertainty may involve things that are completely unknown, whereas risks are often understood via calculable probabilities. For example, though you don't know exactly what will happen after placing a bet on a roulette table, technically the risk of you losing when you bet on red is just slightly over 50 percent. It also must be noted that uncertainty doesn't necessarily imply risks -- something undesirable might happen, but it might be that any of the possible outcomes is OK. This is seldom the case, though, so uncertainty and risk usually run hand-in-hand.

(b) Uncertainty is a major factor in matters of science, technology, health, and the environment. New forms of technology, new medical treatments, the impact of certain substances on the air, water, and/or soil – all these things have effects, both long and short term, that cannot be completely predicted. Instead of clear and distinct rules of cause and effect, the best technical knowledge reveals are risk factors – probabilities that certain consequences will occur (for example, the statement that "smokers have a 50 percent greater chance of contracting a deadly form of adult leukemia," according to a recent study). And it is not necessarily the case that, when given enough time, scientists can eliminate uncertainty and risk. Some uncertainty is unavoidable, and even technologies and treatments that are quite old still involve uncertain elements. For example, while the fact that radiation exposure is a serious health risk has been known for decades, the precise level of radiation that a specific person can withstand is still unknown – a level that causes cancer in me may leave you unaffected.

(c) Some decisions involve unavoidable risk and uncertainty. For example, let's say your local government does a study and projects a 100 percent increase in electrical power demands over the next 10 years. If it turns out that, due to some unforeseen events, the power demands in your town don't grow by more than 20 percent, the construction of new power plants promises to be an economic disaster. On the other hand, if they do not build the power plants and the demand does significantly increase, the town may be unable to supply the needed power. There are risks involved in any of the available options.

(b) Convertible Bonds

Ans. In finance, a convertible bond (or convertible debenture) is a type of bond that can be converted into shares of stock in the issuing company, usually at some pre-announced ratio. It is a hybrid security with debt- and equity-like features. Although it typically has a low coupon rate, the holder is compensated with the ability to convert the bond to common stock, usually at a substantial discount to the stock's market value.

From the issuer's perspective, the key benefit of raising money by selling convertible bonds is a reduced cash interest payment. However, in exchange for the benefit of reduced interest payments, the value of shareholder's equity is reduced due to the stock dilution expected when bondholders convert their bonds into new shares.

The convertible bond markets in the United States and Japan are of primary global importance. These two domestic markets are the largest in terms of market capitalisation. Other domestic convertible bond markets are often illiquid, and pricing is frequently non-standardized.

(c) Market Breadth Index

Ans. Market breadth is a technical analysis theory that predicts the strength of the market according to the number of stocks that advance or decline in a particular trading day.

The breadth of market indicator is used to gauge the number of stocks advancing and declining for the day. If the breadth indicator is strong, this theory predicts that the market will be rising and vice versa.

Breadth is the extent of investor participation in stocks, bonds, and commodities. It high lights how widespread a general price increase or decrease is. Breadth indicators track stock, bond, and commodity market trends in order to assess market strength or weakness and market. They show how many issues are participating in a market move.

The trend in market participation is important. In general, breadth is good if two-thirds of the stocks on an exchange are increasing. When breadth is good, the market is likely to last longer, since more investors are participating. With regard to stock, breadth is the net difference between advancing issues and declining ones. The number of advancing stocks are those traded on an exchange (e.g., New York Stock Exchange) that went up in price on that trading day; declining stocks are those that went down. The market is bullish when advancing issues are significantly more than declining issues, bearish if declines outnumber advances.

The fewer issues going in the same direction as the market averages, the more apt there is to be a trend reversal. Further, the longer a price trend is maintained without a follow-up in the overall market, the more vulnerable is the advance.

Breadth relates to the number of sectors (e.g., industry groups such as airline, oil, autos, or technology) with market participation. If many sectors are enjoying an advance, this is a bullish indication. However, if only one or a few market sectors are involved in the advance, this is a bearish sign. In other words, breadth in the market reveals the extent to which a market index is supported by its components.

Market breadth shows whether the environment for stocks is good or bad. Breadth indicators such as positive and negative divergences signal major turning points in the market. Breadth divergences should be confirmed by a trend reversal in the market indices. Market breadth is an advance indicator of major stock price advances or declines.

When the difference between the number of advancing and declining issues is low, there is a market stand-off that probably will lead to fairly stable prices. An extremely high number of advancing issues, particularly based on a 10-day moving average, are very bullish. An extremely high number of declining issues are very bearish.

The broad market usually leads the market averages at market tops, for example, when the broad list of stocks peaks out ahead of a market index. Breadth analysis is not useful to ascertain major reversals at market bottoms because most stocks coincide with or lag behind the major market averages.

In a thin (narrow, inactive) market where trading for

(d) Agency Theory

Ans. Agency theory is the branch of financial economics that looks at conflicts of interest between people with different interests in the same assets. This most importantly means the conflicts between

- shareholders and managers of companies
- Shareholders and bond holders.

Agency theory explains, among other things, why :–

- Companies so often make acquisitions that are bad for shareholders.
- convertible bonds are used and bonds are sometimes sold with warrants
- Capital structure matters.

Agency theory is rarely, if ever, of direct relevance to portfolio investment decisions. It is used to by financial economists to model very important aspects of how capital markets function. However, investors gain a better understanding of markets by being aware of the insights of agency theory.

One particularly important agency issue is the conflict between the interests of shareholders and debt holders. In particular, following a more riskier but higher return strategy benefits the shareholders to the detriment of the debt holders.

It can easily be seen why debt holders lose out: a more risky strategy increases

the risk of default on debt, but debt holders, being entitled to a fixed return, will not benefit from higher returns. Shareholders will benefit from the higher returns (if they do improve), however if the risk goes bad, shareholders will, thanks to limited liability, share a sufficiently bad loss with debt holders.
This conflict can be addressed by the use of debt covenants, or by providing debt holders with a hedge against such action by the shareholders by issuing convertible debt or debt bundled with warrants.

(e) Odd Lot Theory

Ans. A technical analysis theory based on using odd-lot trading behavior as a contrary indicator. This theory assumes that odd lots are traded primarily by small investors, who usually have less experience than institutional investors Historical theory that the Odd Lot investor-the small personal investor who trades in less than 100-share quantities-is usually guilty of bad timing and that profits can be made by acting contrary to odd-lot trading patterns. Heavy odd-lot buying in a rising market is interpreted by proponents of this theory as a sign of technical weakness and the signal of a market reversal. Conversely, an increase of odd-lot selling in a declining market is seen as a sign of technical strength and a signal to buy. In fact, analyses of odd-lot trading over the years fail to bear out the theory with any real degree of consistency, and it has fallen into disfavor in recent years. It is also a fact that odd-lot customers generally, who tend to buy market leaders, have fared rather well in the upward market that has prevailed over the last fifty years or so.

(f) Efficient Frontier

Ans.

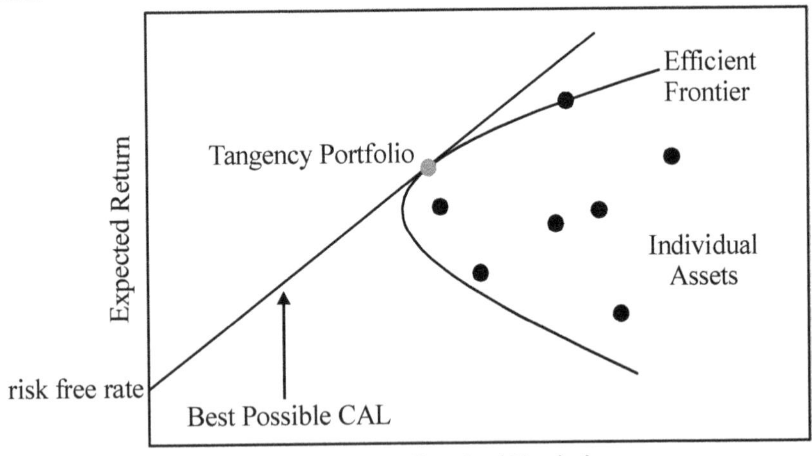

Efficient Frontier. The hyperbola is sometimes referred to as the 'Markowitz Bullet'

Every possible asset combination can be plotted in risk-return space, and the collection of all such possible portfolios defines a region in this space. The line along the upper edge of this region is known as the efficient frontier (sometimes "the Markowitz frontier"). Combinations along this line represent portfolios (explicitly excluding the risk-free alternative) for which there is lowest risk for a given level of return. Conversely, for a given amount of risk, the portfolio lying on the efficient frontier represents the combination offering the best possible return. Mathematically the Efficient Frontier is the intersection of the Set of Portfolios with Minimum Variance (MVS) and the Set of Portfolios with Maximum Return.

The efficient frontier will be convex - this is because the risk-return characteristics of a portfolio change in a non-linear fashion as its component weightings are changed. (As described above, portfolio risk is a function of the correlation of the component assets, and thus changes in a non-linear fashion as the weighting of component assets changes.) The efficient frontier is a parabola (hyperbola) when expected return is plotted against variance (standard deviation).

The region above the frontier is unachievable by holding risky assets alone. No portfolios can be constructed corresponding to the points in this region. Points below the frontier are suboptimal. A rational investor will hold a portfolio only on the frontier.

MS – 44 : Security Analysis and Portfolio Management
December, 2008

Note: Attempt any **five** questions. All questions carry equal marks. Present value and annuity tables are to be provided, if asked for.

Q1. Explain the scope and importance of the Security Analysis and Portfolio Management.

Ans. Security Analysis is the entire process of estimating return and risk for individual securities is known as Security Analysis. Various approaches to Security Analysis are :

1. Traditional Security Analysis : Analysts have attempted to identify undervalued securities to buy, and overvalued securities to sell.
2. Modern Security Analysis : Strongly influenced by Efficient Market Hypothesis. It questions the validity of Traditional Security Analysis.

Portfolio Management : It is the dynamic function of analyzing, selecting, evaluating and revising the portfolio in terms of stated investor objectives. In Traditional Portfolio Management selection of those securities that best fit the personal needs and desires of the investor is done. It may yield less than optimum results.

But, in Modern Portfolio Management, a scientific approach based on estimates of risk and return of the portfolio is used. Analysis of securities is done on the basis of attitudes of investors towards risk-return trade-off.

Most investors, and sadly most investment advisors, have little training or knowledge regarding security analysis and portfolio management. Typically, investor portfolios are built in a hodge-podge manner over time. Securities are chosen without benefit of in-depth analysis and without proper regard as to how they interrelate with one another. Holdings are often spread over numerous accounts held at various locations so there is little way to determine how the overall investment portfolio is performing.

Proper security analysis is required to identify suitable and attractive investments. The level of expertise needed varies between investment types. Stock analysis can be fairly straightforward, but many fixed-income investments incorporate a variety of factors that must be carefully considered. Derivatives, options, futures and commodities are even more complex. Without extensive training, you may find it extremely difficult to ascertain fair value of the many varied security options available. On top of the security selection requirements, you must understand how these individual securities act in concert to form an efficient and effective portfolio. At a minimum, you will need to understand some of the core principles of modern portfolio theory (MPT).

Q2. (a) Distinguish between current yield and yield to maturity of a fixed income security. How are these yields calculated? Discuss.

Ans: Current yield provides a simple way to factor in the effect of a security's market price on the value of coupon payments. However, it doesn't account for two other important sources of return. The first is the additional income that can be earned by reinvesting coupon payments as they are received. The second is the capital gain or loss the market price paid for a security represents against the par value an investor will receive at maturity. The current yield can be calculated by the following formula:

Coupon rate per year = Current Yield / Current market price

Current yield is a superior measure to coupon rate because it is based on current market price. But most widely used measure of fixed income securities is Yield to Maturity.

YTM can be defined as the indicated (promised) compounded rate of return an investor will receive from a bond purchased at current market price and held to maturity. It is the interest rate that equates the bond's price to the discounted cash flows of its promised cash flows.

YTM can be defined as the indicated (promised) compounded rate of return an investor will receive from a bond purchased at current market price and held to maturity. It is the interest rate that equates the bond's price to the discounted cash flows of its promised cash flows. **It takes into account purchase price, redemption value, coupon yield, and the time between interest payments.**

Calculating the YTM is an iterative process, involving repeated calculations that get successively closer to a solution. The exact same formula is used to calculate both YTM and YTC (Yield to Call). The only difference is that, for the YTC, the contractual or estimated call date is used instead of the contractual maturity date.

YTM's Relation with Price: YTM and the price of the Bonds have inverse relations i.e. if YTM goes up the price of the Bonds will come down and when YTM goes down the price of the Bonds will go up. The following table gives an indication between the YTM and current yield, when bonds are quoted at discount or at a premium or at par:-

Bond Selling At.	**Relationship**
Discount	Coupon Rate < Current Yield < YTM
Premium	Coupon Rate > Current Yield > YTM
Par Value	Coupon Rate = Current Yield = YTM

Thus, the YTM will be greater than the current yield when the bond is selling at a discount and will be less if it is selling at a premium.

The calculation of YTM is identical to the calculation of internal rate of return.

· If the yield to maturity for a bond is less than the bond's coupon rate, then the market value of the bond is greater than the par value.

· If a bond's coupon rate is less than its YTM, then the bond is selling at a discount.

· If a bond's coupon rate is more than its YTM, then the bond is selling at a premium.

· If a bond's coupon rate is equal to its YTM, then the bond is selling at par.

There are two methods used for YTM:

(i) Linear interpolation method and

(ii Approximation method.

Interpolation Method: Under this method YTM is similar to calculating Internal Rate of Return. To use this method help of computer and calculator is better. Under this method two rates of return are assumed to find the value of YTM.

Illustration 1 : An investor purchased a 12% Rs. 600 bonds at par five years ago. The current market price is Rs. 750. The YTM can be estimated as follows:

$$Mp = \sum_{t=1}^{n} \frac{I_t}{(1+YTM)^t} + \frac{TV}{(1+YTM)^n}$$

$$\text{Rs. } 750 = \frac{72}{(1+YTM)^1} + \frac{600}{(1+YTM)^6}$$

MP = Market price, TV = Terminal value, I = yearly interest

What is now required is the value of YTM which equates Rs. 750 with the Sum of present values of Rs. 72 for 5 years and of Rs. 600 receivable at the end of fifth year.

A process of trial and error is used. Two rates are assumed say 15% and 20%. The PV at 20% is Rs. 72 x 2.9906 + Rs. 600 x 0.8333 = Rs. 715.32 and

At 15% PV is Rs. 72 x 3.39223 + Rs.600 x 0.86057 = Rs. 760.58.

NOW the estimate can be made by linear interpolation method.

Note: The PV @ 12% is Rs. 795.25, which is higher than MP Rs. 750. So a higher rate 15% is selected. At 15% PV is Rs. 760.58, which is higher than MP. At 20% PV is Rs. 715.32, which is lower than MP. So it means YTM lies between these two rates.

$$\text{YTM} = 20\% + \frac{760.58 - 750}{760.58 - 715.32} \times (20\% - 15\%)$$

$$\text{YTM} = 20\% + \frac{10.58}{45.26} \times (20\% - 15\%)$$

YTM = 20% + 1.16
YTM = 21.16
YTM =20% + 1.16
YTM =21.16

The procedure for linear interpolation is as follows :

1) Find the difference between PV at lower rite and MP is (10.58)
2) Divide step I by the difference between present values at two rates (45.26)
3) Lastly, add to the lower rate the product of step 2 and then multiply by the difference between both rates.

Approximation Method

$$\text{YTM} = \frac{I + (FV - MP)/n}{(FV + MP)/2}$$

FV = face value
MP = market Price
n = number of years
I = annual interest payment

Yield-to-maturity is more complex. It includes all three ways investors generate return: coupon payments, reinvestment of coupon payments, and capital gains or losses. Because it is more complete, yield-to-maturity is the valuation measure commonly used by professional investment managers.

Comparing Current Yield with Yield-to-Maturity

Below is a comparison of current yield and yield-to-maturity, based on a hypothetical two-year note at par with a coupon of 10% paid quarterly and reinvested at the same rate.

Yield to Maturity

Coupon payments	Reinvestment of coupon payments	capital gain / loss Vs. Par	YTM
10%	2.92%		0%
9.75%			
10%	2.92%		-5%
7.10%			

10% 2.92% +5%
12.60%

Current Yield

Coupon Reinvestment capital gain / YTM
payments of coupon payments loss Vs. Par

10% NA NA
10%

Reinvestment of Capital Gain/
Payments Coupon Payments Loss vs. Par YTM

Keep in mind that the investor will only realize the yield-to-maturity if the security is held until maturity and if the coupons are reinvested at the same interest rate. If the investor sells the security prior to maturity at a price other than par, or if interest rates change and the coupons are not reinvested at the same rate, the yield-to-maturity will not change or vary.

(b) Prashanth Ltd., is intending to acquire substantial shares in GVK Ltd. To acquire control in the company. The beta factor of GVK Ltd.'s shares is 1.60 and its current market price is Rs. 190 and the company is consistently paying a dividend of Rs. 46 p.a. The risk free market rate of interest is 12% and the rate of return expected on such securities in the market is 18%.

You are required to value the share of GVK Ltd.

Dividend paid by the firm = Rs. 46

Current market price = Rs.190

So, the expected return :

190= 46/ Ke

Ke= 24.21%

But the required return expected by the investor is 18%. So, the share of GVK is undervalued.

Q3. What is the purpose of technical analysis? Why does technical analysis receive little support from academically oriented students of Investments?

Ans. Technical Analysis is the forecasting of future financial price movements based on an examination of past price movements. Like weather forecasting, technical analysis does not result in absolute predictions about the future. Instead, technical analysis can help investors anticipate what is "likely" to happen to prices over time. Technical analysis uses a wide variety of charts that show price over time.

Technical analysis is applicable to stocks, indices, commodities, futures or any tradable instrument where the price is influenced by the forces of supply and demand. Price refers to any combination of the open, high, low, or close for a given security over a specific time frame. The time frame can be based on intraday (1-minute, 5-minutes, 10-minutes, 15-minutes, 30-minutes or hourly), daily, weekly or monthly price data and last a few hours or many years. In addition, some technical analysts include volume or open interest figures with their study of price action.

The beauty of technical analysis lies in its versatility. Because the principles of technical analysis are universally applicable, each of the analysis steps above can be performed using the same theoretical background. You don't need an economics degree to analyze a market index chart.

Technical analysis is a security analysis discipline for forecasting the future direction of prices through the study of past market data, primarily price and volume. In its purest form, technical analysis considers only the actual price and volume behavior of the market or instrument. Technical analysts may employ models and trading rules based on price and volume transformations, such as the relative strength index, moving averages, regressions, inter-market and intra-market price correlations, cycles or, classically, through recognition of chart patterns.

Technical analysis is widely used among traders and financial professionals, and is very often used by active day traders, market makers, and pit traders. In the 1960s and 1970s it was widely dismissed by academics. Long-term investors often shun technical analysis because it is thought to be a tool used solely for short-term speculation. In fact, a large part of the literature of technical analysis is devoted to short-term timing, which confirms this belief.

Many individual investors have experimented with various charting techniques and have dropped the technical approach after a few "bad" experiences.

The random nature of stock price movements has led to the development of a primarily academic theory called the Efficient Market Hypothesis. The EMH is highly critical of professional investment management and is often used to justify a passive indexed approach to portfolio management. Most of the assumptions that make up the foundations of the efficient market hypothesis seem unrealistic to me – especially the ideas that new information is disseminated throughout the market instantly and that all investors interpret new information accurately and that stocks are always priced correctly. I have observed instances that are almost exactly opposite to this proposition so frequently as to represent a common occurrence.

Students of Investments are often completely indoctrinated in the belief that the market is "efficient" and that technical analysis is of no practical value since the day-to-day fluctuations of stock prices are random. There can be little argument that the day-to-day movements of stock prices are random. And yet, the movements of individual stocks and the broad market demonstrate an uncanny ability to anticipate future fundamental developments and other factors that influence stock prices. Short-term randomness of stock prices does not seem to diminish the ability of the market to more-or-less consistently act as a long-term discounting mechanism.

Q4. What is a diversified portfolio? What type of risk is reduced through diversification? How many securities are necessary to achieve this reduction in risk?

Ans. A portfolio that includes a variety of assets whose prices are not likely all to change together. In international economics, this usually means holding assets denominated in different currencies.

A risk management technique that mixes a wide variety of investments within a portfolio. The rationale behind this technique contends that a portfolio of different kinds of investments will, on average, yield higher returns and pose a lower risk than any individual investment found within the portfolio. Diversification strives to smooth out unsystematic risk events in a portfolio so that the positive performance of some investments will neutralize the negative performance of others. Therefore, the benefits of diversification will hold only if the securities in the portfolio are not perfectly correlated.

It's a portfolio strategy in which you spread your money around among different investments in order to reduce the risk of loss from a decline in the investments. Its goal is to reduce the risk in a portfolio. When diversification is properly applied, then it is expected that volatility or fluctuations in portfolio value become subdued and limited. The act of diversification reduces a portfolio's swings as well as both upside and downside potential, and allowing for more consistent performance under a wide range of economic conditions.

Studies and mathematical models have shown that maintaining a well-diversified portfolio of 25 to 30 stocks will yield the most cost-effective level of risk reduction. Investing in more securities will still yield further diversification benefits, albeit at a drastically smaller rate.

Further diversification benefits can be gained by investing in foreign securities because they tend be less closely correlated with domestic investments. For example, an economic downturn in the U.S. economy may not affect Japan's economy in the same way; therefore, having Japanese investments would allow an investor to have a small cushion of protection against losses due to an American economic downturn.

With a diversified stock portfolio, risk is reduced because different stocks rise and fall independently of each other. On a broader scale, combinations of different investment assets may well cancel out each other's fluctuations in price, reducing the overall risk.

Categorizing risk: The ultimate goal in a diversification strategy is to improve investment performance while reducing risk. One way to categorize risk is to distinguish between unsystematic risk and systematic risk.

Unsystematic risk is risk that is specific to a company. Often, this risk involves some kind of dramatic event such as a strike, a fire or some natural disaster. A company's slumping sales also fall within this category. Diversification among the stocks of many companies reduces unsystematic risk because, of course, it's highly unlikely that every one of the unhappy events listed above will occur in all companies.

Conversely, some events can affect all companies at the same time. This systematic risk includes such occurrences as inflation, war and fluctuating interest rates—generally, those events that influence the entire economy. Of course, diversification cannot eliminate the likelihood of these events happening. Systematic risk accounts for most of the risk in a diversified portfolio. However, in exchange for enduring systematic risk, investors may be rewarded in terms of their investment return. There is no reward for taking on unneeded or unsystematic risk.

A diversified stock portfolio: how much? One way that academic researchers measure investment risk is by looking at stock price volatility. A classic 1968 study by J.L. Evans and S.H. Archer, "Diversification and the Reduction of Dispersion," concluded that an investor who owned 15 randomly chosen stocks would have a portfolio no more risky than the market as a whole. This research confirmed earlier advice, coming from instinct and experience, that Benjamin Graham gave to investors in his 1949 book, The Intelligent Investor. Graham recommended owning from ten to 30 stocks to achieve proper diversification.

Diversification–spreading your investments over many different securities–is a basic principle of sound investing. When you own a large number of securities, the impact of any one on the overall return of your portfolio is reduced. Moreover, if two securities have comparable long-term returns but are exposed to different sets of risks, so that their performances move in the opposite direction from each other (called "negative correlation"), a portfolio that holds both will be less risky than a portfolio exposed only to one. (See the illustration below.)

Figure 1: Two negatively correlated hypothetical investments

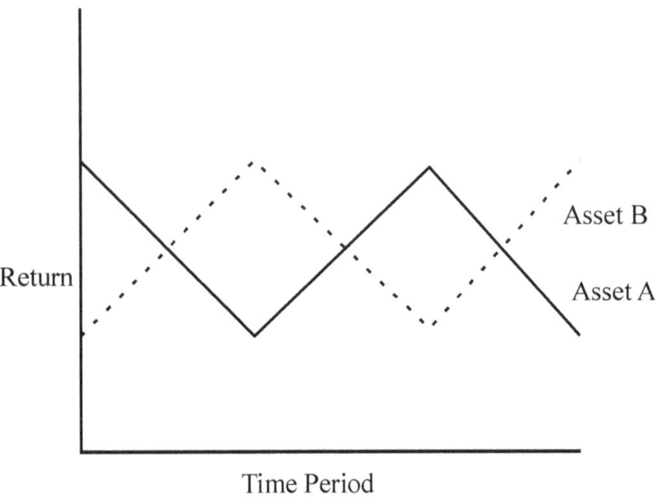

When two or more investments are poorly or negatively correlated, as in this hypothetical example, a portfolio including both, illustrated in Figure 2, can have a similar return with substantially less volatility.

Figure 2: Both investments together

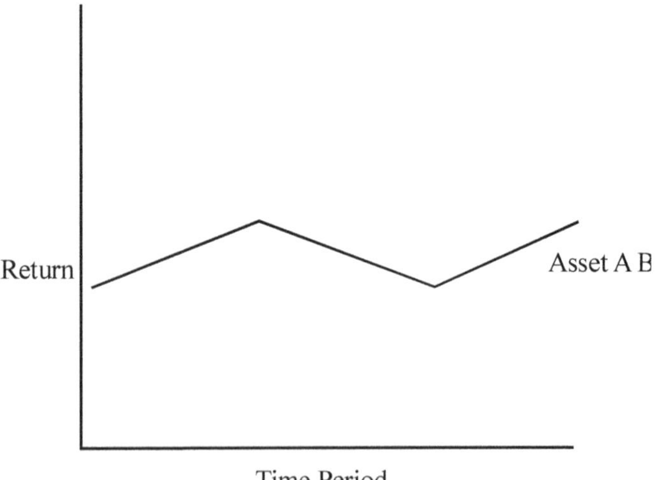

Because of the benefits of diversification, a portfolio of 20-30 securities generally will be less risky than a portfolio holding only one or two securities. Mutual funds are a way to diversify across securities with one purchase decision. For the same reasons, depending upon the risk profiles of the asset classes, a portfolio of two or more asset classes may be less volatile than one asset class with comparable long-term returns. Investors often balance stocks with bonds, domestic securities with international, value stocks with growth stocks, stocks of large companies with those of small firms, stocks and bonds with "hard assets" such as real estate or commodities, and exposure to economically sensitive securities with exposure to relatively insensitive (or "defensive") securities.

Q5. (a) Describe how the Jensen measure of performance is calculated. Under what conditions should it give a similar set of portfolio rankings as the Sharpe and Treynor measures?

Ans: Jensen Measure: The Jensen measure is also based on CAPM. Named after its creator, Michael C. Jensen, the Jensen measure calculates the excess return that a portfolio generates over its expected return. This measure is also known as alpha.

The Jensen ratio measures how much of the portfolio's rate of return is attributable to the manager's ability to deliver above-average returns, adjusted for market risk. The higher the ratio, the better the risk-adjusted returns. A portfolio with a consistently positive excess return will have a positive alpha, while a portfolio with a consistently negative excess return will have a negative alpha.

The formula is broken down as follows:

Jensen's Alpha = Portfolio Return – Benchmark Portfolio Return

Where: Benchmark Return (CAPM) = Risk Free Rate of Return + Beta (Return of Market – Risk-Free Rate of Return)

So, if we once again assume a risk-free rate of 5% and a market return of 10%, what is the alpha for the following funds?

Manager	Average Annual Return	Beta
Manager D	11%	0.90
Manager E	15%	1.10
Manager F	15%	1.20

First, we calculate the portfolio's expected return:
ER(D)= .05 + 0.90 (.10-.05) = .0950 or 9.5% return
ER(E)= .05 + 1.10 (.10-.05) = .1050 or 10.50% return
ER(F)= .05 + 1.20 (.10-.05) = .1100 or 11% return
Then, we calculate the portfolio's alpha by subtracting the expected return of the portfolio from the actual return:
Alpha D = 11%- 9.5% = 2.5%
Alpha E = 15%- 10.5% = 4.5%
Alpha F = 15%- 11% = 4.0%
Which manager did best? Manager E did best because, although manager F had the same annual return, it was expected that manager E would yield a lower return because the portfolio's beta was significantly lower than that of portfolio F.

The Treynor measure only measures systematic risk—it automatically assumes an adequately diversified portfolio.
Sharpe and Treynor measures are similar in a way, since they both divide the risk premium by a numerical risk measure. The total risk is appropriate when we are evaluating the risk return relationship for well-diversified portfolios. On the other hand, the systematic risk is the relevant measure of risk when we are evaluating less than fully diversified portfolios or individual stocks. For a well-diversified portfolio the total risk is equal to systematic risk. Rankings based on total risk (Sharpe measure) and systematic risk (Treynor measure) should be identical for a well-diversified portfolio, as the total risk is reduced to systematic risk. Therefore, a poorly diversified fund that ranks higher on Treynor measure, compared with another fund that is highly diversified, will rank lower on Sharpe Measure.

Jenson Model: Jenson's model proposes another risk adjusted performance measure. This measure was developed by Michael Jenson and is sometimes referred to as the Differential Return Method. This measure involves evaluation of the returns that the fund has generated vs. the returns actually expected out of the fund given the level of its systematic risk. The surplus between the two returns is called Alpha, which measures the performance of a fund compared with the actual returns over the period. Required return of a fund at a given level of risk (Bi) can be calculated as:
Ri = Rf + Bi (Rm - Rf)
Where, Rm is average market return during the given period. After calculating it, alpha can be obtained by subtracting required return from the actual return of the fund.

Higher alpha represents superior performance of the fund and vice versa. Limitation of this model is that it considers only systematic risk not the entire risk associated with the fund and an ordinary investor can not mitigate unsystematic risk, as his knowledge of market is primitive.

In my opinion the Jensen measure is the most stringent. It is testing for statistical significance, whereas the other methods are not. The other methods are also examining average returns, whereas the Jensen measure uses actual returns during each observation period.

The Shape measure, therefore, implicitly evaluates the portfolio manager on the basis of return performance, but also takes into account how well diversified the portfolio was during this period.

Jensen's Differential Return Measure: Jensen's measure of portfolio performance is based on the capital asset pricing model (CAPM). The basic versions of the CAPM is expressed by the equation:

$$E\left(\tilde{R}_p\right) = T + \beta_{pm}\left[E\left(\tilde{R}_m\right) - T\right]$$

where:

$E\left(\tilde{R}_p\right)$ = expected return of a portfolio

T = risk-free interest rate

$E\left(\tilde{R}_m\right)$ = expected return of a market index

β_{pm} = beta of a portfolio

The equation expresses ex ante relationships. If expectations are realized the equation is empirically valid and it can be stated in empirical form as:

$$\tilde{R}_p = T + \beta_{pm}\left(\tilde{R}_m - T\right)$$

Jensen's approach to evaluating portfolio performance involves two steps. First, using equation, he calculates what the return of a given portfolio should be on the basis of β_{pm}, $\tilde{R}_m$ and T. Second, he compares the actual realized return of the portfolio, with the calculated or predicted return. The greater the excess of realized return over the calculated return, the better the performance of the portfolio.

For example assume we are comparing the performance of three portfolios and the market index is represented say by XYZ composite. The actual results of portfolios and the market index in the last three years were as follows:

Portfolio	*Return on Portfolio R_p*	*Portfolio Beta p*	*Risk-Free interest rate*
1	13%	1.2	5%
2	10%	0.8	5%
3	16%	1.5	5%
Market Index of XYZ composite	11%	1.0	5%

The return of the three portfolios on the basis of the CAPM should be:

Portfolio 1 $5\% + (11\% - 5\%) \times 1.2 = 12.2\%$

Portfolio 2 $5\% + (11\% - 5\%) \times 0.8 = 9.8\%$

Portfolio 3 $5\% + (11\% - 5\%) \times 1.5 = 147\%$

The difference between actual realized returns and the calculated return for the three portfolios are:

Portfolio 1 $13\% - 12.2\% = 0.8\%$

Portfolio 2 $10\% - 9.8\% = 0.2\%$

Portfolio 3 $16\% - 14.0\% = 2.0\%$

The risk-adjusted performance of the three portfolios based Jenson's approach indicate that portfolio 3 was the best, portfolio 1 second-best and portfolio 2 the worst.

Using Treynor's approach, the performance index of each portfolio would be

$$\text{Portfolio 1} = \frac{\widetilde{R}_p - T}{\beta_p} = \frac{13\% - 5\%}{1.2} = 6.67$$

$$\text{Portfolio 2} = \frac{10\% - 5\%}{.8} = 6.25$$

$$\text{Portfolio 3} = \frac{16\% - 5\%}{1.5} = 7.33$$

Treynor's approach indicates the same ranking of the three portfolios as Jensen's approach. The two approaches are related, because they both use beta to represent risk of a portfolio.

(b) KAR Portfolio Ltd. has three investments in its portfolio, its details are given below:

Investment	E (R)	B	Proportion of invested funds
X	14%	1.6	50%
Y	16%	1.2	20%
Z	12%	0.8	30%

Calculate the weighted average of expected return and Beta factor of the portfolio.

Weighted average of expected return= 0.14*0.5+ 0.16*0.2+0.12*0.3
=0.138
=13.8%
Beta factor of the portfolio.= 0.5*1.6+ 0.2*1.2+0.3*0.8
=1.23

Q6. What do you understand by a Mutual Fund? Discuss the various types of mutual fund schemes available in the Indian capital market. How is the Net Asset Value (NAV) of a Mutual Fund Unit calculated?

Ans. Mutual funds are that organisation which pools the funds from small investors and invest in diversified portfolio. A mutual fund is a company that brings together money from many people and invests it in stocks, bonds or other assets. The combined holdings of stocks, bonds or other assets the fund owns are known as its portfolio. Each investor in the fund owns shares, which represent a part of these holdings.

Different types of mutual fund schemes: There are a wide variety of Mutual Fund schemes that cater to your needs, whatever your age, financial position, risk tolerance and return expectations. Whether as the foundation of your investment programme or as a supplement, Mutual Fund schemes can help you meet your financial goals.

(A) By Structure

Open-Ended Schemes: These do not have a fixed maturity. You deal directly with the Mutual Fund for your investments and redemptions. The key feature is liquidity. You can conveniently buy and sell your units at net asset value ("NAV") related prices.

Close-Ended Schemes: Schemes that have a stipulated maturity period (ranging from 2 to 15 years) are called close-ended schemes. You can invest directly in the scheme at the time of the initial issue and thereafter you can buy or sell the units of the scheme on the stock exchanges where they are listed. The market price at the stock exchange could vary from the scheme's NAV on account of demand and supply situation, unitholders' expectations and other market factors. One of the characteristics of the close-ended schemes is that they are generally traded at a discount to NAV; but closer to maturity, the discount narrows. Some close-ended schemes give you an additional option of selling your units directly to the Mutual Fund through periodic repurchase at NAV related prices. SEBI Regulations ensure that at least one of the two exit routes are provided to the investor.

Interval Schemes: These combine the features of open-ended and close-ended schemes. They may be traded on the stock exchange or may be open for sale or redemption during pre-determined intervals at NAV related prices.

(B) By Investment Objective

Growth Schemes: Aim to provide capital appreciation over the medium to long term. These schemes normally invest a majority of their funds in equities and are willing to bear short- term decline in value for possible future appreciation.

These schemes are not for investors seeking regular income or needing their money back in the short-term.

Ideal for:

* Investors in their prime earning years.
* Investors seeking growth over the long-term

Income Schemes: Aim to provide regular and steady income to investors. These schemes generally invest in fixed income securities such as bonds and corporate debentures. Capital appreciation in such schemes may be limited.

Ideal for:

* Retired people and others with a need for capital stability and regular income.
* Investors who need some income to supplement their earnings.

Balanced Schemes: Aim to provide both growth and income by periodically distributing a part of the income and capital gains they earn. They invest in both shares and fixed income securities in the proportion indicated in their offer documents. In a rising stock market, the NAV of these schemes may not normally keep pace, or fall equally when the market falls.

Ideal for:

* Investors looking for a combination of income and moderate growth.

Money Market Schemes: Aim to provide easy liquidity, preservation of capital and moderate income. These schemes generally invest in safer, short-term instruments, such as treasury bills, certificates of deposit, commercial paper and inter- bank call money.

Other Schemes

Tax Saving Schemes: These schemes offer tax rebates to the investors under tax laws as prescribed from time to time. This is made possible because the

Government offers tax incentives for investment in specified avenues. For example, Equity Linked Savings Schemes (ELSS) and Pension Schemes. Recent amendments to the Income Tax Act provide further opportunities to investors to save capital gains by investing in Mutual Funds. The details of such taxsavings are provided in the relevant offer documents. Ideal for: * Investors seeking tax rebates.

Sector Funds: Sector funds are those with the objective to invest only in the equity of those companies existing in a specific sector, as laid down in the fund's offer document. For example, an FMCG sector fund shall invest in companies like HLL, Cadbury's, Nestle etc., while a technology fund will invest in software companies like Infosys Technologies, Satyam Computers etc. There are also funds that invest in basic sectors/industries such as Cement, steel and petrochemicals.

Index Funds: Index Funds try to mirror the performance of a particular index such as the BSE Sensex or the NSE 50. Index funds will invest in only those scrips that constitute a particular index. Investment in these scrips is also made in proportion to each stocks weight in the index.

Exchanged Traded Funds: ETFs are a phenomenon which impart a lot of liquidity to an existing market. They are passively Managed Funds tracking and investing in the stocks of a particular benchmark index. ETFs offer the best features of an open and close end funds. They represent units of beneficial interest in Unit Investment Trusts that hold the component stocks of the representative index. As the name suggests they are listed and traded on an exchange like a common stock - the biggest advantage. Today ETFs with different names are traded in the world in different countries. The total assets in ETFs globally are over $ 70 Billion USD.

ETFs	INDEX	SPONSORS
SPDRs	S&P 500	AMEX
WEBS	MSCI	Morgan Stanley, Barclays
DIAMONDS	DOW JONES	AMEX
TRACKET FUND	HANG SENG INDEX	Goldman Sachs, ING Barings Jardine Fleming
CUBES or QQQ's	NASDAQ 100	NASDAQ, AMEX

The largest ETF is the SPDR having over $ 25 billion USD in assets.

Computation of Net Asset Value

(1) Every Mutual Fund shall follow a formula, approved by the Board, for computing the Net Asset Value (NAV) for each of its schemes.

(2) The Net Asset Value shall be calculated and published atleast in two daily newspapers at intervals of not exceeding:

a) One month in respect of open-ended schemes: and

b) Three months in respect of close-ended schemes.

Net Asset Value is the market value of the assets of the scheme minus its liabilities. Per unit NAV is the net asset value of the scheme divided by the number of units outstanding on the Valuation Date.

Sale Price: **Is the price you pay when you invest in a scheme. Also called Offer Price. It may include a sales load.**

Repurchase Price: Is the price at which a close-ended scheme repurchases its units and it may include a back-end load. This is also called Bid Price.

Redemption Price: Is the price at which open-ended schemes repurchase their units and close-ended schemes redeem their units on maturity. Such prices are NAV related.

Sales Load: Is a charge collected by a scheme when it sells the units. Also called, 'Front-end' load. Schemes that do not charge a load are called 'No Load' schemes.

Repurchase or 'Back-end' Load: Is a charge collected by a scheme when it buys back the units from the unitholders.

Q7. Write short notes on any *four* of the following:

(a) Efficient Market Hypothesis

Ans. The Efficient Market Hypothesis (EMH) has been consented as one of the cornerstones of modern financial economics. Fama first defined the term "efficient market" in financial literature in 1965 as one in which security prices fully reflect all available information. The market is efficient if the reaction of market prices to new information should be instantaneous and unbiased. Efficient market hypothesis is the idea that information is quickly and efficiently incorporated into asset prices at any point in time, so that old information cannot be used to foretell future price movements. Consequently, three versions of EMH are being distinguished depends on the level of available information. The weak form EMH stipulates that current asset prices already reflect past price and volume information. The information contained in the past sequence of prices of a security is fully reflected in the current market price of that security. It is named weak form because the security prices are the most publicly and easily accessible pieces of information. It implies that no one should be able to outperform the market using something that "everybody else knows". Yet, there are still numbers of financial researchers who are studying the past stock price series and trading volume data in attempt to generate profit. This technique is so called technical analysis that is asserted by EMH as useless for predicting future price changes.

The semi strong form EMH states that all publicly available information is similarly already incorporated into asset prices. In another word, all publicly available information is fully reflected in a security's current market price. The public information stated not only past prices but also data reported in a company's financial statements, company's announcement, economic factors and others. It also implies that no one should be able to outperform the market using something that "everybody else knows". This indicates that a company's financial statements are of no help in forecasting future price movements and securing high investment returns.

The strong form EMH stipulates that private information or insider information too, is quickly incorporated by market prices and therefore cannot be used to reap abnormal trading profits. Thus, all information, whether public or private, is fully reflected in a security's current market price. That's mean, even the company's management (insider) are not able to make gains from inside information they hold. They are not able to take the advantages to profit from information such as take over decision which has been made ten minutes ago. The rationale behind to support is that the market anticipates in an unbiased manner, future development and therefore information has been incorporated and evaluated into market price in much more objective and informative way than insiders.

The random walk model of asset prices is an extension of the EMH, as are the notions that the market cannot be consistently beaten, arbitrage is impossible, and "free lunches" are generally unavailable.

(b) Securities Market

Ans. The capital market is the market for securities, where companies and governments can raise long term funds. It is a market in which money is lent for periods longer than a year. The capital market includes the stock market and the bond market. Financial regulators, such as SEBI, oversee the capital markets in their designated countries to ensure that investors are protected against fraud.

The capital markets consist of the primary market and the secondary market. The primary markets are where new stock and bonds issues are sold (underwriting) to investors. The secondary markets are where existing securities are sold and bought from one investor or speculator to another, usually on an exchange.

In every economic System, some units which may be individual or Institution are surplus-generating while others are deficit- generating. Surplus-Generating Units are called Savers while Deficit-generating units are called spenders. Households are surplus-generating and Corporates and Government are deficit generators. By placing the surplus funds in Financial claims or Financial securities the Spending community gets funds at a cost and saving community gets various benefits like interest, dividend, capital appreciation, Bonus etc. The Surplus generating units (Savers) are investors and Deficit generating units (spenders) are issuers. These investors and issuers of financial securities constitute two important elements of the securities markets. The third critical element of markets is the intermediaries who act as conduits between the investors and issuers. Regulatory bodies, which regulate the functioning of the securities markets, constitute the last but very significant element of securities markets.

Thus the four important elements of securities markets are:

Investors

Issuers

Intermediaries

Regulators

Securities market can be

Government or Industrial

Long-term or short-term

Primary Market or Secondary Market

Primary Market is the segment in which new issues are made whereas secondary market is the segment in which outstanding issues are traded. It is for this reason that the Primary Market is called the New issues Market and the secondary market is called Stock Market.

(c) Dollar Cost Averaging

Ans. Dollar cost averaging is a timing strategy of investing equal dollar amounts regularly and periodically over specific time periods (such as $100 monthly) in a particular investment or portfolio. By doing so, more shares are purchased when prices are low and fewer shares are purchased when prices are high. The point of this is to lower the total average cost per share of the investment, giving the investor a lower overall cost for the shares purchased over time. Dollar cost averaging is also called DCA and constant dollar plan in the US, pound-cost averaging in the UK, and by the currency-neutral term cost average effect.

In dollar cost averaging, the investor decides on three parameters: the fixed amount of money invested each time, and investment frequency and the time horizon over which all of the investments are made. With a shorter time horizon, the strategy behaves more like lump sum investing. One study has found that the best time horizons when investing in the stock market in terms of balancing return and risk have been 6 or 12 months.

(d) Dow Theory

Ans. Dow Theory is a heterodox theory on stock price movements that includes what is now called technical analysis as well as some portion of sector rotation. The theory was derived from 255 Wall Street Journal editorials written by Charles H. Dow (1851–1902), journalist, founder and first editor of the Wall Street Journal and co-founder of Dow Jones and Company. Following Dow's death, William P. Hamilton, Robert Rhea and E. George Schaefer organized and collectively represented "Dow Theory," based on Dow's editorials. Dow himself never used the term "Dow Theory," nor presented it as a trading system.

The six basic tenets of Dow Theory as summarized by Hamilton, Rhea, and Schaefer are described below.

Six basic tenets of Dow Theory

1. The market has three movements: The "main movement", primary movement or major trend may last from less than a year to several years. It can be bullish or bearish. (2) The "medium swing", secondary reaction or intermediate reaction may last from ten days to three months and generally retraces from 33% to 66% of the primary price change since the previous medium swing or start of the main movement. (3) The "short swing" or minor movement varies with opinion from hours to a month or more. The three movements may be simultaneous, for instance, a daily minor movement in a bearish secondary reaction in a bullish primary movement.

2. Market Trends have three phases: Dow Theory asserts that major market trends are composed of three phases: an accumulation phase, a public participation phase, and a distribution phase. The accumulation phase (phase 1) is a period when investors "in the know" are actively buying (selling) stock against the general opinion of the market. During this phase, the stock price does not change much because these investors are in the minority absorbing (releasing) stock that the market at large is supplying (demanding). Eventually, the market catches on to these astute investors and a rapid price change occurs (phase 2). This occurs when trend followers and other technically oriented investors participate. This phase continues until rampant speculation occurs. At this point, the astute investors begin to distribute their holdings to the market (phase 3).

3. The stock market discounts all news: Stock prices quickly incorporate new information as soon as it becomes available. Once news is released, stock prices will change to reflect this new information. On this point, Dow Theory agrees with one of the premises of the efficient market hypothesis.

4. Stock market averages must confirm each other: In Dow's time, the US was a growing industrial power. The US had population centers but factories were scattered throughout the country. Factories had to ship their goods to market, usually by rail. Dow's first stock averages were an index of industrial (manufacturing) companies and rail companies. To Dow, a bull market in industrials could not occur unless the railway average rallied as well, usually first. According to this logic, if manufacturers' profits are rising, it follows that they are producing more. If they produce more, then they have to ship more goods to consumers. Hence, if an investor is looking for signs of health in manufacturers, he or she should look at the performance of the companies that ship the output of them to market, the railroads. The two averages should be moving in the same direction. When the performance of the averages diverge, it is a warning that change is in the air.

Both Barron's Magazine and the Wall Street Journal still publish the daily performance of the Dow Jones Transportation Index in chart form. The index contains major railroads, shipping companies, and air freight carriers in the US.

5. Trends are confirmed by volume: Dow believed that volume confirmed price trends. When prices move on low volume, there could be many different explanations why. An overly aggressive seller could be present for example. But when price movements are accompanied by high volume, Dow believed this represented the "true" market view. If many participants are active in a particular security, and the price moves significantly in one direction, Dow maintained that this was the direction in which the market anticipated continued movement. To him, it was a signal that a trend is developing.

6. Trends exist until definitive signals prove that they have ended: Dow believed that trends existed despite "market noise". Markets might temporarily move in the direction opposite to the trend, but they will soon resume the prior move. The trend should be given the benefit of the doubt during these reversals. Determining whether a reversal is the start of a new trend or a temporary movement in the current trend is not easy. Dow Theorists often disagree in this determination. Technical analysis tools attempt to clarify this but they can be interpreted differently by different investors.

(e) Holding Period Return

Ans. In finance, holding period return (HPR) is the total return on an asset or portfolio over the period during which it was held. It is one of the simplest measures of investment performance.

HPR is the percentage by which the value of a portfolio (or asset) has grown for a particular period. It is the sum of income and capital gains divided by the initial period value (asset value at the beginning of the period).

HPR = ((Present Value, or face Value, End-Of-Period Value) + (Any Intermediate Gains eg. Dividends) - (Initial Value)) /(Initial Value)

The total return received from holding an asset or portfolio of assets. Holding period return/yield is calculated as the sum of all income and capital growth divided by the value at the beginning of the period being measured.

$$\text{Holding Period Return} = \frac{\text{Income} + (\text{End of Period Value} - \text{Initial Value})}{\text{Initial Value}}$$

To calculate holding period return/yield over multiple years we calculate the annualized holding period return:

$$\text{Annualized HPR} = \left(\frac{\text{Income} + (\text{End of Period Value} - \text{Initial Value})}{\text{Initial Value}}\right)^{\frac{1}{\text{Years}}} - 1$$

Example

Example: Stock with low volatility and a regular quarterly dividend				
End of:	**1st Quarter**	**2nd Quarter**	**3rd Quarter**	**4th Quarter**
Dividend	$1	$1	$1	$1
Stock Price	$98	$101	$102	$99
Quarterly ROI	-1%	4.08%	1.98%	-1.96%
Annual ROI				**3%**

To the right is an example of a stock investment of one share purchased at the beginning of the year for $100. At the end of the first quarter the stock price is $98. This is a capital loss. The stock share bought for $100 can only be sold for $98, which is the value of the investment at the end of the first quarter. The first quarter return is:
($98 - $100 + $1) / $100 = -1%
Since the final stock price is $99, the annual ROI is:
($99 ending price - $100 beginning price + $4 dividends) / $100 beginning price = 3% ROI.
If the final stock price had been $95, the annual ROI would be:
($95 ending price - $100 beginning price + $4 dividends) / $100 beginning price = -1% ROI.

(f) Beta Coefficient

Ans. The beta coefficient is a key parameter in the capital asset pricing model (CAPM). It measures the part of the asset's statistical variance that cannot be mitigated by the diversification provided by the portfolio of many risky assets, because it is correlated with the return of the other assets that are in the portfolio. Beta can be estimated for individual companies using regression analysis against a stock market index.

In finance, the beta (â) of a stock or portfolio is a number describing the relation of its returns with that of the financial market as a whole.

An asset with a beta of 0 means that its price is not at all correlated with the market; that asset is independent. A positive beta means that the asset generally follows the market. A negative beta shows that the asset inversely follows the market; the asset generally decreases in value if the market goes up and vice versa.

The formula for the beta of an asset within a portfolio is

$$\beta_a = \frac{Cov(r_a, r_p)}{Var(r_p)}$$

where r_a measures the rate of return of the asset, r_p measures the rate of return of the portfolio, and $Cov(r_a, r_p)$ is the covariance between the rates of return. In the CAPM formulation, the portfolio is the market portfolio that contains all risky assets, and so the r_p terms in the formula are replaced by r_m, the rate of return of the market.

MS-44 : Security Analysis And Portfolio Management
June, 2009

Note: *Attempt any five questions. All questions carry equal marks. Present value and annuity tables are to be provided, if asked for. Use of calculator is allowed.*

SECTION I

Q1. What do you understand by investment? Explain the steps involved in the investment decision process.

Q2. (a) Define risk and explain the types of risks involved in investment?
(b) The common stock of G S Ltd. is currently selling for Rs. 70 per share. Dividend per share has grown from Rs. 2 to the current level of Rs. 6 over the past ten years and this dividend growth is expected to continue in future also. What is the required rate of return of the G S Ltd.?

Q3. What are the basic premises of technical analysis? Explain the differences between technical analysis and fundamental analysis.

Q4. What is Capital Asset Pricing Model? Explain how is it helpful for measurement of portfolio risk?

Q5. (a) What do you understand by Formula Plans? Critically examine the formula plans and discuss their limitations.
(b) Consider the following data for a particular period:

	Portfolio P	Market M
Average return	35%	28%
Beta	1.2%	1.0%
Standard deviation	42%	30%
Non-systematic risk	18%	-

Calculate the following performance measures for portfolio P and the market: Sharpe, Jensen and Treynor. The T-bill rate during the period was 6%. By which measures did portfolio P outperform the market?

Q6. "The portfolio of a Mutual Fund Scheme depends on the objectives of the scheme." Explain this statement and discuss the various aspects which a Fund Manager takes into consideration while investing the fund's money. Are there any regulatory guidelines in this respect? Discuss.

Q7. Write short notes on any four of the following:
(a) Risk-Return Trade off
(b) Yield-to-Maturity
(c) Efficient Set
(d) Sharpe's Index
(e) Odd Lot Theory
(f) Dollar Cost Averaging

Q8. Explain the salient features of the Securities Contracts (Regulation) Act 1956. How are the stock exchanges regulated in India? Discuss.

MS-44 : Security Analysis And Portfolio Management
December, 2009

Note:

(i) Attempt any five questions.
(ii) All questions carry equal marks.
(iii) Present value and annuity tables are to be provided, if asked for.
(iv) Use of calculators is allowed.

Q1. What are the objectives of security analysis? How do you measure the risk of a security?

Q2. (a) "Systematic risk cannot be controlled, but unsystematic risk can be reduced". Discuss.

(b) Mr. Ranga owns Rs. 1,000 face value bond with five years to maturity. The bond has an annual coupon of Rs. 75. The bond is currently priced at Rs. 970. Given an appropriate discount rate of 10%, should Ranga hold or sell the bond.

Q3. Explain and illustrate the economy-industry-company (EIC) framework of analysis for equity investment.

Q4. What is Efficient Market Hypothesis? How is the Markowitz model useful in portfolio selection?

Q5. (a) Discuss the various Formula Plan that are available to an investor for portfolio revision.

(b) A security pays a dividend of Rs. 3.85 and sells currently at Rs. 83. The security is expected to sell at Rs. 90 at the end of the year. The security has a beta of 1.15. The risk free rate is 5 per cent and the expected return on market index is 12 percent. Assess whether the security is correctly priced.

Q6. What is portfolio performance evaluation? Explain the various methods of portfolio performance evaluation.

Q7. Write short notes on any four of the following:
(a) Risk and Uncertainty
(b) Zero Coupon Bonds
(c) Efficient Frontier
(d) Filter Test
(e) Sharpe's Index Model
(f) Odd Lot Theory

Q8. Explain the various steps involved in the public issue of securities. Give salient features of the guidelines issued by SEBI regarding IPOs.

MS-44 : Security Analysis And Portfolio Management
June, 2010

Note:

(i) Attempt any five questions.
(ii) All questions carry equal marks.
(iii) Present value and annuity tables are to be provided, if asked for.
(iv) Use of calculators is allowed.

Q1. What do you understand by 'Investment'? Explain the steps involved in the investment process.

Q2. (a) Define risk. What are the statistical tools that are used to measure risk of securities return?

(b) Mr. Vamsi is considering the purchase of a bond currently selling at Rs. 875.50. The bond has four years to maturity, face value of Rs. 1,000 and 8% coupon rate. The next annual interest payment is due after one year from today. The required rate of return is 10%.
(i) Calculate the intrinsic value (present value) of the bond. Should Vamsi buy the bond?
(ii) Calculate the yield to maturity of the bond.

Q3. Discuss the various measures that have been adopted in India to protect investors' interest in securities market.

Q4. What is market efficiency? Explain the various anomalies in efficient market hypothesis.

Q5. (a) In the context of Risk Adjusted returns, briefly explain:
(i) Treynor's Ratio
(ii) Sharpe's Ratio

(b) Puja and Devika re the two mutual funds Puja has a mean success of 0.15 and Devika has 0.22. The Devika has double the beta of Puja fund's 1.5. The standard deviations of Puja and Devika funds are 15% and 21.43%. The mean return of market index is 12% and its standard deviation is 7. The risk free rate is 8%.
(i) Compute the Jensen Index for each fund.
(ii) Compute the Treynor and Sharpe indices for the funds. Interpret the results.

Q6. What is portfolio revision? Why does it arise? Discuss the various constraints in portfolio revision.

Q7. Distinguish between any four of the following:

(a) Growth Fund and Balanced Fund Ex-dividend and Cum-dividend Commercial Paper and Commercial Bill of Exchange

(b) Self-regulation and Legislative regulation

(c) Buy-back of Shares and Surrender of Shares

(d) Money Market and Capital Market

Q8. Write short notes on any four of the following:

(a) Investment Vs. Speculation

(b) Bullish market

(c) Capital market line

(d) Technical analysis

(e) Efficient portfolio

(f) Price-earnings approach

MS-44 : Security Analysis And Portfolio Management
December, 2010

Note:

(i) Attempt any five questions.
(ii) All questions carry equal marks.
(iii) Present value and annuity tables are to be provided, if asked for.
(iv) Use of calculators is allowed.

Q1. Explain the principles of Portfolio Management. Distinguish between Security Analysis and Portfolio Management.

Q2. (a) Discuss the various measures taken by the SEBI for increasing liquidity in the stock markets.

(b) Mr. Prashanth holds a debenture of ₹100 carrying a coupon rate of 12% p.a. The interest is payable half - yearly on 30th June and 31st December every year. The maturity period of the debenture is 6 years and it is to be reduced at a premium of 10%. The investor's required rate of return is 14% p.a. Compute the value of the debenture.

Q3. "Estimation of equity price is the main challenge in the entire process of equity investment decision". Discuss.

Q4. Define Capital Asset Pricing Model. What are the basic assumptions underlying Capital Asset Pricing Model?

Q5. (a) Explain the Markowitz Theory of Portfolio Analysis. Is Sharpe's Model an improvement over Markowitz Theory?

(b) Mr. Vijay is having units in a mutual fund for the past three years. He wants to evaluate its performance by comparing it to the market.

	Fund	Market
Return	70.60	41.40
Standard deviation	41.31	19.44
Risk free rate	2%	2%
B	1.12	–

Find out Sharpe and Treynor indices. Comment.

Q6. What do you understand by Portfolio Revision? Discuss the various constraints in portfolio revision.

Q7. Distinguish between any four of the following:

(a) Index fund and fund of funds.

(b) Load fund and No load fund.

(c) Open-ended fund and close-ended fund.

(d) I.P.O. and private placement.

(e) Merchant banking and Commercial banking.

(f) Net assets value and net present value.

Q8. Write short notes on any four of the following:

(a) Systematic and Non-systematic risks.

(b) Deep discount bond.

(c) Security market line.

(d) Dow theory.

(e) Efficient frontier.

(f) Benchmark portfolio.

MS-44 : Security Analysis And Portfolio Management
June, 2011

Note:

(i) Attempt any five questions.
(ii) All questions carry equal marks.
(iii) Present value and annuity tables are to be provided, if asked for.
(iv) Use of calculators is allowed.

Q1. What do you understand by 'investment'? Explain the various factors, which form the basis of the investment process.

Q2. (a) Discuss the main provisions of the Securities Contracts (Regulation) Act, 1956 governing the Stock Exchange in India.

(b) The company GVK's next year dividend per share is expected to be ₹3.50. The dividend is expected to grow at a rate of 10 percent per year in subsequent years. If the required rate of return is 15 percent per year, what should be the price of its shares? The prevailing market price is ₹75 per share.

Q3. What is Fundamental Analysis? Bringout its relevance to the security analyst.

Q4. What is Efficient Market Hypothesis (EMH)? Explain the techniques for testing the various forms of E.M.H.

Q5. (a) What do you mean by Formula plans? Critically examine the formula plans and discuss their limitations.

(b) Compute the risk of the portfolio from the following information.

Security	Proportion of portfolio	Standard deviation	Coefficient of correlation
A	0.20	0.2	r_{AB}0.5
B	0.20	0.3	r_{BC}0.3
C	0.60	0.5	r_{AC}0.1

Q6. Compare and contrast Capital Asset Pricing Model Arbitrage Pricing Theory (CAPM) and (APT) which of the two is a better model for pricing risky assets and why?

Q7. Write short notes on any four of the following:
(a) Systematic and unsystematic risk
(b) Dow Theory
(c) Efficient Frontier
(d) Sharpe's Single Index Model
(e) NSDL
(f) Treyner's Index

Q8. "Mutual funds provide stability to share prices, safety to investors and resources to prospective entrepreneurs". Comment.

(b) Briefly discuss the different types of Mutual Fund Schemes introduced in India.

"It doesn't matter who you are, where you come from. The ability to triumph begins with you – always".

-Oprah Winfrey

MS-44 : Security Analysis And Portfolio Management
December, 2011

Note:

(i) Attempt any five questions.
(ii) All questions carry equal marks.
(iii) Present value and annuity tables are to be provided, if asked for.
(iv) Use of calculators is allowed.

Q1. 'The investment environment has undergone several changes in India since 1991'. Discuss this statement and explain the three elements of investment environment.

Q2. (a) What are the objectives and functions of Securities Exchange Board of India?

(b) A bond has a par value of ₹1,000. It has a coupon rate of 9%. It matures after 8 years. Its current market price is ₹800. What is the yield to maturity of the bond?

Q3. Differentiate between fundamental analysis and technical analysis. Discuss the usefulness of odd of theory and Elliot wave theory on stock market prediction.

Q4. Explain the concept of 'efficient market'. Discuss the implications of 'efficient market hypothesis' for security analysis.

Q5. (a) What are the basic assumptions behind the Markowitz Portfolio theory?

(b) Rotari Holdings Ltd., an investment company has invested in equity shares of a blue chip company. Its
Risk free return (Rd = 9%
Expected total return (R_m) = 16%
Market sensitivity index (B_i) = 0.8
Calculate the expected rate of return on the investment made in the security.

Q6. What are formula plans? How is a constant rupee value plan different to a constant ratio plan? Discuss.

Q7. Write short notes on any four of the following:

(a) Warrant
(b) Industry analysis
(c) Filter rule
(d) Capital market line
(e) Arbitrage pricing theory
(f) Beta

Q8. (a) "Depository Service is another major development in the Indian Stock Market". In the light of this statement explain the function and significance of depository service in India.

(b) Distinguish between (i) Private Placement and Rights Issue and (ii) Listing of Securities and Rating of Securities.

MS-44 : Security Analysis And Portfolio Management
June, 2012

Note:

(i) Attempt any five questions.
(ii) All questions carry equal marks.
(iii) Present value and annuity tables are to be provided, if asked for.
(iv) Use of calculators is allowed.

Q1. "An investment decision is essentially a choice between current and future consumption". Explain with suitable examples.

Q2. (a) Why is regulation necessary over the securities market? Describe the three main types of regulatory framework relating to financial services.

(b) Prashanth has bought shares of the Everest Company which has paid ₹3.00 per share as dividend per share during the last financial year. He anticipates two situations either a 5 per cent decline in the dividend or a 5% growth in the dividend in the next year. His anticipated rate of return is 20%. You are required to calculate the price of the share in both the situations.

Q3. In what respects technical analysis is superior to fundamental analysis? List out the major technical indicators applicable to: (i) individual stocks and (ii) the markets.

Q4. What is Efficient Market Hypothesis? How is the Markowitz model useful in portfolio selection?

Q5. (a) Compare and contrast the constant - dollar - value plan, constant - ratio plan, and variable - ratio plan.

(b) Prashanth's Holdings Ltd., an investment company has invested in equity shares of a blue chip company. Its
Risk free return (Rf) = 9%
Expected total return (Rm) = 16%
Market sensitivity index (Bi) = 0.8
Calculate the expected rate of return on the investment made in the security.

Q6. What are the basic assumptions of Arbitrage Pricing Theory (APT)? Discuss the problems associated with the empirical testing of APT.

Q7. Write short notes on any four of the following:
(a) Risk and Uncertainty
(b) Yield to maturity (YTM)
(c) Security market line (SML)
(d) Filter Rule
(e) Treyner's Index
(f) Naive Diversification

Q8. (a) Discuss the concept of Mutual Fund and explain the restrictions imposed by SEBI on the investments made by Mutual Funds.

(b) Explain the different types of Mutual Fund schemes available to the Indian investors. What are the reasons for floating different types of schemes?

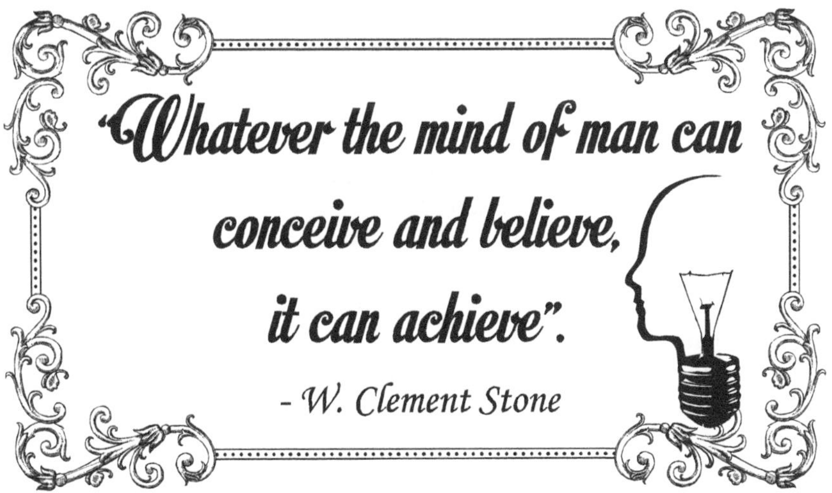

MS-44 : Security Analysis And Portfolio Management
December, 2012

Note: *Attempt any five questions. All questions carry equal marks. Present value and annuity tables are to he provided, if asked for. Use of calculators in allowed.*

Q1. Explain the concept of investment. Discuss in detail the steps involved in the investment process.

Q2. (a) Critically evaluate the role of SEBI as stock market developer and regulator.

(b) The common stock of GVK Ltd. is currently selling for ₹70 per share. Dividend per share has grown from ₹2 to the current level of ₹6 over the past ten years and this dividend growth is expected to continue in future also. What is the required rate of return of the GVK Ltd.?

Q3. "Economic forecasting is the heart of economic analysis." Explain this statement and describe the various techniques of economic forecasting.

Q4. Explain the Dow Theory. Is it useful in predicting the price behaviour of stocks? Is the Dow Theory applicable to the Indian stock market?

Q5. (a) What are benchmark portfolios? How are they used to evaluate the performance of a portfolio manager? Discuss with suitable examples.

(b) Consider the following data for a particular sample period:

	Portfolio P	Market M
Average return	35%	28%
Beta	1.2	1.0
Standard deviation	42%	30%
Non-systematic risk	18%	

Calculate the following performance measures for portfolio P and the market: Sharpe, Jensen, and Treynor. The T - bill rate during the period was 6%. By which measures did portfolio P outperform the market?

Q6. Discuss the CAPM and its application in portfolio selection. Explain the relationship between SML, CML and Characteristic Line.

Q7. Write short notes on any four of the following:
(a) Risk-return trade off
(b) Duration and Immunization
(c) Efficient Frontier
(d) Elliot Wave Theory
(e) Arbitrage Pricing Theory
(f) Random Walk Hypothesis

Q8. (a) 'Mutual funds provide stability to share prices, safety to investors and resources to the prospective entrepreneurs'. Critically evaluate this statement.

(b) Distinguish between:
(i) Sector Fund and Index Fund
(ii) Systematic Investment Plan and Re-investment Plan.

MS-44 : Security Analysis And Portfolio Management
June, 2013

Note: *Attempt any five questions. All questions carry equal marks. Use of calculators is allowed.*

Q1. Define investment. Describe the steps involved in the investment process.

Q2. (a) How is the present value of a bond determined? What effect does the use of semi annual discounting have on the value of a bond as compared to annual discounting? How can an investor eliminate the re-investment rate risk inherent in bonds?

(b) A bond of ₹1000 face value bearing a coupon rate of 12% will mature after 7 years. What is the value of the bond if the discount rates are 14% and 12% (PVIFA 14%, 7 years 2.88, PVIFA 12%, 7 years 4.564, PVIF 14%, 7 years .400, PVIF 12%, 7 years .452)

Q3. What do you understand by Earning Per Share? Explain the various traditional and modern methods of forecasting EPS.

Q4. Define the various forms of the market efficiency. State the anomalies in the Efficient Market Hypothesis.

Q5. How is the expected return for one security and a portfolio determined? What is the relationship between correlation coefficient and the covariance, both Qualitatively and Quantitatively.

Q6. Explain the Sharpe Index model. How does it differ from the Markowitz model?

Q7. Describe the basic Arbitrage Pricing Theory Model of two factors. What are the advantages of APT over CAPM?

Q8. Discuss briefly the concept of 'Mutual Fund'. Describe the role of Registrar, Custodians and the Fund managers in a mutual fund.

MS-44 : Security Analysis And Portfolio Management
December, 2013

Note: *Attempt any five questions. All questions carry equal marks.*

Q1. What do you understand by investment risk? Classify the traditional sources of investment risk and mention whether they are general sources of risk or specific sources of risk. How is interest rate risk related to inflation risk?

Q2. (a) Explain the importance of earnings, dividend payout and required rate of return in estimating the theoretical value of the stock.

(b) Anil has bought Everest Company stock, that has paid ₹3.00 dividend per share during the last financial year. He anticipates two situations either a 5% decline in the dividend or 5% growth in the dividend in the next year. His anticipated rate of return is 20%. Fix the price for both the situations.

Q3. Explain the utility of economic analysis and state the economic factors considered for this analysis. What is the effect of economic growth on stock prices?

Q4. Write short notes on:
(a) Moving Average
(b) Moving Average Convergence Divergence (MACD) indicator.
(c) Relative Strength index
(d) Dow theory

Q5. Define Markowitz diversification. Explain the statistical method used by Markowitz to obtain the risk reducing benefit.

Q6. Explain the CAPM theory. What are the advantages of adopting CAPM model in the portfolio management?

Q7. What is portfolio revision? Describe the various formula plans used for portfolio revision.

Q8. Distinguish between performance measurement and performance evaluation of an investment portfolio. Describe the Sharpe, Treynor and Jensen measures of portfolio returns.

MS-44 : Security Analysis And Portfolio Management
June, 2014

Note: *Attempt any five questions. All questions carry equal marks. Present value and annuity tables are to be provided, if asked for.*

Q1. Define Investment. Discuss the effect of changes in investment environment on investment decisions.

Q2. What do you understand by Initial Public Offer (I.P.O.)? Who are allowed to make an I.P.O.? Discuss the salient features of the SEBI guidelines on I.P.O.

Q3. (a) What is meant by Yield-To-Maturity (YTM)? How is it different from current yield and coupon rate?

(b) Mr. Prashanth owns ₹1,000 face value bond with five years to maturity. The bond has an annual coupon of ₹75. The bond is currently priced at ₹970. If the appropriate discount rate is 10%, should Prashanth hold or sell the bond?

Q4. "Fundamental analysis provides an analytical framework for rational investment decisionmaking". Discuss.

Q5. (a) What are the various limitations of Markowitz model? How the Sharpe's single index model simplifies the selection process of portfolio investment?

(b) Stocks X and Y have the following parameters:

	Stock X	Stock Y
Expected return	20%	30%
Expected variance	25	36
Covariance X Y	30	

Is there any advantage of holding a combination of X and Y?

Q6. Explain the logic of the Arbitrage-Pricing Theory (APT). How does it compare and contrast with the Capital Asset Pricing Model (CAPM)?

Q7. What is the essential difference between the Sharpe and Treynor Indexes of portfolio performance? Which one do you think is preferable and why?

Q8. How are the returns on managed portfolio attributed to stock selection and market timing? Discuss with illustrations.

MS-44 : Security Analysis And Portfolio Management
December, 2014

Note: *Attempt any five questions. All questions carry equal marks. Present value and annuity tables are to be provided, if asked for.*

Q1. Define investment. Describe the steps involved in the investment process.

Q2. (a) Define risk. What are the different types of risks? Explain the methods of risk handling.

(b) A Bond with ₹1,000 face value, bearing a coupon rate of 12% will mature after 7 years. What is the value of the bond if the discount rates are 14% and 12%?

Q3. "Effective regulation is an essential condition for orderly growth of securities market". Explain this statement and discuss the broad classification of regulatory frame-work relating to financial services.

Q4. What is market hypothesis? Explain the different forms and anomalies of efficient market hypothesis.

Q5. (a) What is technical analysis? Explain the techniques and limitations of technical analysis.

(b) A financial analyst is analysing two investment alternatives of X and Y. The estimated rates of return and their chances of occurrence for the next year are given below.

Probability of Occurrence	Rates of Return	
	X	Y
0.20	22%	5%
0.60	14%	15%
0.20	–4%	25%

(i) Determine each alternative's expected rate of return, variance and standard deviation.
(ii) Is alternative 'X' comparatively riskless?
(iii) If the financial analyst wishes to invest half in alternative Y and another half in X, would it reduce risk? Explain with reason.

Q6. Explain the Principle of Dominance. Define the Efficient Portfolio and Efficient Frontier.

Q7. Describe the portfolio management services offered by stock brokers and merchant banks?

Q8. "In the Indian context, buy-and-hold is a better strategy compared to any of the portfolio revision strategies". Comment.

MS-44 : Security Analysis And Portfolio Management
June, 2015

Note: *Attempt any five questions. All questions carry equal marks. Present value and annuity tables are to be provided, if asked for.*

Q1. Define 'Investment'. Explain the process and purposes of investment by the investors.

Q2. What are the objectives of listing of securities? Discuss the requirements for listing of securities in stock exchange.

Q3. (a) Discuss the different approaches for valuation of Common Stock.
(b) The book value per share of a company is ₹145.50 and its rate of return on equity is 10 percent. The company follows a dividend policy of 60% pay out. What is the price of its share if the capitalisation rate is 12 percent?

Q4. How does technical analysis differ from fundamental analysis? Discuss the various assumptions underlying in technical analysis.

Q5. (a) What is Capital Asset Pricing Model? What are the assumptions of the Capital Asset Pricing Model?

(b) From the following details, evaluate the performance of the portfolios of A and B by using Treynor's and Sharpe's Indexes and rank them.

Portfolio	Return	Sd.	Riskless return	Beta
(A)	6.00	15.24	3.0	1.00
(B)	3.30	4.92	3.0	2.85

Q6. Explain the logic of the Arbitrage - Pricing Theory (APT). How does it compare and contrast with CAPM?

Q7. Critically examine the applicability of Jenson and Treynor's measures of portfolio performance to Indian Mutual Funds.

Q8. Critically evaluate the three formula plans and suggest modification, if any, to make them useful for investors in Indian Stock Market.

MS-44 : Security Analysis And Portfolio Management
December, 2015

Note: *Attempt any five questions. All questions carry equal marks. Present value and annuity tables are to be provided, if asked for.*

Q1. "Higher the return, higher will be the risk". Discuss the various types of risks involved in investment.

Q2. What is 'Primary Market'? Discus the important developments that have taken place recently in Indian primary market.

Q3. (a) What is electronic settlement of trade? Explain the procedure for purchasing and selling of dematerialised securities.
(b) A company decides that it will not pay any dividends for 20 years. After that time it is expected that the company could pay dividend of ₹15 per share indefinitely. However, the company at present could pay ₹3 per share. The required rate of this company's shareholders is 10 percent. What is the loss to each shareholder as a result of the policy of the company? Calculate the value of the equity share.

Q4. Critically evaluate the fundamental analysis. How is it useful to a prospective investor?

Q5. (a) What is Markowitz Portfolio Theory? Explain the basic assumptions of Markowitz Theory.
(b) Three Mutual Funds have reported the following rates of return and risk over the last five years.

Growth Fund	Return	St. Deviation (Risk)	Beta
Shriram	15%	16%	1.15
Birla	13%	18%	1.25
ICICI	12%	11%	0.90

Rank each fund by Sharpe's and Treynor's performance evaluation criteria, given the Risk free Return (Rf) as 7%.

Q6. What are the various techniques of technical analysis? Explain the various challenges to technical analysis.

Q7. "Mutual funds provide stability to share prices, safety to investors and resources to prospective entrepreneurs". Comment.

Q8. Compare and contrast constant-dollar-value plan, constant-ratio plan and variable-ratio plan. You may use imaginary data.

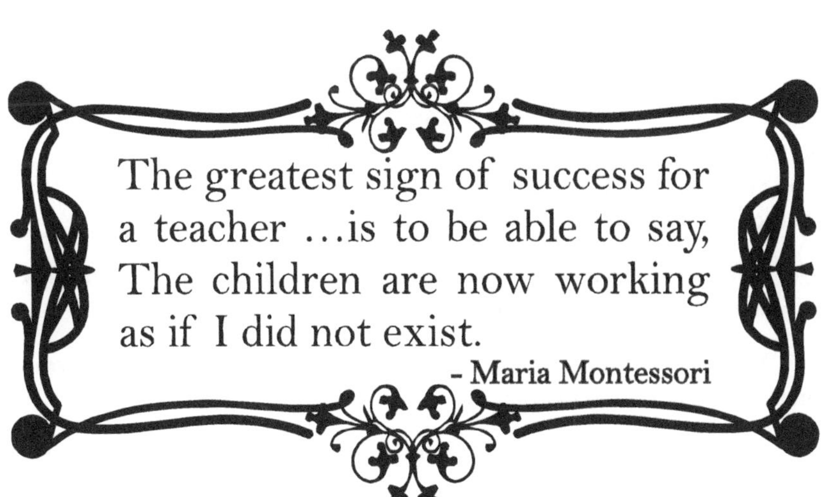

MS-44 : Security Analysis And Portfolio Management
June, 2016

Note: *Attempt any five questions. All questions carry equal marks. Present value and annuity tables are to be provided, if asked for.*

Q1. Define investment. State and explain the elements and objectives of investment.

Q2. (a) Explain the importance of risk and return in security analysis. How would you estimate risk and return for a common stock?
(b) A firm has paid a dividend of ₹5 per share last year. The growth in the dividends is expected to be 5% per annum. Determine the estimated market price of the equity share if growth rate of dividend:
(i) rises to 10% and
(ii) falls to 2%
(iii) Find the present market price of the share, if required rate of return of the investor is 15%.

Q3. "Fundamental analysis provides an analytical framework for rational investment decisions". Discuss.

Q4. Define Markowitz diversification. Explain the statistical methods used by Markowitz to obtain the risk reducing benefit.

Q5. (a) What is Capital Market Theory? Explain how security market line will be determined.
(b) Calculate the Sharpe's Index for Portfolios X, Y and Market (M) from the following data:

	X	Y	M
Standard deviation	18%	16%	8%
Return	14%	20%	20%

The risk free rate is 10%
Which of the above portfolios you would prefer and why?

Q6. Define the Efficient Market Hypothesis. What kinds of empirical evidence were produced to reject the efficient market hypostasis?

Q7. What is portfolio performance evaluation? Explain the Treynor's measure of portfolio evaluation.

Q8. What is portfolio revision? Explain the active and passive strategies in portfolio revision.

MS-44 : Security Analysis And Portfolio Management
December, 2016

Note: *Attempt any five questions. All questions carry equal marks. Present value and annuity tables are to be provided, if asked for.*

Q1. Distinguish between Investment, Speculation and Gambling. What is the usefulness of a Sound Investment Plan?

Q2. (a) Why do companies issue shares in primary market? What is the relationship between the new issue market and the secondary market?
(b) ABC company stock is currently selling at ₹25 per share. The stock is expected to pay ₹1 as dividend per share at the end of the next year. It is reliably estimated that the stock will be available at ₹29 at the end of one year.
(i) If the forecast about the dividend and price are accurate, is it advisable to buy at the present price, if the required rate of return is 20%.
(ii) If the investor's required rate of return is 15% and the dividend remains constant, what should be the price at the end of the first year? You are required to calculate the value of the firm's shares in (i) and (ii) situations above.

Q3. "Stock Exchanges are institutions of economic growth, liquidity and industrial support". Discuss.

Q4. How is Sharpe model an improvement over Markowitz model? Explain the procedure for portfolio risk measurement under Sharpe model.

Q5. (a) Discuss about the techniques employed for testing market hypothesis.
(b) Consider the following data for a particular sample period:

	Portfolio P	Market M
Average return	0.35	0.28
Beta	1.2	1.0
Standard Deviation	0.42	0.30
Non-systematic risk	0.18	0

Calculate the following measures for portfolio P and the Market M, the risk free rate of return is 0.06.
(i) Sharpe, Treynor and Jensen
(ii) By which measures did portfolio P outperform the market?

Q6. What are oscillators? How are they different from moving averages? Would you recommend the usage of an oscillator? Explain.

Q7. Describe the restrictions placed by Securities and Exchange Board of India on Investments by Mutual Funds. Discuss the norms which Mutual Fund Manager takes into consideration while buying the Non-convertible debentures and the equity shares.

Q8. What do you mean by Formula plans? Critically examine the formula plans and discuss their limitations.

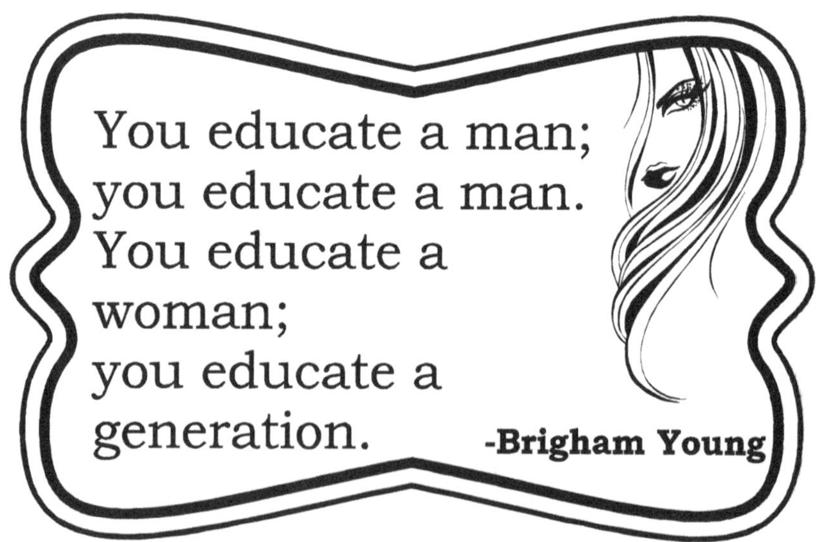

MS-44 : Security Analysis And Portfolio Management
June, 2017

Note: *(i) Answer any five questions. (ii) All questions carry equal marks.*

Q1. What are the factors affecting investment environment in India? Discuss the issues related to securities trading.

Q2. Explain the guidelines of SEBI regarding appointment of brokers and public issue.

Q3. (a) Explain the concept of risk and return and its applications in investment management.

(b) A company is currently paying a dividend of ₹4.24 per share. The dividend is expected to grow at 18 per cent annual rate for 5 years, then at 12 per cent rate forever. What is the PV of the share, if the capitalisation rate is 14 per cent ? The PV Factor at 14% for year 1 to 5 are .877, .769, .675, .592, .519 respectively.

Q4. 'Economy-Industry-Company (EIC) framework provides a useful approach to equity investment decisions.' Explain and illustrate.

Q5. (a) Describe the Markowitz Theory of portfolio selection. Rationalise the holdings of different portfolios by different investors at the same point of time.

(b) From the following data calculate portfolio return and portfolio risk:

Security	Expected Return	Standard Deviation	Proportion of funds invested
ACC	8.89	19.55	0.10
TCS	5.12	7.99	0.40
HLL	3.42	6.18	0.50

Variance - convariance

Security	ACC	TCS	HLL
ACC	382.09	68.73	39.87
TCS	68.73	63.82	68.87
HLL	39.87	68.87	38.25

Q6. What do you understand by portfolio risk? Under what conditions the portfolio risk can be minimised?

Q7. "Mutual funds provide stability to share prices, safety to investors and resources to the prospective entrepreneurs." Explain.

Q8. Write short notes on:
(a) Tradability
(b) Capitalisation
(c) Credit rating
(d) Market breadth

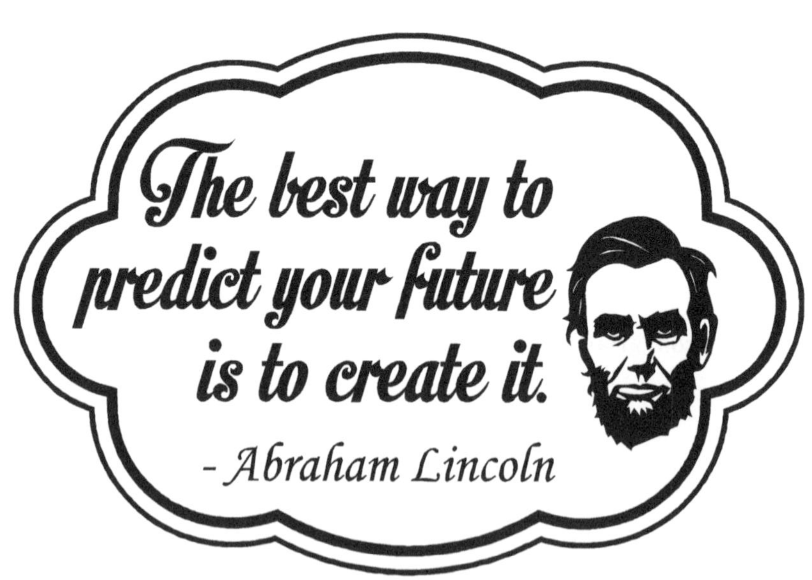

MS-44 : Security Analysis And Portfolio Management
December, 2017

Note: *(i) Answer any five questions. (ii) All questions carry equal marks.*

Q1. Describe the role of SEBI in regulation of mutual funds and investors protection in India.

Q2. (a) What are the features of common stock? Briefly explain the dividend capitalisation model of common stock valuation.
(b) A company is currently paying a dividend of ₹2.12 per share. The dividend is expected to grow at a 9 per cent annual rate for 3 years, then at 6 per cent rate for ever. What is the PV of the share, if the capitalisation rate is 7 per cent? The PV factor at 7% for year 1 to 5 are .935, .873, .861, .763, .713 respectively.

Q3. Distinguish between fundamental and technical analysis. What are the various tools used in technical analysis of investment?

Q4. Explain the significance of the co-variance in calculating portfolio risk. Under what circumstances will the variance of a very large portfolio diminish to zero?

Q5. (a) What is efficient portfolio? Discuss the various steps involved in selecting an optimal portfolio.

(b) A portfolio consists of four securities (A), (B), (C) and (D). Basic data is shown below. Calculate return and risk.

Security	Proportion of Investment	Alpha ( )	Beta ( )	Residual Variance
(A)	0.3	2.50	1.8	270
(B)	0.2	0.75	0.9	140
(C)	0.4	3.25	2.3	195
(D)	0.1	1.00	0.5	098
Market return =15%; Market return variance =130				

Q6. Distinguish between Treynor and Sharpe indices of portfolio performance. Which one do you recommend? Why?

Q7. What are Formula Plans? Critically examine the formula plans and discuss their limitations.

Q8. Write short notes on:
(a) Security Analysis
(b) Asset Management Company
(c) Dis-investment
(d) Moving average

A teacher who is attempting to teach without inspiring the pupil with a desire to learn, is hammering on a cold iron.
-Horace Mann

MS-44 : Security Analysis And Portfolio Management
June, 2018

Note: *(i) Answer any five questions. (ii) All questions carry equal marks. (iii) Use of calculators allowed.*

Q1. What do you understand by investment? Discuss the different alternatives available to investors for making an investment?

Q2. Discuss the trading system in stock exchanges. Mention some of the recent reforms in the trading system.

Q3. (a) What are basic valuation models of bonds? How to calculate the yield on bonds?

(b) Amrutha Ltd, recently paid ₹4.00 per share as dividend for the last year. Its dividend is expected to grow by 15 per cent every year for the next three years, thereafter it will continue a normal growth rate of 6 percent per annum. If the required rate of return is 16 percent, what is the intrinsic value of the equity share of Amrutha Ltd?

Q4. Explain Dow Theory. Analyse the various charts and trends used by technical analysts to exercise the option of buying/ selling securities in the stock market.

Q5. (a) What is "Random Walk Hypothesis"? Explain the basic assumption underlying technical analysis and how they differ with the weak form of Efficient Market Theory.
(b) Security A offers an expected return of 14 percent with a standard deviation of 8 percent. Security B offers an expected return of 11 percent with a standard deviation of 6 percent. If you wish to construct a portfolio with a 12.8 percent expected return, what percentage of the portfolio will consist of security A?

Q6. Distinguish among the performance measures, viz., Sharpe ratio, Treynor measure and Jenson alpha. Describe how each of these three performance measures is calculated. Explain how each of the measures relates excess return and relevant risks.

Q7. Many people advocate mutual funds for small investors. They suggest that the best strategy for small investors is to invest in good mutual fund and put them away. What do you think is preferable? Why?

Q8. Write short notes on:
(a) Investment Vs. Speculation
(b) Sharpe's Performance Measure
(c) EIC Framework
(d) Earnings Multiplier

The art of being wise is the art of knowing what to overlook.

MS-44 : Security Analysis And Portfolio Management
December, 2018

Note: *(i) Answer any five questions. (ii) All questions carry equal marks.*

Q1. Define investment. Explain the risk return trade-off of investment decisions and discuss in detail the investment decision process.

Ans. Refer to Chapter-1, Q.No.-1, Q.No.-4 and Q.No.-5

Q2. Discuss the General Valuation Framework for valuation of securities. Explain how the valuation of preferential share is done.

Ans. General valuation framework consists of basic valuation model, value price relationship, Cootner Hypothesis and dynamic valuation process.

Now, Refer to Chapter-3, Q.No.-2 and Q.No.-3

Cootner Hypothesis

Cootner adds one more dimension to the general view of investor action and buy-sell pressures. He classifies active investors further into two groups viz., 'professional investors' and `unsophisticated investors'. The former are resourceful enough to discover news and develop estimates of intrinsic value even before the unsophisticated investors get the news. They will, therefore, be the first to commence market action the moment a value-price mismatch is discovered. 'Unsophisticated investors' including hasty speculators who act on 'hot tips' would not get any news other than public news and will not have the skill to interpret even such public news. They will however, act in the market but such an action would be incompatible with true changes in intrinsic value. For instance, some of them might have got retirement benefits and would desperately want to invest in shares and securities. And unfortunately, such an action may come up at a time when price is more than value. Likewise, some such investors may have to finance a marriage in the family and would have to sell shares held by them even if price is already ruling at a level lower than the intrinsic value. It is obvious that the action of unsophisticated investors would cut against the trading pressures needed to rectify the disequilibrium between value and price.

It is only when their irrational action takes prices to substantial 'highs' or 'lows' that the professional investors re-enter the scene and pocket enormous profits even while attempting to realign the errant prices to intrinsic values.

Paul Samuelson has supplemented the Cootner formulation of the valuation model by stressing the state of continuous equilibrium. Such a situation would be formed when prices adjust at high speed to values. Instantaneously adjusting prices to 'vibrating values' would be known as perfectly efficient prices, which would be assumed to reflect all information. A security with perfectly efficient prices would be in continuous equilibrium.

Valuation of preferential share

Now, Refer to Chapter-3, Q.No.-5(c)

Since dividends from preference shares are assumed to be perpetual payments, the intrinsic value of such shares will be estimated from the following equation valid for perpetuities in general:

$$V_p = \frac{C}{(1+K_p)} + \frac{C}{(1+K_p)^2} + \ldots = \frac{C}{K_p}$$

Where V_p = the value of a perpetuity today

C = the constant annual payment to be received

K_p = the required rate of return appropriate for the perpetuity.

Now Refer to Chapter-3, Q.No.-6

Q3. What are the objectives of listing of securities? Discuss the requirements for listing of securities in stock exchange.

Ans. We know that the commodities in which transactions in a stock exchange take place are Government Securities, Corporate securities, stocks, bonds, debentures, etc. But the stock exchange will not allow all the securities to deal within it. Every stock exchange maintains a list containing the names of selected companies in whose securities the stock exchange will deal. This list is called "**Official trade list**".

Only those securities whose name appears on the official trade list can only be traded in the stock exchange. Unlisted securities cannot be dealt with in the stock exchange. The company, which wants its securities to be dealt with in a recognized stock exchange, should apply to the stock exchange and get its name included in the official trade list.

Listing means the admission of securities of a company to trading on a stock exchange. Listing is not compulsory under the Companies Act. It becomes necessary when a public limited company desires to issue shares or debentures to the public. When securities are listed in a stock exchange, the company has to comply with the requirements of the exchange.

The major objectives of listing are:

(1) To provide ready marketability and liquidity of a company's securities.

(2) To provide free negotiability to stocks.

(3) To protect shareholders and investors interests.

(4) To provide a mechanism for effective control and supervision of trading.

Listing requirements

A company which desires to list its shares in a stock exchange has to comply with the following requirements:

(1) Permission for listing should have been provided for in the Memorandum of Association and Articles of Association.
(2) The company should have issued for public subscription at least the minimum prescribed percentage of its share capital (49 percent).
(3) The prospectus should contain necessary information with regard to the opening of subscription list, receipt of share application etc.
(4) Allotment of shares should be done in a fair and reasonable manner. In case of over subscription, the basis of allotment should be decided by the company in consultation with the recognized stock exchange where the shares are proposed to be listed.
(5) The company must enter into a listing agreement with the stock exchange. The listing agreement contains the terms and conditions of listing. It also contains the disclosures that have to be made by the company on a continuous basis.

Q4. Define 'Fundamental Analysis'. Critically evaluate the relevance of Economic-Industry-Company (EIC) framework for equity investment decisions.

Ans. Refer to Chapter-6, Q.No.-1 and Q.No.-2 & Refer to Chapter-3, Q.No.-1

Q5. What is company level analysis? Discuss the various quantitative analysis methods used for equity investments.

Ans. Refer to Chapter-7, Q.No.-1

The two method commonly used under quantitative analysis approach are:

(1) Dividend Discounted Method

The dividend discount method is based on the premise that the value of an investment is the present value of its future cash dividends. The present value (PV) is calculated by discounting the future cash dividend at cost of equity. The formula, thus, is

$$PV = \frac{D_1}{(1+K)} + \frac{D_2}{(1+K)^2} + \text{.........} + \frac{D_n}{(1+K)^n}$$

If the dividend grows at a constant rate and the term "n" approaches infinity, then the above equation can be rewritten as under:

$$PV = \frac{D_1}{k-g}$$

Where, k = discount rate or cost of equity
g = growth rate of dividend
D1 = expected dividend

Dividend discount model assumes that the growth rate of future dividend is mainly arising out of retained earnings. That is if the firm grows because of retained earnings, it will have additional earnings, which in turn leads to higher dividend. This is basic assumption of constant dividend growth model. If the dividend growth is fueled by other reasons like cost reduction or increase in productivity or increase in market price, etc., the model may not reflect the correct value. Another reason for the failure of the model is when the growth rate is more than discounting rate.

Though it looks that the value of shares can be increased by increasing dividend, it may not have the desired impact since an increase in payout will reduce the growth rate arising out of retained earning and thus negatively affect the value. In fact, the growth rate of dividend under constant growth model is equal to Return on Investment (ROI) times the ratio of retained earnings to net profit. Thus any increase in the numerator of the valuation equation will be offset by an increase in the value of denominator and one can't expect the value to increase because of a mere increase in dividend rate or dividend payout ratio. Of course one has to look into cost of equity also. If cost of equity is equal to ROI, then changes in payout or retained earnings ratio will have no impact on the price. On the other hand, if the cost of equity is less than ROI, then an increase in payout ratio will adversely affect the value. If the cost of equity is higher than ROI, then value is positively affected if there is an increase in payout ratio.

The following inferences is drawn:

(1) If the return on investment is equal to discounting rate, changes in payout ratio fail to have an impact on the value of the firm.

(2) If the return on investment is greater than discounting rate, then value is positively affected if the company cuts the payout ratio.

(3) If the return on investment is less than discounting rate, then value is positively affected if the company increases the payout ratio.

While applying this approach, one has to be careful about using the discount rate, K.

A higher value of discount rate would unnecessarily reduce the value of an equity while a lower value would unreasonably increase it, that will have implications to invest/disinvest the shares. A discount rate is based on the risk free rate and risk premium.

That is,

Discount Rate = Risk Free Rate + Risk Premium

$$K = R_f + R_P$$

Thus, higher the risk free interest rate with R_p remaining the same would increase the discount rate, which in turn would decrease the value of the equity. In the same way, higher risk premium with R_f remaining the same would increase the overall discount rat and thus decrease the value of the equity.

(2) Price-Earnings Approach

According to this method, the future price of an equity is calculated by multiplying the P/E ratio by the expected EPS. Thus,

P = EPS × P/E ratio

The P/E ratio or multiple is an important ratio frequently used by analyst in determining the value of a share. It is frequently reported in the financial press and widely quoted in the investment community. The P/E ratio essentially reflects the amount that the shareholders are willing to pay for every Rupee of earnings. As such it should reflect the risk associated with the earnings: The inverse of P/E is equal to capitalisation rate.

As in DDM, the P/E model also fails to consider the future potential of earnings of the company since growth rate of earnings is not deducted from the capitalisation rate to get the value of the firm.

This approach seems to be quite straight and simple. There are, however, important problems with respect to the calculation of both P/E ratio and EPS. Pertinent questions often asked are:

- How to calculate the P/E ratio?
- What is the normal P/E ratio?
- What determines P/E ratio?
- How to relate company P/E ratio to market P/E ratio?

The problems often confronted in calculating this ratio are: which of the earningspast, present or future to be taken into account in the denominator of this ratio? Like wise, which price should be put in the numerator of this ratio? These questions need to be answered while using this method.

P/E ratio is broadly determined by:

- Dividend pay out
- Growth
- Risk free rate
- Business risk
- Financial risk

Thus, other things remaining the same,

(1) Higher would be the P/E ratio, if higher is the growth rate or dividend payout or both.

(2) Lower would be P/E ratio, if higher is

(a) Risk free rate,

(b) Business risk,

(c) Financial risk.

Q6. Define market efficiency and describe the differences in various forms of market efficiency. Explain some of the anomalies in Efficient Market Hypothesis (EMH).

Ans. Refer to Chapter-8, Q.No.-1 and Q.No.-4

Q7. Define Markowitz diversification model. Explain the statistical methods used by Markowitz to obtain the risk reducing benefit.

Ans. Refer to Chapter-10, Q.No.-5

We can now proceed to learn how to find an optimal portfolio. This requires an application of quadratic programming.

Minimise Variance of Portfolio $Z: \sum_{i=1}^{n} \sum_{j=i}^{n} Cov_{ij} W_i W_j$

Subject to: $\sum x_i E(R_i) - E^* = 0$

$\sum x_i - 1 = 0$

Combining the above three equations, we get an optimisation equation to minimise the risk:

$$Z = (\sum \sum Cov_{ij} w_i w_j) + (\lambda_1 \sum X_i E(R_i) - E^*) + (\lambda_2 \sum X_i - 1)$$

For a three securities portfolio, the optimisation equation is as follows:

$$Z = X_1^2 \sigma_{11} + X_2 \sigma_{22}^2 + X_3^2 \sigma_{33} + 2X_1X_2\sigma_{12} + 2X_1X_3\sigma_{13} + 2X_2X_3\sigma_{23} + \lambda_1$$

$$(X_1E_1 + X_2E_2 + X_3E_3 - E^*) + \lambda_2(X_1 + X_2 + X_3 - 1)$$

Setting partial derivatives of Z with respect to all variables equal to zero (dz/dx_1, dz/dx_2, dz/dx_3, $d\lambda_1$ and $dz/d\lambda_2$), we get a set of five euqations and solving the five linear equations for the unknowns X_1 X_2 and X_3, the proportion of investment to be made in each of the stocks to get the desired return. The above quadratic programming results will be in the form of three equations in the form of

$$X_1 = a + b_1 E(R)$$
$$X_2 = a + b_2 E(R)$$
$$X_3 = a + b_3 E(R)$$

Where 'a' and 'b', are known and one has to substitute the expected rate of return to know the investment to be made in the three stocks.

The portfolio selection process as described above is not something new; the model was presented by Harry Markowitz briefly in 1952 and later in a complete book entitled Portfolio Selection-Efficient Diversification of Investment (1959). One important concept that Markowitz emphasised for the first time was that some measure of risk, and not just the expected rate of return, should be considered when dealing with investment decision.

Q8. Critically examine the applicability of Jenson and Treynor's measures of portfolio performance to Indian Mutual Funds.

Ans. Refer to Chapter-14, Q.No.-4

MS-44 : Security Analysis And Portfolio Management
June, 2019

Note: *Attempt any five questions. All questions carry equal marks.*

Q1. What do you understand by Investment Risk? List and explain the various components of investment risk.

Ans. The word 'risk' is common vocabulary and is widely used in the world of investments. In normal life, the term risk often means a negative outcome. If you say that it is risky to drive vehicle in a particular road, you actually mean that driving in that road may cause an accident. However, the term risk in investments has a different meaning. It not only refers to a scope of negative occurrence but also implies the chance of positive return.

Investment risk can be defined as the probability or likelihood of occurrence of losses relative to the expected return on any particular investment. Stating simply, it is a measure of the level of uncertainty of achieving the returns as per the expectations of the investor. It is the extent of unexpected results to be realised.

Components of investment risk:

Now, Refer to Chapter-2, Q.No.-8, Q.No.-9, Q.No.-10 and Q.No.-13 (Pg. No.-13, 14, 15)

Q2. What do you understand by valuation of securities? Explain the three step valuation process. How is the valuation of fixed income securities done?

Ans. Securities Valuation means determining the market value of equity instruments (viz. common stock and preferred stock), debt instruments (viz. bonds and bills of exchange), derivatives (viz. options and futures) issued by government agencies, financial institutions and corporate organisations.The main factors driving the securities market value include liquidity, demand and supply of similar instruments, stock market rates of similar securities, present value of future cash flows etc.

Security valuation is important to decide on the portfolio of an investor. All investment decisions are to be made on a scientific analysis of the right price of a share. Hence, an understanding of the valuation of securities is essential. Investors should buy underpriced shares and sell overpriced shares. Share pricing is thus an important aspect of trading.

Three step valuation process: Refer to Chapter-3, Q.No.-1 (Pg. No.-20)

(1) Economy Analysis: All firms are parts of the overall system known as the general economy', which witnesses ups and downs. It is logical to begin the valuation process with projections of the 'macro economy'. What you should grasp is the vast number of influences that affect the 'general economy'. To give only a few examples: Fiscal policy affects spending both directly and through its multiplier effects. For example, tax cuts can encourage spending whereas additional taxes on income or products can discourage spending. Similarly an increase or decrease in government spending also influence the economy. For example, increases in road building increases in road building increases the demand for earthmoving equipment and concrete materials.

(2) Industry Analysis: All industries are not influenced equally by changes in the economy nor they are affected by business cycles at just one single point of time. For example, in an international environment of peace-treaties and resolution of cold war, profits of defence-related industries would wane. The upturn in construction industry generally lags behind the economy. Similarly, a boom or expansion of the economy is not likely to benefit industries subject to foreign competition of product obsolescence. The equipment manufacturing industry will perform well towards the end of economic cycle because the buyer firms typically increase capital expenditure when they are operating at full capacity. On the other hand, cyclical industries such as steel and auto, typically do much better than aggregate economy during expansion but suffer more during contractions. In contrast, non-cyclical industries like food processing or drugs would show neither substantial increase nor substantial decline during economic expansion and contraction.

(3) Company Analysis: After determining that an industry's outlook is good, an investor can analyze and compare individual firms' performance within the entire industry. This involves examining the historical performance of the company, the firm's standing in the industry and future prospects. The last one is critical for estimation of cash flows and hence value. It should be noted that a good Stock or Bond for investment need not come from the best firm or market leader in the industry because the Stock or Bond of such firms may be fully valued or overvalued and hence there is no scope for earning additional return. Thus, investors always look for firms which are undervalued for investments than looking for firms, which are best in respective industries.

(4) Empirical Support for the Valuation Sequence: You may at this stage, ask a question: "Why should the 'company-level' be the last stage in the valuation sequence?" The valuation sequence can be defended and your question aptly answered if it could be shown that earnings, rates of return, prices, and risk levels of a company bear relationships with the economy or with the market which is used as a substitute factor for the 'general economy'. Many studies are available on the subject and it may not be out of place to provide an overview of their basic findings.

Valuation of fixed income securities: Refer to Chapter-3, Q.No.-4 (Pg. No.-22)

Q3. What do you understand by Initial Public Offer (IPO)? Discuss the salient features of the SEBI guidelines on IPOs.

Ans. Initial Public Offer is a process which enables unlisted or private companies to go public so as to raise capital either to repay debt or business expansion or for promoters to dilute stake in the company. It is a great way through which an individual can buy a stake in the company which previously was not possible.

IPO basically represents the first time, a company will financially benefit by the issue of its stock. However, post the Initial Public Offer, the underlying company will not receive any compensation but the share transfer will take place between buyers and sellers in the open market.

Now, Refer to Chapter-4, Q.No.-3 (Pg. No.-38)

Q4. "Fundamental analysis provides an analytical framework for rational investment decisions." Discuss.

Ans. Refe to Chapter-6, Q.No.-2, Q.No.-4 and Q.No.-5 (Pg. No.-54, 57, 61)

Company Analysis: Company analysis is the first stage of fundamental analysis. The economy analysis provides the investor a broad outline of the prospects of growth in the economy. The industry analysis helps the investor to select the industry in which investment would be rewarding. Now he has decide the company in which he should invest his money. Company analysis provides answer to this question.

Company analysis deals with the estimation of return and risk of individual shares. In company analysis he may evaluating short and long term financial position by applying various ratios. The prosperity of a company would depend upon its profitability and financial health. For knowing profitability of the company the investor may calculate profitable ratios, operating ratios etc.

Q5. What do you understand by Earning Per Share (EPS)? Explain the various methods of forecasting EPS. Which one do you consider the best and why?

Ans. Earnings per share or EPS is an important financial measure, which indicates the profitability of a company. It is calculated by dividing the company's net income with its total number of outstanding shares. It is a tool that market participants use frequently to gauge the profitability of a company before buying its shares.

EPS is the portion of a company's profit that is allocated to every individual share of the stock. It is a term that is of much importance to investors and people who trade in the stock market. The higher the earnings per share of a company, the better is its profitability. While calculating the EPS, it is advisable to use the weighted ratio, as the number of shares outstanding can change over time.

Now, Refer to Chapter-7, Q.No.-4 (Pg. No.-67)

Q6. Define market efficiency. Describe the various forms of market efficiency and discuss the different tests of the weak form of efficient market hypothesis.

Ans. Refer to Chapter-9, Q.No.-1, Q.No.-2 (Pg- No.-86, 88)

Q7. Explain the logic of the Arbitrage Pricing Theory (APT). How does it compare and contrast with the Capital Asset Pricing Model (CAPM)?

Ans. Refer to June-2008, Q.No.-4 (Pg. No.-195)

Q8. Critically evaluate the three formula plans and suggest modifications, if any, to make them useful for investors in Indian Stock Market.

Ans. Refer to Chapter-13, Q.No.-3 (Pg. No.-128)

MS-44 : Security Analysis And Portfolio Management
December, 2019

Note: *Attempt any five questions. All questions carry equal marks.*

Q1. Describe the nature of investment decisions and explain the investment decision process. List the various kind of financial instruments available for investment and discuss the risk return profile of each.

Ans. Investment decisions are premised on an important assumption that investors are rational and hence prefer certainty to uncertainty. They are risk-averse which implies that they would be unwilling to take risk just for the sake of risk. They would assume risk only if an adequate compensation is forthcoming. And the dictum of 'rationality' combined with the attitude of 'risk aversion' imparts to investments their basic nature.

Now, Refer to Chapter-1, Q.No.-4, Q.No.-5 and Q.No.-7 (Pg. No.-2, 3, 6)

Q2. (a) Explain major eligibility guidelines recommended by SEBI for the issuers in the primary market.

Ans. Refer to Chapter-4, Q.No.-3 (Pg. No.-38)

(b) Do you consider SEBI as an effective regulator of capital market? Comment.

Ans. Refer to Dec-2007, Q.No.-2(a) (Pg. No.-169)

Q3. (a) Explain the different types of risks. How do you measure the different types of risks?

Ans. Refer to Chapter-2, Q.No.-3, Q.No.-8, Q.No.-9, Q.No.-10 and Q.No.-13 (Pg. No.-11, 13, 14, 15)

(b) Mr. A has a perpetual bond of the face value of ₹1,000 . He receives an interest of ₹60 annually and its current value is ₹600. What is the yield to maturity?

Ans. Same as Chapter-3, Q.No.-5(b) (Pg. No.-23) and Refer to Dec-2008, Illustration-1 (Pg. No.-206)

Q4. As a fundamental analyst, which aspects of a stock would you like to analyse before recommending it to the investors?

Ans. Refer to June-2008, Q.No.-3 (Pg. No.-194)

Q5. (a) Discuss in detail, Capital Asset Pricing Theory. Explain the Capital Asset Pricing Model with suitable examples.

Ans. Refer to Chapter-12, Q.No.-1 and Q.No.-7 (Pg. No.-117, 122)

(b) Assume that the risk free rate of return in 7%; the market portfolio has an expected return of 14% and a standard deviation of return of 25%. Under the equilibrium condition as described by the CAPM, what would be the expected return for a portfolio having no unsystematic risk and 20% standard deviation of return?

Ans. Same as Chapter-11, Illustration-2 (Pg. No.-115)

Q6. From the following information relating to three mutual funds of Avanesh Limited and the market index, calculate Treynor measure, Sharpe's measure and Jenson's measure:

Fund	Mean Return (in %)	Standard Deviation (in %)	Beta
ABC	30	22	1.3
XYZ	23	15	0.9
Gold	22	24	1.2
Market index	15	18	

Risk free rate is 6%.

Ans. Same as Dec-2007, Q.No.-5(a) (Pg. No.-180)

Q7. What do you mean by portfolio revision? When is portfolio revision needed? Critically appraise various portfolio revision plans.

Ans. Refer to Chapter-13, Q.No.-1 and Q.No.-3 (Pg. No.-127, 129)

Q8. Write short notes on the following:

(a) Systematic vs. Unsystematic Risk

Ans. Refer to Chapter-2, Q.No.-5 (Pg. No.-12)

(b) Single Index Model

Ans. Refer to Chapter-11, Q.No.-3 and Q.No.-7(f) (Pg. No.-111, 114)

(c) Dow Theory

Ans. Refer to Chapter-8, Q.No.-2 (Pg. No.-73)

(d) Balanced Funds

Ans. Refer to Chapter-16, Q.No.-3 (Pg. No.-151)

MS-44 : Security Analysis And Portfolio Management
June, 2020

Note: *(i) Attempt any five questions.*
(ii) All questions carry equal marks.

Q1. (a) What do you mean by Investment? Discuss the different channels or alternatives available to an investor for making investment.

(b) "The investment process involves a series of activities starting from the policy formulation." Discuss.

Q2. Describe the various recent initiatives taken by the Securities and Exchange Board of India (SERI) to protect the interest of the investors.

Q3. (a) Distinguish between systematic risk and unsystematic risk. How do you measure these risks?

(b) Face value of a Debenture = ₹ 1,000
Annual Interest Rate of Debenture = 12 per cent
Maturity Period = 5 years

What is the value of the Debenture, if :
(i) Required rate of return is 12 per cent
(ii) Required rate of return is 15 per cent
(iii) Required rate of return is 10 per cent

Q4. (a) Make a comparison between Fundamental Analysis and Technical Analysis. Which one is more helpful to the investors, when they want to invest in capital market?

(b) What are the tools of Technical Analysis? Discuss about the various reversal and continuation price patterns found in Technical Analysis.

Q5. (a) What is Markowitz Diversification? Explain the statistical method used by Markowitz to reduce the risks.

(b) An investor purchases an equity share at a price of ₹100 now. Its expected year end price with relevant probabilities and expected year end dividend are as follows:

Probability	Share Price (₹)	Dividend (₹)
.20	125	5
.40	120	3
.30	115	2
.10	105	Nil

Find out the expected return and variability of return of equity share.

Q6. What do you mean by Portfolio Revision? When is portfolio revision needed? Critically appraise the various portfolio revision plans.

Q7. Discuss the different types of mutual fund schemes in India. Which one would you like to suggest for better investment?

Q8. Write short notes on the following:

(a) Sharpe's Single Index

(b) Efficient Frontier

(c) Elliot Wave Theory

(d) Arbitrage Pricing Theory

MS-44 : Security Analysis And Portfolio Management
December, 2020

Note: *Attempt any five questions. All questions carry equal marks.*

Q1. As an investment advisor what factors would you suggest while deciding the investment portfolio of a client? Explain briefly.

Q2. (a) Explain the mean-variance approach to estimation of return and risk of a security.

(b) A bond of ₹1,000 was issued five years ago at a coupon rate of 6 per cent. The bond had a maturity period of 10 years as of today; therefore, five more years are left for final repayment at par. The market interest rate currently is 10 per cent. Determine the value of the bond.

Q3. What do you understand by Trading System of Stock Exchanges? Explain the various features of National Exchange for Automated Trading (NEAT) system.

Q4. (a) Elucidate, how is company analysis undertaken in fundamental analysis.

(b) Discuss industry analysis using the relative valuation approach.

Q5. Explain Random Walk Hypothesis. What are the various levels of market efficiency?

Q6. (a) What are the advantages of adopting CAPM model in the portfolio management?

(b) How can securities be evaluated with the help of the CAPM theory?

Q7. Consider the following information for four mutual funds A, B, C and D:

	Mean return (%)	S. D. (%)	Beta
A	12	15	0.80
B	16	22	0.76
C	21	37	1.15
D	13	24	1.32

The risk-free rate of return is 10% and face value is ₹100 each. Evaluate the performance of these mutual funds using Sharpe and Treynor ratios. Comment on the evaluation after ranking the funds.

Q8. Write short notes on the following:

(a) Systematic vs. Unsystematic risk

(b) Japanese candlesticks

(c) CML

(d) Portfolio revision strategies

MS-44 : Security Analysis And Portfolio Management
June, 2021

Note: *Attempt any five questions. All questions carry equal marks.*

Q1. Explain how investment opportunities should be evaluated on the basis of risk-return trade-off. Explain with example.

Q2. (a) Describe the multiplier approach to share valuation.

(b) A company has an EPS of ₹ 20·67. Its return on equity is 15% and it follows a policy of retaining 60% of its earnings. If the opportunity cost of capital is 18%, what would be the price of the share today?

Q3. Discuss the trading system in stock exchanges. Mention some of the recent reforms in the trading system in India.

Q4. What are the premises of technical analysis? What are the differences between technical and fundamental analysis?

Q5. Define Markowitz diversification and also explain the statistical method used by Markowitz to reduce the risks.

Q6. The following data are available to you as portfolio manager:

Security	Estimated return (%)	Beta	SD (%)
A	30	2·0	50
B	25	1·5	40
C	20	1·0	30
D	11·5	0·8	25
Market Index	15	1·0	18
Govt. Security	7	0	0

In terms of the security market line, which of the securities listed above are underpriced?

Q7. What do you mean by Portfolio Revision? Describe the major constraints in portfolio revision.

Q8. What are the various types of mutual fund schemes available in India? Explain their features.

MS-44 : Security Analysis And Portfolio Management
December, 2021

Note: *Attempt any five questions. All questions carry equal marks.*

Q1. "The investment process involves a series of activities starting from the policy formulation." Discuss.

Q2. (a) What is risk? Distinguish between systematic and unsystematic risk.

(b) Determine the price of ₹1,000 zero coupon bond with yield to maturity of 18% and 10 years to maturity. What is YTM of this bond if the price is ₹220?

Q3. "Stock Exchanges Act as barometers of the health of economy." Discuss.

Q4. (a) What are the differences between fundamental analysis and technical analysis? How do you make use of both of them?

(b) Discuss the concept of Price Indicators. Elaborate various charting techniques.

Q5. Discuss the different forms of Efficient Market Hypothesis (EMH) with empirical evidence.

Q6. (a) Distinguish between Capital Assets Pricing Model (CAPM) and Arbitrage pricing theory.

(b) How does Markowitz's theory help in planning an Investor's portfolio?

Q7. The following table provides information regarding portfolio return and risks:

Portfolio	Expected return E (R)	σ
1	10	4
2	12	7
3	13	5
4	16	12
5	20	14

(i) The Treasury bill rate is 5%. Which portfolio is best?

(ii) Would it be possible to earn 12% return with standard deviation (S.D.) of 4%?

(iii) If S.D. is 12%, what would be the expected return?

Q8. Write short notes on the following:

(a) Superfluous Diversification

(b) Dow theory

(c) SML

(d) Portfolio revision strategies

MS-44 : Security Analysis And Portfolio Management
June, 2022

Note: *Attempt any five questions. All questions carry equal marks.*

Q1. What are the different attributes to be considered before investing? Discuss.

Q2. (a) How is multiple year holding stock prices estimated with two-stage and three-stage growth models?

(b) A bond of ₹1,000 was issued five years ago at a coupon rate of 6 percent. The bond had a maturity period of 10 years and as of today, five more years are left for final repayment at par. The current market interest rate is 10 percent. Determine the value of the bond.

Q3. What do you understand by "Order Books"? Explain in detail the order matching rules followed to execute trades on Indian Stock Exchanges.

Q4. (a) Elucidate how company analysis is performed through fundamental analysis.

(b) Compare and contrast efficient market hypothesis with fundamental and technical analysis.

Q5. Describe the valuation of stocks using Capital Asset Pricing Model (CAPM).

Q6. (a) Define Markowitz diversification and also explain the statistical method used by Markowitz to reduce the risks.

(b) Explain the concept of Efficient Frontier in the context of Portfolio Selection.

Q7. Vijay Enterprise has a beta of 1.5. The risk free rate is 7% and the expected return on the market portfolio is 14%. The company pays a dividend of ₹2.50 per share and the investor expects a growth in dividend of 12% per annum for many years to come. Compute the required rate of return on the equity according to CAPM. What is the present market price of the equity share assuming the computed return is the required return?

Q8. Write short notes on the following:

(a) Odd Lot Trading

(b) Point and Figure Charts

(c) Serial Bond

(d) Market Risk

MS-44 : Security Analysis And Portfolio Management
December, 2022

Note: *Attempt any five questions. All questions carry equal marks.*

Q1. What is 'Investment'? Discuss the nature of investment decisions and describe the investment decision process.

Q2. Explain the fundamentals of valuations as applied to fixed income securities. Describe the three-step valuation process used in investment analysis of equity shares.

Q3. What do you understand by Economic Analysis? Describe the various variables used as a measure of economic activities.

Q4. Explain the following:

(a) Moving Average

(b) Moving Average Convergence-Divergence (MACD) Indicator

(c) Relative Strength Index (RSI)

(d) Basic Tenets of Dow Theory

Q5. Define 'Market Efficiency' and describe the differences in various forms of market efficiency.

Q6. What do you understand by 'Portfolio Risk'? Under what conditions:

(a) Portfolio risk can be minimised?

(b) Variance of very large portfolio diminishes to zero?

Q7. What is Portfolio Performance Evaluation? Describe Treynor's and Sharpe's indices of portfolio performance. Which one do you recommend? Why?

Q8. What do you understand by Formula Plans? Critically examine the various formula plans and discuss their limitations.